Who
Really
Matters

Who Really Matters

The Core Group Theory of Power, Privilege, and Success

Art Kleiner

CURRENCY

DOUBLEDAY   NEW YORK   LONDON   TORONTO   SYDNEY   AUCKLAND

A CURRENCY BOOK
PUBLISHED BY DOUBLEDAY
a division of Random House, Inc.

CURRENCY is a trademark of Random House, Inc., and DOUBLEDAY is a
registered trademark of Random House, Inc.

Book design by Chris Welch

Library of Congress Cataloging-in-Publication Data
Kleiner, Art.
Who really matters : the core group theory of power,
privilege, and success / Art Kleiner.—1st ed.
p. cm.
Includes bibliographical references and index.
1. Corporate power.   2. Organizational behavior.
3. Success in business.
I. Title.
HD2741.K478   2003
650'.01—dc21   2003053100

ISBN 0-385-48448-8

SPECIAL SALES
Currency Books are available at special discounts for bulk purchases for
sales promotions or premiums. Special editions, including personalized
covers, excerpts of existing books, and corporate imprints, can be created
in large quantities for special needs. For more information, write to Special
Markets, Currency Books, specialmarkets@randomhouse.com

1 3 5 7 9 10 8 6 4 2

To Faith, Frances, Elizabeth, and Constance
—my Core Group.

CONTENTS

Part 1

The

Reality of

Organizations

CHAPTER 1

The Customer Comes Eighth

ack in the early 1980s, when writing mission statements was just an infant management fad, a division of the Exxon Oil Company held an employee conference to announce their new "core values." Enshrined as number one on the list was this simple sentence: "The customer comes first."

That night, the division executives met for dinner, and after a few drinks, a brash young rising star named Monty proposed a toast. "I just want you to know," he said, "that the customer does *not* come first." Then Monty named the president of the division. "*He* comes first." He named the European president. "He comes second." And the North American president. "He comes third." The Far Eastern president "comes fourth." And so on for the fifth, sixth, and seventh senior executives of that division, all of whom were in the room. "The customer," concluded Monty, "comes eighth."

Said the Exxon retiree who told me this story: "There was an agonized silence for about ten seconds. I thought Monty would get fired on the spot. Then one of the top people smiled, and the place fell apart in hysterical laughter. It was the first truth spoken all day."

"The customer comes first" is one of the three great lies of the modern corporation. The other two are: "We make our decisions on behalf of our shareholders" and "Employees are our most important asset." Government agencies have their own equivalent lies: "We are here to serve the public interest." Nonprofits, associations, and labor unions have theirs: "Above all else, we represent the needs of our members."

Of course, if organizations were really set up on behalf of these interests, then they would do a better job, by and large, in serving them. When organizations fail, people tend to assume that their leaders are inept, overwhelmed, or corrupt. But suppose instead that all organizations are doing precisely what they're supposed to be doing. What, then, is their objective? Judging not from their rhetoric, but from their actual behavior and accomplishments, what purpose are most organizations seeking to fulfill?

This book is an effort to answer that question. It starts with the premise that, in every company, agency, institution, and enterprise, there is some Core Group of key people—the "people who really matter." Every organization is continually acting to fulfill the perceived needs and priorities of its Core Group. It's sometimes hard to see this, because the nature and makeup of that Core Group varies from workplace to workplace, and so do the mission statements and other espoused purposes that get voiced to the rest of the world. But everything that the organization might do—meeting customer needs, creating wealth, delivering products or services, fulfilling promises, developing the talents of employees, fostering innovation, establishing a secure workplace, making a better world, and, oh yes, returning investment to shareholders—comes second. Or maybe "eighth." What comes first, in every organization, is keeping the Core Group satisfied.

Core Group dynamics explain why some corporations spend years scrambling frugally for profit, and then squander it on ill-advised mergers, disproportionate pay for their senior executives, or hidden and improper deals. Core Group dynamics also explain why some government agencies block efforts to reform themselves, even when their reputation and potential survival depends on reform. And why some nonprofit organizations persevere against enormous odds to fulfill their idealistic missions, while complacently dismissing potential partnerships that might genuinely help them. Indeed, every organization seems to have its own forms of Core Group–related folly or corruption.

It's because of Core Group dynamics that a depressing number of business corporations have evolved into organizations with one primary purpose: To extract wealth from all constituents (not just the shareholders, but the employees, customers, and neighbors as well) and give it essentially to the children and grandchildren of some of its senior executives. And yet Core Groups are not inherently bad or dysfunctional. Indeed, they represent probably the best hope we have for ennobling humanity—at least in a world like ours, in which organizations have the lion's share of power, capital, and influence. An organization's Core Group is the source of its energy, drive, and direction. Without an energetic and effective Core Group, all efforts to spark creativity and enthusiasm sputter out.

If you work in an organization, then all this may be second nature to you, so obvious and taken for granted that it barely even registers as important. But when you take a step back, the significance for all of us, even those who don't work in organizations, is unavoidable. We live in a civilization composed of organizations. Indeed, in industrialized countries, the organizational birthrate exceeds the human birthrate. Even though organizations are continually merging, swallowing each other up, or dwindling into inactivity, there are more organizations each year than there were the year before.

People have always used organizations to amplify human power. Individuals didn't build pyramids or cathedrals; tribal and feudal organizations did. But since the industrial revolution, and in the past 150 years in particular, organizations have become powerful in unprecedented ways. They are faster than they have ever been, operating with the perpetual acceleration of computers and wireless communication. They are interconnected through vast global webs of trade and distribution, webs that (among other things) make most human beings virtually dependent on organizations for food, shelter, and transportation. They are pervasive; there are almost no sustainable ways of making a living without organizations, and organizations dominate the political system, instead of paying fealty to it.

It's as if some giant invisible species suddenly invaded the Earth around 1850, reshaping civilization in its image, obviously here to stay—and yet almost nobody seems to see it clearly. Nobody really knows how it works, or even what it does. Some people go to business school to master these new creatures, and end up being mastered by them.

The left protests against globalization, capitalism, big corporations, and Wall Street; the right excoriates big government, corrupt labor, or liberal media. But when you strip away the rhetoric, both sides seem to be driven by the same basic dynamic. They feel excluded from, rejected by, opposed to, and trampled on by the Core Groups of organizations associated with the other side.

If we are going to act effectively in a society of organizations, we need a theory that helps us see organizations clearly, as they are. We need to observe this new species in its natural habitat, to track its behavior, and to study its relationships with predators and prey. Only then can we ask: Why does it operate this way? And what, if anything, could be different? Only then can we learn to use organizations, instead of feeling like we are being used by them. Only then can we move organizations away from being simply the property and tools of the few, and develop their potential for the rest of us. Only then can we form real relationships with the members of this new species, as employees, neighbors, cocreators, participants, leaders, and even lovers of organizations.

In short, if we want to not just live within society, but establish ourselves as leaders and creators, then we have to understand the dynamics of the Core Group.

The root of the word "core" is the Latin *cor*, or heart, and the Core Group is the genuine heart of an organization. Management writer Arie de Geus, in his book *The Living Company*, calls the Core Group the "we" of the organization—the central proprietors of its interests. They usually include most, but not all, of the people at the top of the organization chart. Plus others. The Core Group members are the center of the organization's informal networks, and symbolic representatives of the organization's direction. Maybe they got into the Core Group because of their position, their rank, or their ability to hire and fire others; maybe because they control a key bottleneck, or belong to a particular influential subculture. Maybe their personal charisma or integrity got them in. In the end, it probably doesn't matter that much how they got in. What matters is that they matter.

The Core Group won't be named in any formal organization chart, contract, or constitution. It exists in people's hearts and minds. Its power is derived not from authority, but from legitimacy. Its influence is not always conscious, or even visibly apparent, but it is always present in the implementation of actual decisions. It is the fundamental aspect of organizational culture that makes visitors to a workplace scratch their heads sometimes: "What *are* those people thinking?"

It is impossible to imagine an organization without a Core Group. And if you could imagine one, why would you want to create it? Start-ups need entrepreneurial Core Groups who put themselves at risk for the company's future. (People start organizations in the first place precisely because they want to be in a Core Group, if only to see what it would be like. I should know; I cofounded a consulting firm largely for that reason.) Large, well-run companies need a Core Group of senior leaders who can permanently merge their identities with that of the organization. Government agencies and nonprofits need Core Groups that can take a visible stand on behalf of the organization's principles. Even the most hierarchically strict organizations, like military units, depend on their Core Groups to maintain, among other things, the level of mutual respect that soldiers need to operate above and beyond the limits of their orders.

As we'll see throughout this book, there is always an implicit, somewhat unconscious bargain of mutual commitment in organizations: The people of the organization agree to make decisions on behalf of the Core Group, while the Core Group members agree to dedicate themselves as leaders to the organization's ultimate best interests. When it works, the result of this arrangement is greatness. Indeed, behind every great achievement, there is almost certainly a great organization (even when it seems like the achievement is that of a single individual). And behind every great organization there is certainly a great Core Group.

Great or miserable or in-between, the Core Group sets the organization's direction. *The organization goes wherever its people perceive that the Core Group needs and wants to go. The organization becomes whatever its people perceive that the Core Group needs and wants it to become.* If a goal is perceived as irrelevant to the Core Group, then it will not be reached, no matter how worthy it is, how ardently it is advocated, or even how stringently it is mandated by law or regulation. (At most, the organization will pretend to pursue it, grudgingly complying with the rules.) If a goal is perceived as close to the heart of the Core Group, then the organization will get there, come hell or high water. Moreover, just as every coherent human group comes to embody a set of values, ideas, and attitudes, the Core Group nearly always becomes an unconscious microcosm of the whole. If Core Group members think or act in a particular manner, or with particular attitudes, those percolate throughout the hierarchy. If Core Group members are cold to each other and to employees, then the whole enterprise becomes like a frozen wasteland. If the Core Group somehow warms up, then a little Santa's Workshop begins to develop amidst the tundra.

Thus, if you want to know what an organization stands for, start by exploring the characteristics and principles of its Core Group. If you want to invest in a company, look not just at its business prospects and trading history, but at the quality and reliability of its Core Group. If you want to lead an organization to great new things, start by fostering the kind of environment in which a great new Core Group can emerge. If you need to change or influence an organization, you can't do it unless you understand which aspects of the Core Group are open to change, in what ways, and by whom. Finally, if you remain unaware of the nature of an organization's particular Core Group, then that organization will be opaque, ungovernable, and dangerous to you—even if you are ostensibly the person in charge. You may go through your career, for instance, thinking that "the customer comes first," acting as if that premise were true, and wondering why you never seem to get the rewards and recognition you think you deserve.

The Core Group theory emerged from watching organizations at play. Trained as a journalist, in 1979, I began covering Silicon Valley and the emerging precursors to the Internet for the counterculture publication that Stewart Brand had founded, the *Whole Earth Catalog*. Every once in a while, a corporation invited some of us Whole Earthers to advise them on the prospects for these strange new technologies. At one such meeting in 1982, some senior executives of the Atari Corporation asked for advice on the potential value of their new product, a home computer. I remember walking out still puzzled by two questions: Why would this buttoned-down organization (which Atari had become after its purchase by Time-Warner) want advice from Whole-Earth-Catalog-style hippies? And why wouldn't these leading-edge technology executives already know their own business? (Now, of course, I know the answer to both questions; this company, which had ejected its technology-savvy founder and been acquired by Time-Warner, had a new Core Group in place that was in over its head.)

By 1985, when Atari had already entered its inevitable decline, I had grown bored with writing about technology. Behind every technology story, after all, was a much more interesting business story, and behind every business story was a much more interesting story about management culture. I drifted to writing about advertising and then management, covering the quality movement and other business fashions of the late 1980s. This in turn led to a consulting job helping an MIT lecturer named Peter Senge develop a book about systems thinking in organizations—a book which ultimately became the 1990 best-seller *The Fifth Discipline*. Around the same time, I spent six years researching and writing my own book, *The Age of Heretics,* about the social movement to change large corporations from within.

As part of these and other endeavors—cocreating several *Fifth Discipline* follow-up "Fieldbooks," writing regularly on "Culture and Change" for the business magazine *strategy+business,* working part-time as a management consultant, helping develop a series of organizational oral histories called "learning histories" at Massachusetts Institute of Technology, and conducting a course on the future at New York University's Interactive Telecommunications Program—I have interviewed more than a thousand people in depth, from a wide variety of organizations, about their aspirations, experiences, and frustrations in the workplace. The Core Group theory sums up the common threads I've perceived in all of those conversations. It also reflects a series of in-depth conversations conducted during the past five years with leading organizational thinkers and thoughtful organizational participants about the Core Group concept and its implications.

In the rest of the chapters of this book, I hope to articulate "who really matters" in a way that transcends both cynicism and naiveté, charting the boundaries and influence of the Core Group and discovering the most effective ways to manage it, live with it, and influence organizations for the better.

Several chapters will focus on the topics that come to mind when people think of hierarchy and authority: Power (especially in Chapter 9, "Power and Legitimacy"), Privilege (which is discriminatory by nature because it's a kind of love, with all the hope and abuse that this implies; see Chapter 4, "A Very Special Kind of Love"), and organizational or business Success (which is intimately linked with the distinctive knowledge of the Core Group, as discussed in Chapter 7, "A Core Group Way of Knowledge").

I'll feel that this book is successful if it helps some readers through the thickets of Core Group–dominated office politics and if it inspires a few CEOs or senior managers to rethink their organizational practices. If the role of Core Groups is as prevalent and significant as I think it is, then perhaps this book can help spark new forms of dialogue about the nature of corporate governance and the role of Core Groups and organizations in society at large.

Most of all, I'd love to see this book help bring some great Core Groups into being. There's a great deal at stake: the profitability and health of the organizations around us, and the life, liberty, and pursuit of happiness of the rest of us who must live with them.

CHAPTER 2

How Organizations
Think

For more than a year, the new consulting firm had been planning its divestiture, and it was finally time to cut loose. Formerly a division of a much larger high-tech corporation, it would now be free, for example, to pursue contracts with its former competitors. The board was still working out the details of separation on a December evening in the mid-1990s, when the top 350 people gathered together in a Boston hotel ballroom to launch their bold adventure. Marianne, the CEO, made a forty-minute valedictory speech in which she thanked all the people who had helped engineer the shift; then Brad, a gifted Texas storyteller and human resources executive, recounted the tribulations that had occurred along the way.

In the back of the room, with a half-smile on his face, stood Lothar, the director of research. He was young, only in his mid-30s, and he had been one of the few skeptics about the divestiture. But once its inevitability became clear, he had signed on wholeheartedly. To be sure, he had ducked out of the organizing work of the new enterprise, cheerfully explaining that there were plenty of other people who could handle those tasks. "They need me to focus on research in the meantime, so that as soon as we're set up, we can show clients that we know what we're doing." He felt confident about his place in the new company; after all, he had been at the center of the old division. Whenever there had been a major change, one thought on everyone's mind had been: "What will Lothar think of this?" The company continually acted as if it had his best interests at heart and was continually watching out for him.

Now, however, as Lothar listened to the valedictories, his smile faded and his back stiffened. For neither Marianne nor Brad, both of whom considered him a friend, mentioned his name in any part of their recitals. When they were finished, amidst the applause and the serving of dessert, Lothar silently slipped out a side door and went home.

Lothar is a close friend of mine as well, and I happened to be at that dinner. With another colleague, I went up to Marianne and Brad and confronted them: "What about Lothar?" Their faces fell. They hadn't even realized the omission. They had completely forgotten about him.

During the next few months, most of the influential people in the organization continued to treat Lothar with friendship and respect. They met him for lunch; they went on ski trips together; they asked his advice. But his status had changed. He did not get the job he had been promised, managing research for the new organization. Worse still, he was told about this only at the last possible moment, which meant that (in order to keep his benefits), he had to scramble back to the old parent company to take any job they would give him.

Once, it would have been a priority for the consulting firm to make sure he had whatever he needed; now, he discovered he could not rely on anyone whom he had trusted. It was almost as if the organization itself was a sentient creature, a creature with a mind of its own. And this creature was rejecting him.

Seeing Lothar's story unfold was one of the experiences that propelled me to write this book, but I have also conducted dozens of interviews over the years with other people enmeshed in similarly inexplicable dynamics. Some have been cast adrift. Others, including the developers of many corporate skunk works, see their brilliant ideas and strategies ignored. Some are senior executives who put forth a bold new move, expecting it to cascade down the hierarchy as usual, but discover that while the organization is loyal to *them*, it has no interest in the changes they have in mind.

Is the organization actually sentient? Is it thinking for itself? It doesn't matter. The organization is, in effect, making a collective choice, and all of us who work there, even if we disagree, are as independent as neurons in a larger brain.

To make sense of this, we need to understand how organizations act and think. The basic building block of organizational action isn't the job, the team, the project, the process, the share, or even the dollar: It's the *decision*. Organizations are essentially the sum of all the decisions made in them over time. Some decisions, made at the top of the hierarchy, are visible and obviously influential. They have an immense pull on the direction of the whole system. The decision to close a plant or start a new product line affects many other decisions at many levels. But even a decision to change an order of paper clips from Staples to a local stationer (or vice versa) may help chart the course of the organization's future in some small but significant way. Put all these decisions together and you end up with a coordinated movement, evolving into its own emergent form.

Writer Kevin Kelly calls this phenomenon a "hive mind," and he associates it with a form of computer game called Cinematrix. Invented by Loren Carpenter at Lucasfilm in the mid-1980s, it gives an entire audience shared control of a cursor on the screen. As it happens, I was a member of one of the early audiences for this technology in 1984. We played a large-screen version of a computer game called BallBlazer, a kind of virtual one-on-one soccer. The object was to use your electronic paddle to propel the "ball" (a dot of light) past the end zone of the other team. Half the audience controlled one electronic paddle; the other half controlled the other paddle. Everybody had a joystick at their seat. The paddles moved according to the aggregate pull of everyone connected to them. If you moved your joystick, you would see your team's paddle echo your motion—but only if enough people moved it in the same direction along with you. If people moved the paddle in different directions, their efforts canceled each other out.

Before long, a kind of two-way feedback manifested itself. The crowd didn't just move the paddle; the paddle also moved the crowd. Each of us, as individuals, found ourselves becoming attuned to the paddle's direction, and we acted accordingly. The easiest and most natural thing to do was to move our own joysticks along with the paddle; to ape it with our own gesture and feel the instinctive pleasure that comes from operating in tune with the crowd. If we felt contrary, we could move the joystick in a different direction and enjoy the moral righteousness of seeing our contributions virtually ignored. And those of us who were truly gifted at the game could get out on the cutting edge of the paddle's movement, a little bit ahead of the crowd. We could be the first to see the direction the ball was going and the first to turn the paddle to meet it. That gave us the satisfaction of recognizing the hive mind taking shape behind our own mind and following.

That's what organizational decision-making is like.

People in organizations make hundreds of thousands of decisions each day, for a variety of motives, usually without knowing exactly how the results will turn out. Sometimes we make decisions for intrinsic reasons—because we want something. Sometimes we make the decisions we think we are supposed to make. Sometimes we are guided by the knowledge that others around us will suffer if we let them down. All these decisions add up, without anyone coordinating them, to an overall purpose: a collective imperative for the organization's every move. And as we continue to work for an organization, like the players of Cinematrix BallBlazer, we become attuned to the direction that the hive mind is already taking. We learn to tack with the wind, or sometimes to step out in front of it; we may also have the temperament to oppose it from time to time. But we are always aware of it.

Hence the importance of the Core Group. If you have ever worked in an organization, then you know that every critical decision is made amidst a maelstrom of conflicting priorities, constraints, competitors, and constituents. (Some call this the "business environment.") We have to bring it down to manageable size in our minds, or we couldn't function.

Core Groups are a collective invention, emerging from the hive mind (or, as philosopher Mary Douglas calls it, the "thought world") of any organization or community. The Core Group gives people a way to manage the complexity of decisions. In the same way that infants recognize faces more easily than other objects, we who work in organizations find it easy to attune ourselves to other people. We let a relatively small group of people stand as simple symbols for complicated goals, motives, and consequences. In other words, we anthropomorphize our business environment and the choices we have to make. We convert them, in our minds, to human form.

When faced with a complex decision, you might ask yourself: How comfortable would so-and-so be with this decision? There is probably a range of "so-and-so's." How will this sit with your boss? How would your boss's boss feel? What would the executive team think? And the board? And the union? And the person in charge of some critical function, like a key factory or region? Would Irene and Frank over in the next office let you get away with it? Do you want Joe or Sally walking in your door next week, saying, "I wish you hadn't done that"? Do you care if it means more work for your administrative assistant? And what about the fact that unless the executive VP approves of your decision, we'll be forced to go back to square one and start all over?

Even if you don't personally go through such a litany when you make a decision, your colleagues and fellow employees do—and that's what sets the direction of the organization. The influence of these key people trumps all other concerns, not because of some mystical resonance, but simply because of the cumulative effect of the decisions made throughout the organization. If people believe the Core Group needs and wants something to happen, they assume that making it happen is part of their job. Even those who resent or disapprove of the Core Group will fulfill its members' perceived wants, at least to some extent, for they feel it is their job to do so, and everyone around them continually reinforces that feeling. (And, as we'll see in Chapter 9, the rewards and recognition structures of the organization are set up to reinforce this.)

You can hear the influence of the Core Group in the way people talk. When debating a new plan, they make their case in Core Group terms. We say, "John is really excited about it." Or, "Larry has a lot of heartburn about it." Or, "I don't want to be the one to tell Kevin we can't make it happen." (These are real quotes from an employee of Cisco Systems, describing how decisions are made there.) On one level, those comments are merely statements about the emotions of a Core Group member. But on a more important level, they are hard-edged assessments of the organization's willingness to act. The speaker doesn't care how good the plan is; if Larry has heartburn, it's not going to happen. And it's not just because of the Johns, Kevins, and Larrys as individuals (or the Anitas, Carlys, and Lindas in other organizations), but because of what they stand for. They are living symbols of tighter cost controls, more stringent quality, bolder moves, greater customer focus, or whatever it may be. When you mess around with Larry, you also mess around with the company's future.

Now imagine that, for any organization, you could make a list of all the "so-and-so's" in *everyone's* mind in aggregate—all the people who influence all the decisions made through the course of a year. Some names would stand out as significant, but only for subparts of the organization. The head of Asian sales might be carried in the minds of anyone in Tokyo, but not at all significant to decisions made in Brussels. Other names would be important to the whole organization: the CEO, of course, but also some other critical people in the hierarchy. And there would also be some classes of people (like "large stockholders" or "key customers" or "oversight figures" or "labor union leaders") that take on significance for the whole organization. Each of these individuals or groups represent not just themselves, but an image of the direction of the organization: a view of where it may go.

Those are the members of the Core Group. They aren't all the decision-makers; they are all the people whom decision-makers keep in mind. If you could somehow map the decisions made all year on a two-dimensional grid, as arrows going in various directions, and you could "solve" for the result, the entire grid would end up moving the Core Group's way.

For example: You and I might work for the same company in a "new products" division. You might decide to introduce two new products. I may be in charge of evaluating those products, charged with blocking them if they don't meet the company's financial criteria. Chances are, if I think the Core Group will approve of it, even if it doesn't meet the criteria, I will let it pass. This won't happen because I am a sycophantic toady; it will happen because I believe that it is part of my job to pass through items that the Core Group will approve of. Chances are, the perks and incentives in the organization, along with other communications from my boss and other bosses, reinforce that belief. Moreover, others in my department are also making decisions on the same basis. In the face of all that pressure, no wonder that most decisions are made to satisfy the perceived needs and wants of the Core Group.

Remember Lothar, my friend who had been research director

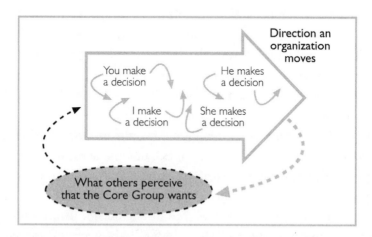

A generic map of the "thought world" or "hive mind" of a typical organization: a perpetual dynamic between other's perception of the Core Group and the aggregate of organizational decision-makers.

of the consulting firm? His sudden expulsion makes sense only from the perspective of Core Group theory. Of all the senior managers in the new company, he had been *most* closely associated with the old parent company. In fact, he had spoken out against the divestiture. More important, he was the only manager still championing a vision of research as the core of the company's activity: a key part of the old culture, but a cost center that the new consulting firm was hoping, subliminally, to escape. In the back of the minds of Marianne and Brad (and lots of other people as well) was a lingering question about Lothar: As a living reminder of the old parent company, even though he has changed his tune, will he be embarrassing to the people who count around here? The Core Group members themselves said no; Lothar should stay. But to the hive mind, the answer was yes. Lothar must exit.

As individuals, some of us learn not to give in to the hive mind's signals. We may even be valued (in some enlightened organizations) because we think differently than everyone else. But even so, we will use the Core Group to calibrate the fit between our own views and the overall direction of the organization. We talk about "agreeing with David" or "not wanting to go faster than Alice will go." The Core Group's priorities are the standard, in other words, against which we measure our own.

In a paradoxical way, the less hierarchical and more fluid an organization is, the more influence the Core Group has. In a tight hierarchy, where you are supposed to follow orders to the letter and the boss checks up on you, there isn't much complexity to deal with. But when everybody's decision makes a difference, and people at every level make a lot of decisions, the Core Group becomes critically important. Otherwise, no one would get anything done. In the worst organizations, the Core Group becomes a set of mental shackles that people put on themselves. They feel bound to do what the boss wants, and they spend their time guessing about what that might be. Since there's safety in numbers, they often guess together—a phenomenon called "groupthink." But in the best organizations, there isn't much groupthink. People are conscious of their point of view, and of the Core Group's. The Core Group and the rest of the organization continually learn from each other.

But those organizations are relatively rare. Let's look first at the kinds of organizations, and the people in them, that we're likely to run into.

CHAPTER 3

A Field Guide to Some
Common Core Groups

Ever since it was founded in the 1830s, the consumer products giant Procter & Gamble has enjoyed a stable, slowly evolving management structure. At first a family business (with four generations of Procters and Gambles in management positions), by the 1920s it had evolved a system of promotion from within. For years, nearly all senior executives started their careers at P&G in the marketing function. They came direct from college, then worked their way up the ladder to assistant brand manager, brand manager, and finally to executive. It was a tough route, and deservedly so; P&G is so renowned for its genius in marketing and product development that the preeminent trade magazine *Advertising Age* once devoted an entire double-sized issue as a tribute to the company. It is said that only a sixth of the young marketers who join P&G ever serve a full career there; the rest are driven out through fierce inner competition.

Those who make it have joined an elite. They are not just at the top of the hierarchy; they dominate the company's culture. People in the rest of the company will admit, when pressed, the extent to which the perceived priorities of the marketing group drive their decisions. For example, P&G has one of the most innovative factory production operations in the world—in its own way, as remarkable as P&G's genius for marketing. American team-based management, with its tremendous breakthroughs in productivity and employee creativity, is largely descended from the "sociotech-nical" designs that the company began to develop in the 1960s. But until relatively recently, all this occurred under a cover of darkness. Even as late as the mid-1990s, P&G's operations executives were reluctant to talk openly about their methods, not only among out-siders, but within the company itself.

The old rationale for this secrecy—preventing outsiders from learning P&G's production secrets—no longer applied. The wis-dom of team management had long since been made public and applied in other companies (often by P&G alumni). Why, then, the secrecy? The production executives whom I talked with perceived that it was part of their job to make sure they did not overshadow their marketing-oriented counterparts. Their own careers de-pended on not making the Core Group suspicious of them. (I've been told that this dynamic changed during the mid-1990s, when the boundaries among P&G functions loosened up and people moved more easily among them.)

Different companies have very different Core Group patterns. Take Boeing, for instance. Only in the 1990s did Boeing diversify from its aircraft division, which still earns sixty percent of its rev-enues, into telecommunications, satellites, and rocketry. The air-craft engineers—who were the core of the Core Group during their heyday in the 1950s, the era of Boeing's B-52 bomber—have gradually seen their Core Group status erode. By the 1980s, it had deteriorated to the point where aircraft engineers worked in huge bull pens, with monitors on catwalks clocking their bathroom breaks. (In 2000, when 16,000 engineers went on strike, one of their primary demands was to get more "respect." They won the strike, but when it was over, they went back to the bull pens.)

Today, if you were to draw the Boeing Core Group, you'd show a deep split between the financially oriented core executives (sym-bolized by CEO Philip Condit) and the long-standing leaders of the aircraft division's bureaucratic management. A few years hence, that might change, for in 2001, Boeing moved its headquar-ters from Seattle, home of its aircraft business, to Chicago. Phil

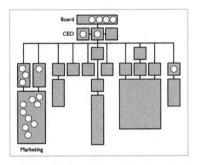

These diagrams portray the Core Groups of four (fictional but typical) organizations: A consumer products company, in which people in marketing join the Core Group early in their careers . . .

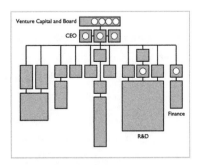

. . . a high-tech start-up with a small Core Group that includes a very influential board of venture capitalists . . .

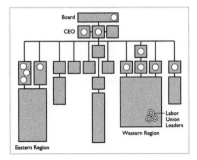

. . . a large manufacturer and military contractor with a fragmented Core Group and labor union leaders among the members . . .

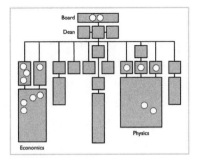

. . . and a research university with a strong faculty Core Group (and a weak dean).

Condit said he personally loved the Puget Sound region; he had lived there for thirty-six years. But he had concluded, he said, that "if you are [placed] directly with any one of your business units, it changes the dynamic of the way you view that business." In other words, he moved two thousand miles just to push the aircraft business further out of the Core Group. Whether that move succeeds or not is still to be seen.

Every organization has its own evolving Core Group story, its own favored categories of people, shifting either with lightning speed or glacial slowness, depending on the history and nature of the organization. At McKinsey, the Core Group is heavy with ex-Naval officers. In the Navy, the Core Group consists of the "rising stars" (officers who are singled out at very junior levels and continually picked for plum assignments thereafter) and the "gray-beards" (influential officers nearing retirement). At Microsoft, famously, the Core Group consists of employees whose stock has matured (and who are thus independently wealthy) and of people who have been personally recognized by "billg," the e-mail tag for Bill Gates. (A Microsoft employee once told the *New York Times*, "Of the 34,000 employees here, there are 5,000 who really count.") In the late 1980s and early 1990s at one publishing company I know, there was a group of editors known as the "A Team," favored with assignments, budgets, and invitations to select parties. At a public middle school I know of, the most favored teachers were called the "chosen ones." In some Silicon Valley companies, staffers speak of the "rock stars."

At Royal Dutch/Shell, at least during the 1980s and early 1990s, it was people with "letter-grade" potential (i.e., potential to reach the higher management ranks, which were denoted with letters of the alphabet instead of numbers). The most prized "letter-grade" quality, other than good performance records and a collegial un-flappability, was "helicopter" sensibility: the ability to focus on minute details one moment and zoom up to the big picture in the next. There was a risk in being tagged as "letter-qualified": Those who fell from that status into mere "number-qualified" potential were generally asked to leave the company.

In Silicon Valley start-ups, the Core Group often consists of the few high-tech engineers who had the original vision for the technology, plus the two or three financial angels who (in the best of cases) are there to build the business, and (in the worst of cases) are there to sell out and cash in. (*Built to Last* author Jim Collins calls these latter companies "built to flip," because the Core Group has no interest in sustaining the kind of steady, deliberate growth that can produce a lasting enterprise.) In large, complex organizations like GE or Exxon, there may be hundreds of interlocking Core Groups for suborganizations, each active in its own division or department. They vie with one another for the attention of the ultimate Core Group common to all of them, consisting perhaps of the CEO and his kitchen cabinet, as well as (in both cases) some highly visible people who have come to develop influence across all the various businesses and operations of the enterprise.

In fluid organizations, the Core Group may shift in membership from year to year or even from month to month; people may get used to the discomfiting feeling of being in the "in crowd" one month and the "out crowd" the next. In some family firms, by contrast, the membership of the Core Group is fixed enough to last for generations, with outsiders finding no way in, no matter how hard they work and how indispensable and loyal they become. A manager at the Ford Motor Company told me that, during the days when Ford advertised that "Quality is Job One," his boss pulled him aside and told him, "Remember. Your real job here is creating wealth for the Ford family." A host of Ford executives over the years, including Lee Iacocca and Jac Nasser, have apparently been forced out over the years for forgetting this principle.

At most magazines I've known, either the production staff has Core Group status (in which case deadlines are sacrosanct) or the editorial staff does (in which case the magazine is exceptionally current and tolerant of last-minute changes). In oil companies, the Core Group tends to be dominated by "upstream" people (who started their careers as geologists, exploring for oil or extracting it from the ground), rather than "downstream" people (like refiners or marketers). In most large companies, it helps to be a man, but at

The Body Shop, the global natural cosmetics corporation, the Core Group has been nearly all women. (Flexible time for mothers, naturally, is a companywide practice.)

Occasionally one finds an organization where the chief executive is barely a member of the Core Group at all. For instance, at some universities, nothing happens without the approval of long-standing faculty members in critical departments. The president or dean has a limited term or limited power, and if he or she tries to change the organization, people simply say yes but ignore the changes. "Headmasters come and go," say the faculty members at one private school, "but we'll be here forever." (Harvard professor Robert Kegan, educational chair of Harvard's Institute for Management and Leadership in Education, says that two favorite jokes come up again and again. Faculty members ask: "What is an associate dean? A mouse training to be a rat." And deans ask: "What's the difference between a tenured faculty member and a terrorist? You can negotiate with a terrorist." In other words, the faculty members are in the Core Group, and the deans are not.)

Similarly, one sometimes finds an organization where the people who make the most money are not necessarily in the Core Group. These tend not to last very long. Companies with commodities-trading divisions, for instance, have sometimes been forced to pay their traders more than their chief executives make. (That's why some industrial companies get rid of their trading divisions.) And at the nonprofit Point Foundation, where I worked when it published both *CoEvolution Quarterly* and the *Whole Earth Software Review*, the *Software* staffers made much more money than the *CoEv* staffers. But the *CoEv* staffers, who had been there first, were much closer to the heart of the enterprise. Ultimately, they defined the Core Group, and they lasted much longer.

In some organizations, Core Group members are the people who control hiring, firing, and incentives—pure and simple. In others, they operate primarily through cultural channels, as living embodiments of a way of thinking or a set of values. (Bill O'Brien, the legendary president of 1980s-era Hanover Insurance whom Peter

Senge wrote about in *The Fifth Discipline*, tended to foster this kind of Core Group in the companies he managed.) In some organizations, Core Group members consist of the founders and the first to enter (which also means the last to be laid off). And in still others, like IBM under Lew Gerstner, they came into an established organization, engineered a Core Group coup of sorts, and acquired legitimacy and influence by setting a new direction. The Core Group in some organizations can include critical outsiders: stock analysts, major customers (Wal-Mart installs Core Group members at key suppliers), bankers, institutional investors, politicians, labor leaders, and even outside agitators (at Royal Dutch/ Shell, some activists became so persistent and capable at mobilizing public opinion after the Brent Spar and Ken Saro-Wiwa incidents that some insiders regarded them as Core Group members).

The size of the Core Group can be huge, or it can be tiny. Quite a few "new economy" and Internet businesses perished in the late 1990s because they tried to use Core Group status to attract employees. They distributed so many stock options and other perquisites that they created an enormous de facto Core Group that the cash flow of the business could not support.

Those are just a few ways of categorizing Core Groups by membership. But you could also categorize them by their recurring behaviors. There could be a Core Group catalog bestiary, listing the types of patterns that occur in organizations large and small, public and private, time and time again. For example:

- **The Deceptively Subservient Bureaucracy:** A long-standing Core Group remains in place forever while putative bosses come and go. The goal of the enterprise is to protect the position and status of the civil service, tenured faculty, established executive layer, or whoever the bureaucracy might be. The British writer and television producer Anthony Jay (who once wrote a book called *Management and Machiavelli*) satirized this dynamic in his 1980s television series *Yes, Minister*, in which Nigel Hawthorne played the wily obfuscator Sir Humphrey Applebee. Sir Humphrey is not a *bad* individual at heart, but he is preoccupied with the perpetual bureaucratic chess game of jockeying for allies, perks, and rank—the small gains that are almost imperceptible to outsiders but massively compelling to the cognoscenti. The minister he reports to, James Hacker, was elected on the Thatcheresque platform of cleaning up the bureaucracy. Hacker's comparative inexperience puts him at a continual disadvantage, but he wins a point or two against Sir Humphrey every third episode or so. Such are the comforts of fiction.

- **The Organization That Is Almost Too Nice for a Core Group:** Some organizations are so downright idealistic that nobody wants to overtly admit they have any power or influence over anyone else. The net result: Everybody senses that someone else has control over the situation, but nobody talks about it out loud, and resentment builds up under the surface. Barbara Waugh, who wrote the wonderful organizational book *The Soul in the Computer*, worked at one nonprofit institute once where, she says, "the students thought the staff was the Core Group, the staff thought the board was, and the board thought the staff was. The center had no center." Nonetheless, there is always a Core Group. Sometimes it can explicitly be established (through collective conversation) as the board, staff, and students together as a whole. Otherwise, one or two people will tend to manipulate their way into the Core, influencing decisions to go their way while maintaining the fiction that everyone is equal.

- **The Indigestible Acquisition:** Lockheed-Martin buys General Dynamics, AOL buys Time-Warner, AT&T buys NCR, Microsoft buys Vermeer, or anyone buys anyone, and there turn out to be significant groups of old-heritage people who simply cannot be brought into the new company. The acquired Core Group remains in place, refusing to be dissolved, still influencing (at least) the people in the acquired part of the business. Often there's no real substantive reason for the difference, only that "our guys" lost and "your guys" won. But that doesn't make the acquisition any more digestible. Gradually, the people of various "heritages" grant legitimacy to each others' Core Group members, and then the differences subside somewhat. Or, if not, then the organizations split again.

- **The Hidden Cabal:** In Joseph Heller's novel *Catch-22*, a postal clerk named Ex-Private-First-Class Wintergreen controlled the Army by meddling with the mail. Every large organization has its Wintergreen equivalent: an administrative assistant or CEO's secretary who is privy to top-secret information and manages (if nothing else) access to the top of the hierarchy. I've noticed that a myth crops up in many organizations about these people. They're the ones secretly running the place, simply because they control the Core Group—aren't they? But in actuality, only a very few secretaries or aides ever rise to a position of genuine Core Group status, where the organization is paying attention to their perceived intentions and directions. More likely, they stand as gatekeepers to the real Core Group members—aware of everything that happens but influencing almost none of it. Meanwhile, behind the scenes, there probably *are* some quiet influencers who know how to shift the direction of people's decision-making and covertly do it. But they're more likely to be members of informal professional networks, like financial or engineering people who met back in school, pass information to each other behind the scenes, and help each other get recognized as important. (I've been told that in some major South African corporations, two ethnically oriented leagues—the Afrikaans Bröderbund and the English-speaking Freemasons—have played this kind of covert role, to the point where managers who wanted to get something done had to essentially clear it with both groups. Since their members detested each other, that wasn't always easy.)
- **The Charismatic Random Star** pattern, often seen in consulting firms, nonprofits, and small partnerships, generally centers around one or two mercurial rainmaking Core Group members who have license to be indulged. The rest of the organization, with varying levels of resentment and amusement, scurries to keep up, tying

up loose ends and complaining about the lack of stability, never quite knowing how they will be regarded or treated by the stars themselves—or by each other. They continually collude, of course, in the same randomness that they complain about. Recently, there was a cash-flow crisis at a consulting firm. The bookkeeper had badgered all the consultants to turn in their billing sheets on time, but no one confronted the most senior partner, who habitually turned in his time sheets late. "You mean," said the partner, "everybody is being told to clean up their act except me?" That was correct. "Everyone else gets someone to ride herd on them," he complained. "I have to do it for myself."

- **Silos, Stovepipes, and Chimneys:** W. Edwards Deming and others in the quality movement often spoke of "sub-optimization," in which different parts of the organization (say, operations, marketing, and finance) all ignore or compete with each other. As a result, they spend more time coping with the problems they cause each other than reaching their collective goals. This is often seen as a symptom of poor organization design, and perhaps it is. But it has more fundamental roots in Core Group politeness. When Core Group members continually avoid conflict by avoiding each other, then the people who report to them and watch them for signals do the same. Each part of the hierarchy, operating on its own, ultimately develops its own Core Group. The legitimacy of each then depends on how well they can show up the cluelessness and intransigence of the others. The more their functions duplicate each other, the more virulent the rivalry tends to be, and if you can get the organization to work only by getting the brand strategy gang and the brand advertising gang to align their interests, then you've got quite a challenge on your hands.

Indeed, most Core Group dynamics tend to replicate themselves all through the organization this way. If the Core Group is fractious, work teams at every level of the hierarchy fight each other. If the Core Group is collegial, so are its minions. At a consulting firm I once worked for, the three senior partners were known for their personality traits: one of them repeatedly tried to manage every detail (even though he knew better); another one withdrew in times of crisis and worked only on his own projects; and a third sat back, observed, and offered commentary from a distance. I joined a team of three subordinates on a new assignment, and lo and behold, I found myself repeatedly trying to manage every detail (even though I knew better). One of my colleagues withdrew in times of crisis and worked only on her own projects, and the other sat back, observed, and offered commentary from a distance.

Of course, all of these categories are gross oversimplifications. Real-world Core Group dynamics are so mutable and indistinct, so much a matter of perception and interrelationship, that a fully accurate map of the Core Group in any good-sized organization would require a three-dimensional computer program to simulate—showing dots for individuals in the organizations and lines depicting the connections and influences that link them to others. People in the Core Group might be placed closer to the center of the model. To collect this information, we'd have to tap into the mind-set of the organization's people, presumably by surveying them: "Whose interests do you consider when you make a decision?"

Even if the results of that survey were accurate, it would still provide just a snapshot of one Core Group moment. To truly get an accurate computer simulation, we would have to track all employees' perceptions and loyalties, through some futuristic brainwave-measuring implant device, and plug the data in real-time into the computer simulation. Then each of the little dots in the program, signifying individuals, would continually be in motion. At any given moment, some would move closer to the center, while others gravitated towards the periphery. Some would burn brightly, picking up more connections, while others would lose their luster. That image, impossible to really produce, would be as close as we could get, I suspect, to a genuine map of the Core Group.

In the absence of such a map, if we're going to get anywhere in influencing that organization, we need to create our own, more appropriate ways of tracking Core Groups.

Diagnostic Exercise 1

Who Really Matters Here?

The longer people work in an organization, the more attuned they become to the nuances of its Core Group: to the reasons why one person has an office near the chairman while another has chosen an office on a different floor, or the reasons why one person is continually talked about while another, seemingly at the same rank in the hierarchy, is shunned. Even junior people have *some* intuitive sense of the makeup of the Core Group. But no one penetrates all its secrets. When it comes to Core Group dynamics, no individual knows everything—not even the individuals who are in the Core Group themselves. (They don't know, for instance, the information being deliberately hidden from them.)

So if we want to tap into that knowledge, we don't want to do it individually. Let's you and I start together with a small group of people trying to achieve something around here—a sympathetic group of people, open to new understanding, ready to challenge each other when necessary, but in the nicest possible way. We'll draw on our collective awareness, intuition, and experience to create a picture of the organization that none of us could develop by ourselves.

We'll need to get some privacy. We're not ready to go public with our discoveries yet; we may never be. Probably the easiest beginning is to find an empty, secure room, and put an organization chart (like Figure 1A) up on the wall.

Now let's answer the following questions about people in the organization:

1. Thinking back to the last five major decisions we made, whose interests did we consider? About whom did we say to ourselves, "What would so-and-so think of this?"
2. Who are the people with the power to get things done—even if it means bypassing the ordinary, day-to-day, rational decision-making process?
3. Who could stop something from happening simply by raising an eyebrow or questioning it?
4. Who are the "heroes" of our organization—the larger-than-life celebrities within the organization about whom stories often circulate?

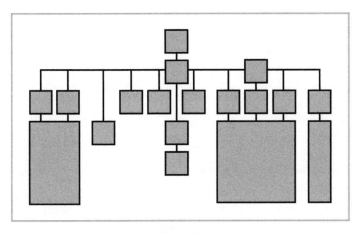

Figure 1A

5. Who makes the highest salaries? If there were a crunch, who would be the last to leave the organization?
6. Who represents key subgroups—a labor union, a plant, a function, a region?
7. Who can convene people into a meeting simply by inviting them?
8. Who is identified as the intellectual, emotional, financial, or moral heart of the organization?
9. Out of all the people we've identified, who's really in the Core Group?

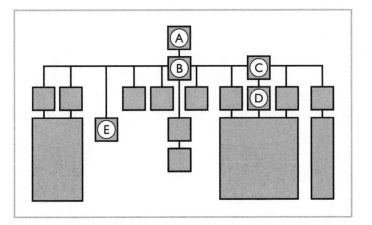

Figure 1B

. . . and that, in turn, represents a starting point for further diagnostics. Once you have a rough map like Figure 1B, the other diagnostic exercises in this book can be used to make sense of the Core Group in your organization and figure out how to intervene accordingly—to make the organization more responsive, the Core Group more effective, and the long-term results more powerful.

Diagnostic Exercise 2
How Is the Core Group Chosen?

Looking at the Core Group as a whole, what signals does it send about the preferred nature of its membership? For example . . .

- Which professions are prominent in the Core Group? Which parts of the organization have a "fast track" into the Core Group?
- How do people get into the Core Group? Is it through merit? By being recognized by existing Core Group members? By being bottlenecks to some indispensable function? Through demonstrated integrity and widespread support? Are they born (or married) into it? Are they rainmakers, bringing in business? Or are they just the kind of people that you'd want to have in your Core Group—and so would everyone else in the organization?
- What do they have that non–Core Group members *don't* have?
- Is the Core Group a microcosm for all the different professions, backgrounds, ethnicities, attitudes, and ways of thinking that are prominent in your organization? Or is it limited to one or two categories of people, with the other categories far less visible?
- How well does the Core Group represent the constituents of your organization? What does it have in common with your most important customers, investors, employees, suppliers, beneficiaries, donors, regulators, governors, and neighbors? How well-positioned is it to learn from them?
- When you see people you've never met before walking down the corridors of your workplace, what cues tell you whether they are members of the Core Group? The clothes they wear? The cars they drive? The colors of their badges? The parties and functions to which they are invited? The clubs they join? Their style of talking? The type of work assigned to them? The manner in which they are treated by others? Or simply their presence?
- Of all these factors (and more), which are the factors that truly made a differ-

ence in *your* organization? Which are the factors that *would* make a significant difference if you could somehow get them to change?

- What's the difference, in other words, between the Core Group as it is, and the unfolding potential of the Core Group as it could be?

- Would everyone (including the Core Group members themselves) agree with your interpretation? How would their view of it differ? And what's the bedrock evidence, the pure data, that everyone would agree was significant in getting these people into this role?

- One final question, just to get a sense of the atmosphere in which you will develop your awareness: Does the Core Group stand out in your organization? Does it blend in? Or does it show up only on certain occasions, like the sun coming out from behind a cloud?

CHAPTER 4

A Very Special
Kind of Love

I was happier than I've ever been in my life," wrote Gail Bentley. She was describing the three years she had spent, starting in 1997, as the CEO of a start-up Internet company called Workingweekly.com—a web portal of advice and connection for young employees trying to figure out their place in the world. "I was living the life I was born to live, and I knew it. I was challenged every day, and while I was exhausted and stressed and overworked, I was incredibly, amazingly happy."

Her children came to the office every day with her, and the other employees played with them. She took pride in being the linchpin of an enterprise that supported not just her own family, but sixty other people. She basked daily in their commitment, their appreciation, and the atmosphere of creativity that followed her around the office. She laid her head down on the pillow every night "knowing that [I] gave everything [I] had that day and [had] gotten everything life had to offer [me] that moment."

Welcome to the Core Group. There is no formal initiation, not even a celebratory lunch. There are no forms to fill out and probably no change in your official job description. But everything is different now. The organization sees you as central to its fate. In return, it is devoted to you. From now on, it will automatically pivot and twist to give you what it thinks you want and need, up to the limits of its capability. You won't even need to ask.

36

If it thinks you need work, it will find work for you. When you travel, it will make the connections easier. (One of the Royal Dutch/Shell managing directors, asked what he would miss most upon retirement, said, "The little man who comes to meet me at the plane and takes care of everything.") If you need money, it will boost your pay (as much as it can without endangering the promises it has made to other Core Group members). If your pay is already so high that you bridle at your taxes, it will manage your accounting. It may even put itself at risk for you, lending you money beyond the bounds of propriety and hiding the loans, as long as possible, from the eyes of investors, debtors, and regulators. If you have children and they need watching, it will set up a child care program. You won't even have to request it; it will be justified as a general benefit for all employees. But when your kids (and those of other Core Group members) no longer need child care, the whole program may be quietly closed down. If you do not want people to think of you as arrogant, the organization will give you opportunities to act humble (and training to help you be convincing). The more you seem to ask of your organization, the more it will do for you. And it will justify all this by claiming, in all sincerity, that it cannot afford to lose you.

It's as if the organization has fallen in love with you, a passionate, head-over-heels kind of love that is present beneath the surface of every conversation you have. The organization does all the things for you that infatuated lovers do. It anticipates your desires and needs before you've even articulated them to yourself. It exalts you; it pays attention to you. You are never far from the center of its thoughts. It is chivalrous toward you and dismissive of all others. At an outdoor party I once attended, an elderly woman sat ignored by everyone else until an elderly man whom she had just met spoke up: "Would someone please see that Sally is served?" My wife, seeing Sally brighten up, said to me, "*That's* the way a man should treat a woman." Whether or not that's true, it *is* the way an organization treats its Core Group members.

If you have ever started an organization, or if you have become part of the Core Group of an existing one, you know how exhilarating this kind of treatment can be. Far too few of us get to experience it. We hear only stories from afar in which the organization lays the world at its lover's feet, glimpses of fairy-tale-like perks and privilege.

In 1989, ITT's chief executive, Rand Araskog, published a book called *The ITT Wars: A CEO Speaks Out About Takeovers.* Some months later, a partner in a media purchasing supply firm got a call from an ITT public relations manager. The book was about to be remaindered—sold at low costs to inexpensive outlets.

"There are 25,000 copies left," said the PR manager. "We don't want Rand, or anyone else from ITT, to walk past the Strand [a New York used-book store] and see his book at the one-dollar table." The media firm purchased the books for a dollar apiece, stored them briefly, and then dumped them.

When McCaw Communications introduced its cellular telephone technology in the United States, those who knew the industry could always tell where the service would be introduced next by tracking the vacation plans of founder Craig McCaw. "Funny places like ferry parking lots and island counties, where Craig was traveling in boat or car, soon had excellent service," recalled industry observer Mark Anderson. Even today, the best way to guarantee that you'll have great cell-phone service, with no dropouts or lost calls, is to buy a home near that of a telephone company executive.

In the 1970s, William H. Whyte (the author of *The Organization Man*) studied corporations that had moved their headquarters from New York City to its suburbs during the previous ten years. Each company had conducted an elaborate relocation research study, rating and ranking the general suitability of potential locales. But Whyte was skeptical. He and his research staff plotted the location of thirty-eight relocated corporations vis-à-vis the homes of their senior executives. The average distance from the CEO's home was eight miles.

"Companies say the top man's preference becomes a factor only after the basic decision to move has been made," wrote Whyte. "The facts suggest the reverse, that it is a prime motivating factor from the beginning. The coincidence is too great to be rationalized otherwise. . . . It was in the locker rooms of the golf clubs that the most important location research may have taken place."

And so on. Mergers and acquisitions with no viable rationale except the aggrandizement of the Core Group . . . clerical staff . . . baseball season tickets . . . salmon fishing trips . . . endowed university chairs in Core Group members' names . . . parking spots . . . and (as we learned after Jack Welch's divorce case) the quiet extension of many of these perks on into retirement. They also extend down the hierarchy. As executive-compensation critic Graef Crystal has noted, when the CEO's salary goes up, so do the salaries of everyone else on the executive committee. Many of these salaries are high enough to create long-lasting dynasties: The great-great-grandchildren of many corporate senior executives will never have to work.

The consequences are so familiar by now that it's almost possible to forget how obscene they can be. Excessive executive salaries drain working capital from the enterprise, deplete the presumption that people of merit will be rewarded accordingly, extinguish morale, shortchange shareholders, and drive the rest of the organization to compensate by boosting short-term profits whatever the cost.

Core Group perks in academia and other nonprofit settings may seem trifling by comparison; as the old joke puts it, academic battles are nasty because the stakes are so low. But from a Core Group perspective, the stakes are immense. A Core Group faculty member can dominate the direction of an entire department, allocating grant money, lab space, and travel budgets—which in turn determine the professional prestige (and thus the future opportunities) of everyone in the department. One of the most prevalent perks is graduate assistants—the indentured servants of university work, whose labor is often essential to producing publishable research.

And even compared to all this, the most significant and irresistible perks are the intangible ones. Core Group members are taken seriously, in a way that few other people enjoy. They are invited to solve problems, even when they don't have any special knowledge or skill. Their solutions work (everyone sees to that). Their virtues are publicly recognized and their mistakes unseen. They are routinely credited with the insights of others. ("Nobody at Citibank was interested in anything," wrote Charles Ferguson in *High Stakes, No Prisoners*, a masterful history of the high-tech industry in the 1990s, "unless John Reed thought of it first.") Finally, and perhaps most significantly, they enjoy the considerable perk of constantly being reminded that they are doing something important. Others are doing it with them, but it remains theirs.

These are not business stories. They are love stories. They describe a very special kind of love, the kind of love that Puff the Magic Dragon had for Little Jackie Paper: a giant organism trying, with all its prodigious might, to make an individual human feel special. The perks are simply the most visible symptom of the organization's infatuated state.

For example, in the thirty-eight cases that William Whyte studied of corporate headquarter relocations to suburbia, did all those CEOs explicitly say, "I want the headquarters near my house"? Some certainly did. (I mentioned Whyte's research at a talk at the headquarters of the scenario consultancy Global Business Network, and immediately the principal founder, Peter Schwartz, put up his hand. "Of *course* I located headquarters near my house," he said. "That was one of the reasons for starting GBN in the first place.") But most of the CEOs probably didn't need to make it so explicit. The Core Group dynamics did the job for them. The people in charge of relocation, the executives who approved it, and the consultants they hired all naturally recognized that moving within eight miles of the CEO's house was a *career-enhancing* thing to do, particularly if they could make it seem unavoidable.

Not that the Core Group members put up a fight. Indeed, the more extreme the organization's love for them, the more likely Core Group members are to take it for granted and demand even more. They don't just want to be fabulously wealthy; they want to be the *most* fabulously wealthy. (Some CEOs admit to scanning other companies' annual reports to find out what kinds of salaries and perks other CEOs are getting, so they can judge how well they're being treated by their own magic dragons.)

It takes a person with an unusual caliber of mind and a remark-able willfulness to withstand an organization's love. And most people don't even see any reason to resist; indeed, those who start organizations are often motivated by the desire to have an organization in love with them for a change. (This may also be the primal impulse behind street gangs. Where else will the members of socially marginalized groups get to be part of an organization that exists, within its capabilities, to give them what they want? To be sure, the Core Group in most gangs is fairly hard to enter. It might require killing someone. But it might be the only Core Group its members will ever find that is open to them.)

You may feel a bit jealous of this kind of love if you are not in the Core Group yourself. You might find yourself saying the kinds of things that bystanders often say: "I just don't understand what General Motors sees in Roger Smith" or "what Metro-Goldwyn-Mayer sees in David Begelman." But the object of the organization's adoration may have been chosen for reasons that no one can easily understand. He or she may embody some kind of organizational shadow, some collective psychological need. (How else could anyone explain the attraction of Robert Maxwell or Al Dunlap?) Or maybe there was never a dark side. Maybe the Core Group member was simply attractive because he or she could get things *done*. And when the relationship unravels, no one can quite put their finger on the reason why. "I *still* don't understand what went wrong with that Ken Lay," says the onlooker ruefully. "He seemed like such a nice boy."

It's important to reemphasize, before we go any further, that there is nothing wrong with Core Groups, per se. In most organizations, the Core Group members are robust, intelligent, capable people. They deserve each individual perk and reward. They generally don't intend the cumulative effect when all the perks are added up, the dysfunctional feeling that some people are loved by the organization and others are not. Moreover, we don't condemn all forms of love just because people sometimes fall into dysfunctional relationships. So why should we condemn all Core Groups just because some are exploitive parasites and others are unconscious of their impact?

But that doesn't mean we should remain indifferent. For, alas, not all love stories have a happy ending. Occasionally, the organization and the love object end up living happily ever after, growing old and raising subsidiaries together. But as often as not, they get caught up in the problematic aspects of love affairs: tedium, jealousy, spite, money troubles, and the pressure of greater and greater responsibilities. Painted wings and giants' rings make way for golden parachutes and shareholder liabilities.

And sometimes the organization simply can't maintain the strength that true love requires. That's what happened to Working weekly.com's Gail Bentley. Fueled by dot-com-bubble-style venture capital, her company went bankrupt. Two million dollars in promised investments fell through, and she had to fire sixty employees in one day. The Core Group she had constructed around herself dissolved that day. She went on to write about the experience in one of her last columns for the enterprise—a grief-filled cry by a bereaved lover. She clearly missed the attention: "While most of the former Working Weekly team seem to be wonderfully supportive of each other and close, very few people call me. I check my e-mail all day, and most days it's just mailing lists." And the affection: "I try playing with my kids and I think of all the people at Working Weekly that they loved so much, that they grew up with, that they'll probably never see again."

Everywhere she went, she saw something that reminded her of the dreams she had shared with her beloved: "I see one of [our] empty green newsstand boxes, and I start thinking about how we have 100,000 magazine prototypes just sitting somewhere, and I can't get them out because we haven't paid the printer." She wondered what she did wrong, and she slogged through the day trying to pick up the pieces left behind: "Every stitch of clothes in the closet, every piece of paper to file or shred, every call that needs to be made, every step is awful and painful and reminds [me] of the way things used to be and the way they are now."

Eventually, she found a buyer for the domain name and another job for herself. She took down the essay from the Web; like many stories of broken hearts, its urgency receded over time. And so it is with people who fall out of the Core Group. They pick themselves up again and start anew. Other organizations fall in love with them after a while, in a kind of entrepreneurial version of serial monogamy.

But something more is at stake here. Serial monogamy is great for a while, but if everyone raised children that way, civilization would fall apart. The future of the species depends on having love affairs that mature into committed, mutually satisfying relationships that last long enough to generate stable families. Similarly, civilization in our time depends on having organizations last long enough to bear and raise the quality of life of the world around them. We can't do this if our Core Groups practice serial infatuation, going from boom to boom, departing at the first wave of collapse or the opportunity to sell out the stock. If we care to create substantial, long-lasting organizations with Core Groups that deserve them, we have to learn to understand why organizations become infatuated in the first place—and what great Core Groups, like great lovers, can provide in return.

Diagnostic Exercise 3

Are You in the Core Group?

- Are you visible to the organization? Do you feel that the organization sees and values you?
- If you say something significant, good or bad, do you hear it repeated until it makes its way back to you?

- Do you find the organization giving you raises, credits, promotions, and perks before you ask for them? Have you ever been surprised by someone saying, "We thought you'd be pleased," and giving you—a set of car keys? a trip? a much larger office?
- Did you receive those gestures when you were being "courted" for a job—and then have them drop away when the organization was able to take you for granted? (Maybe you're not in the Core Group after all.)
- Do you have a basic sense of well-being about where the organization is going, and why? When you think about the ideal kind of organization that you would most like to work for, is it similar to the organization where you currently work?
- Do you get hints from people throughout the organization that they would like to know what you think, but few people actually ask you?
- Is the organization in love with you? What does it find in you to love?
- And do you love it in return?

CHAPTER 5

Power and Legitimacy

By nature, I'm a fairly egalitarian-minded sort of fellow. Back when I was just starting out as a management writer, uncertain whether I'd ever be able to make a living in the field, I was hired by MIT lecturer Peter Senge to help him conceive and edit a book he was writing. It was clear how much more experienced he was than I, but I felt no unusual deference toward him. Nor did he expect any. We maintained a breezy, casual respect for each other. To be sure, he was paying my salary, but we were still basically two artisans working on a project together. When that book, *The Fifth Discipline*, became a best-seller, and when it propelled us both into an ongoing follow-up series (the *Fifth Discipline Fieldbook* series), the sense of collaborative equality only got stronger.

Imagine my surprise, then, a few years later, when I went to work for him in a formal organizational role. Peter invited me to take an editorial job at the institute he directed then, the MIT Center for Organizational Learning. As always, he was friendly and affable when I walked into his office. By now, I had been in the field several years; I was far more confident and comfortable than when Peter and I had first met.

But there were also two subtle, yet undeniable, signals that something was amiss. When I said, "Hello, Peter," my voice cracked. And when I reached to shake his hand, I realized that my palm was sweaty.

These two symptoms were the first clues I had that my relationship with Peter had changed. He had taken on a new status in my
mind—not just my boss, but the man who had founded the
"Learning Center" (as we called it), the place where I would now
be working. And indeed, as soon as I took the job, my contacts with
Peter clicked into a formal pattern that I had never experienced
with him before. When we passed, we exchanged small, respectful
nods and brief smiles. When I needed something from him, I presented the request concisely, avoiding digressions, in a manner
clearly designed to conserve his time and save me from embarrass-
ment. As a collaborator, I had argued and mused freely with him,
in a give-and-take free-for-all. Now, as an employee, I never presented him with an idea that I thought he might turn down. When
I had to solve a problem that required Peter's input, I no longer
consulted Peter himself. Instead, I consulted the mental image I
had of Peter. I grew to know this mental image much better than I
knew the actual person.

I also learned, fairly quickly, that there were other people to
keep in mind, either casually or explicitly. They included Angela
(the administrative staffer who organized the Center's most visible
service, its program of courses), Vickie (who managed Peter's
schedule), Jay and Ed (Peter's mentors at MIT, whose presence
gave the Center more credibility there), as well as Dan, Bill, and
George (three younger but important researchers). Each of these
people had an influence that could not be easily defined, nor could
it be ignored. (Some people, looking back, said Angela was never in
the Core Group at all. But then why did she have one of the largest
offices? And why did so many people connected with the Center
identify her as the living personification of it?)

Except for Peter, none of these people had formal authority over
me. They could not hire me, fire me, give me raises, or make any
formal evaluation of me. Even Peter didn't have that much authority over me, especially as my work with George on "learning histories" took on a life of its own. What, then, accounted for my sweaty
palms and cracked voice? It was the fact, pure and simple, that

Peter was no longer just a colleague. He was also a boss. In small and large ways, I continued to take his interests into account. So did everyone else at the Center. And we all, in one way or another, also perpetuated the Core Group status of Angela, Vickie, Dan, Bill, and George. Some of them were in the Core Group because of their positions; some, because of their informal roles. It didn't really matter how they got there; what mattered was that they mattered. Day after day, in all the small decisions we made, all the employees contributed to keeping these individuals more or less at the center of the Core Group.

The same is true in every organization. As employees, we cannot vote our bosses into the Core Group, as we would vote them into office in a democracy. But we *do* vote in another sense: with the quality and commitment of our decisions. While we depend on the boss for direction, the boss (and others) depend on us for legitimacy.

For example, if we enlist wholeheartedly in an individual's cause, with as much enthusiasm and commitment as we can muster, and make our decisions accordingly, then we have delegated a much stronger kind of power to them. People around the organization will see, and take note of, our enthusiasm. Others may follow. Over time, this will be echoed in tangible results. And if the person we are following is credited with those results, then he or she may well be tapped for a more prominent place in the formal hierarchy. Even if that doesn't happen, he or she may develop a reputation for fostering commitment. If enough other people also respond with commitment, then he or she may even start to "outrank" people who are more senior in the formal hierarchy, at least in the ability to get things done. We have contributed to putting that person closer to the Core Group.

On the other hand, if we comply grudgingly with commands from our boss, we tend to engender an atmosphere of resentment and ennui. People notice that, too. They also notice the relatively meager results that we produce, and the lack of commitment that exists around the boss. All of this makes an impression, and his or her Core Group status grows weaker.

I don't mean that people literally choose their bosses or formally place people in the Core Group. The boss has "positional" power based on his or her spot in the hierarchy. He or she can compel people to follow orders. Bosses without much legitimacy have a number of different ways to get people to do things: Incentives, discipline, threats, rewards, bullying, pleading, and bribery are all popular methods. But none of these, in the long run, are as effective as legitimacy, and they all carry a cost. Especially in crises, it's the legitimate leaders, not the positional leaders, who carry the day. This is true even in the most highly authoritarian organizations, like the military, where officers quickly learn that they cannot command through positional authority alone. Young American Army lieutenants, fresh from ROTC training, discovered this in the Vietnam War when they tried to pull rank. They soon became known as "FNGs." The "NG" stood for "New Guy." The veteran troops razzed them, disobeyed them, and even killed them sometimes.

If legitimacy seems like a thin, evanescent, and relatively unimportant kind of power compared to power of authority, that's in part due to long-standing attitudes about the way power ought to work. In both Eastern and Western traditions of political thought, the inescapability of force and authority is one of the most recurring themes. If it isn't God we must obey, it's the Gods; or the King; or the Emperor; or the Lord; or the Church; or the parents; or the General Will. And there is no choice in a feudal society or tyranny, where power is physical and absolute. But in today's world, at least in democratic societies, authority is relative. We carry our bosses around in our heads.

Why, then, if commitment and legitimacy are so important, do most people in organizations simply go along and "ratify" the status quo? Why do we legitimize bosses who don't really deserve legitimacy, simply because they are our bosses? I think there are two reasons. First, we tend to do what we think we're supposed to do, because we don't think we have a choice. We believe our jobs, incentives, and rewards depend on it.

But there is also a deeper reason. It has to do with cognitive complexity. We legitimize the status quo because to do otherwise taxes our capability.

Consider, for example, the tactic of the "work-to-rule" strike. In this strike, union members show up at work and obey all commands. They follow the rules as precisely as possible. But they suspend all personal commitment, including the judgment they ordinarily exercise. If the rules say that in an emergency the operations people must stop and confer, they do exactly that—for *every* emergency, including the ones they know full well how to deal with without stopping. Several years ago French railroad engineers, forbidden by law from striking, conducted a work-to-rule action in which they painstakingly inspected the safety of every bridge they crossed, just as procedures demanded. No trains ran on time.

Work-to-rule strikes are enormously effective. But they are rare, even in the most intransigent labor-management situations, because they are exhausting. It is terribly hard to make all the decisions. Most of the time, most of us would rather just act in favor of those who have legitimacy in our minds, even if we feel antagonistic to them. It is enormously freeing to have an image in our minds

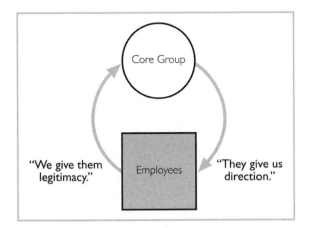

The ongoing implicit bargain between the Core Group members and the rest of the organization, in which legitimacy is exchanged for cognitive simplicity.

of "what the boss would think about this" instead of having to figure it out from scratch each time.

In other words, while the Core Group depends on us for legitimacy, we depend on them for direction. "Direction" doesn't mean control, but the simplicity that allows us to act without having to pay too much attention. This is why many of us in organizations tend to be narrower and less experimental with our power than the Core Group members themselves sometimes expect. "Take initiative!" say the bosses. "Participate in innovation!" As employees, we respond by saying, "Just tell me what to do and I'll do it." Or, "I only want to get back to my desk."

Sometimes employees grant legitimacy to people whose physical type resembles the existing Core Group members, just because that's the way it's always been done around here. (*Dilbert* cartoonist Scott Adams lampooned this tendency by labeling fast-trackers as people who succeed only because they have "executive-style hair.")

Some people, who are tapped to be Core Group members early in their careers, enjoy this kind of legitimacy thereafter. As they're invited to key meetings, given plum assignments, and otherwise favored and fast-tracked, they gradually walk a bit taller and act a bit more authoritative. People recognize the form, if not the substance, of leadership in them, and that increases their legitimacy still further. Meanwhile, nobody thinks to train or develop them systematically; they move from assignment to assignment, never staying put long enough to fully learn how the operations work at the ground level. By the time they reach the top of the hierarchy, they are arrogant, unchallengeable, ignorant—and dangerous.

There is a similar problem with organizational diversity at many companies; executives may unconsciously keep women and people of color out of the Core Group, but everybody else in the organization unconsciously (or consciously) colludes with them in doing so. (We give nicknames to women prominent in the hierarchy, for instance: the "Ice Queen," or the "Iron Maiden.") That's why the "glass ceiling" is so hard to break through, and why breaking through requires not just steady force, but skill and the ability to talk safely about Core Group dynamics. (For more about this, see Chapter 13.)

I've noticed that different types of organizations tend to confer legitimacy on different types of leaders. I once met an editor at a small, community newspaper who continually snapped at his subordinates. Finally, one of his assistants sent him an e-mail with an ultimatum: "Don't you ever tell me to shut up again like that." The next day, she walked in on him while he was chewing out another staffer. He snarled at that person, "Screw you!" and then without missing a beat turned to the assistant and said, "And you—shut up!"

In a commodities-trading company, this wouldn't have affected the boss's legitimacy at all. By lunchtime, both the boss and the assistant would have bragged about it around the company. But at this small, community newspaper, it had a very different effect. Sure, he apologized. Sure, she forgave him. Sure, both of them continued to work there. But both knew that his legitimacy had been eroded. In fact, the word went around the office: There were only a few more lapses permitted to him, or he would, in effect, be kicked out of the Core Group. He would no longer be able to get anyone to do what he asked them to.

In the end, the more conscious we become of the way that we carry our bosses in our heads—the more conscious we become of our ability to confer legitimacy—the more power we can exert in the way we do it.

We may not be able to stop obeying some bosses. (Eventually, my voice stopped cracking at the MIT Learning Center, but I never fully lost my organizationally inspired deference toward Peter Senge, even after I stopped working there.) We will still be subject to the fear of losing our jobs, and we will still be tempted to follow the path of least resistance and continue promoting those with "executive-style hair."

But at the very least, we *can* begin to consciously choose to confer legitimacy on others. And we can set ourselves up to earn legitimacy from others. What people conventionally call "leadership" is, in fact, the ability to get others to confer legitimacy on us—and thus to get others to put us in the Core Group.

Building legitimacy is frequently overlooked as a way to influence organizations, but in the end, it is probably the most effective way—especially when it is grounded in your own authentic persona. Consider, for instance, the story of Linda Pierce. When I first met her, at the MIT Learning Center, she had just taken a job as the executive advisor to the Leadership Council at the Shell Oil Company based in Houston. Shell Oil had just embarked on a wide-ranging organizational change program that they called "transformation," and that had brought them to seek the help of Peter Senge (among others). Linda's job, with no staff except a couple of assistants, was to advise the top ten leaders of the company, to take notes at their meetings, and to help design the next round of change they wanted to create.

The job was as much a potential trap as an opportunity. Linda, then in her late fifties, had spent her entire career at Shell. She was a woman rising in staff positions in an extremely hierarchical oil company run by mostly male technologists. She had trained herself to keep cool and reserved in the face of crisis and provocation. And in the past three years of layoffs and cutbacks, that training had been tested. Furthermore, the job she had was unprecedented: working full-time with all ten men at the core of Shell Oil's Core Group. All of them were formidable; they had each inspired their share of sweaty palms and cracked voices. It would have been natural for anyone in that role to fall back into a reticent position as assistant, taking notes at Leadership Council meetings and carrying out specific commands. In fact, some of the executives of the company expected Linda to do just that.

She didn't. She took a stand on behalf of the changes—both arguing for the best possible company that Shell Oil could be and speaking frankly (but diplomatically) about the current problems in the company. She did this with the Leadership Council members, but more important, she did it with other people throughout the company, building on the years' worth of relationships she had cultivated, and reaching out to others she considered important (including those she hadn't quite gotten along with in the past). Nobody "appointed" her to this role in any formal way. But as it happened, she knew a lot of people; she was what social network theorists call a "hub" or a "connector": someone who is skillful and natural at cultivating networks. She was the kind of person—unflappable and courteous, but steely-solid when she believed in something—whom people naturally respected. Nor were most of the Leadership Council members approachable or easy to talk to. So when people had a problem or a concern about transformation, they went to Linda first. And when people had a decision in mind that related to transformation, they asked themselves: Well, what would Linda think was the right thing to do? They conferred a legitimacy upon her that even the Leadership Council could not confer.

How do I know this? Mostly, from conversation with other people at Shell Oil, and a few clues from her own autobiographical story (which I helped edit for Peter Senge's anthology *The Dance of Change*). But there was also the time when we were working on a project together, for which, at my request, she had asked a few Shell managers to spend two or three hours taking part in a workshop. Then, worrying about the extra hassle I had provoked, I telephoned her with second thoughts. "I guess we don't need these people there after all," I said.

She was silent for a few moments. Then she said, "Art." There was another pause. And then: "I want to say something very deliberately to you. I realize that you don't know our company very well. I have carefully built my relationships with these people. When I ask them to do something, my reputation depends on the fact that they know it will be worthwhile. I don't want to be put in a position of canceling unless there's a good reason, because that would be like telling them their contribution is not important. So I need to know from you—is it valuable for them to be there? And if they come, can you make sure they will be able to see the value they are giving us?"

I said, "Yes, Linda. I think they should come. And I'll make sure they see it." My voice cracked. And the telephone receiver almost slipped out of my hand.

CHAPTER 6

Employees of
Mutual Consent

She always had her dignity, all the way. . . . We both knew exactly
what men are for and what they're not for.

The speaker is Julie Jacquette, a fictional nightclub singer in *Death of a Doxy*, a Nero Wolfe detective novel by Rex Stout. She is talking about a friend who has just been murdered. But she could also be speaking about organizations. If you want your dignity intact, all the way, and you're working at a modern job, then you have to know what organizations are good for, and what they are not good for.

Organizations, as we've seen, are innately set up to fall in love with the Core Group. That's what they're good for.

But what, then, if you're among the ninety-five percent of people in most organizations who are *not* part of the Core Group? Does this mean the organization is not good for you? Does it mean giving up hope of a fulfilling job or career? Hardly. Indeed, in many ways you may be better off having a non–Core Group position, especially if you are not ready to commit your life to any particular organization.

But first you have to recognize your situation for what it is, and not be distracted by an illusory Core Group status that you don't actually share. You may have strong and satisfying relationships with individual *people* in the organization, including people in the Core Group. You may work under a banner, literal or figurative, that says, "We are all one big family here." You may have a variety of perks and benefits, ranging from an employee cafeteria to an open-door supply closet to a 401(k) plan. But even if you have all of the above, you cannot count on the organization to operate on your behalf when it doesn't have to. That is not in its nature.

The organization, as a whole, probably doesn't even see you as an individual. It sees only the results you produce and the demands you make on it. If you leave, individual people may miss you, but once again, the organization will not notice. It will simply fill the vacuum left by your absence. It's nothing personal, after all, just business. Similarly, in tough times, you are subject to being downsized. Again, nothing personal, but the organization has no intrinsic reason to protect you.

In short, if you are not a Core Group member, then to the organization, you are a transactional employee, or (to use the term I prefer) an employee of mutual consent. Your job is defined by an implicit or explicit contract, a basic agreement between you and your employer. You may be asked to provide a level of commitment and interest beyond simply showing up, but both you and your employer know that, underneath the rhetoric, you have the right to withhold your commitment anytime, so long as you do a satisfactory amount of work. And the organization has the right to promote, demote, deploy, and discard you (within limits set by the contract). Either side can break off this relationship at any time (subject to terms of your agreement).

Core Group members, of course, have contracts too, but their contracts are formalities, secondary to the organization's willingness to please them. (Some Core Group members, keenly aware of the fact that their Core Group status may be temporary, take advantage of that status to negotiate great contracts for themselves.) You, by contrast, have a job in which the contract (implicit or not) is everything. You probably have to bargain for (or design) every perquisite and promotion you get, because the organization is keenly aware of the advantage it has in getting the most out of you for the least investment. (Another word for this advantage is "productivity.") Even if the organization is basically good-hearted, you cannot expect it to watch out for you. Most of its members don't have the space or time to pay much attention to you, except on an individual basis. Organizationally, they are all too busy watching the Core Group.

It may sound harsh to say that organizations have merely a transactional relationship with their employees. That implies they don't care about their employees, except as objects to be exploited. But a clear, coherent transaction turns out to be a much more solid foundation for a working, mutually beneficial relationship than an illusory Core Group relationship. People can have tremendous, highly fulfilling careers as employees of mutual consent.

Organizations *are* good for something else besides fulfilling the perceived priorities and desires of the Core Group. They are natural amplifiers of human capability. They are innately set up for allowing people to act together, to produce things and experiment at a scale that would otherwise be unfeasible. You don't have to be in the Core Group to take advantage of this. Organizations are often eager, once you show you are capable of taking some of their resources out for a spin, to let you see what you can do with them.

Your challenge is not to protest against the Core Group's existence, but to become more conscious of the dynamics of your particular organization, until you can see more clearly the choices you have: to find a route into the Core Group yourself (if that's possible and it fits your own temperament); to leave for a different organization in which you feel more fulfilled; to start an organization of your own (and thus create your own Core Group); or to build an effective career as a transactional employee, taking advantage of the myriad ways in which working for an organization can improve your life and work.

It's relatively easy to accept this reality intellectually. But it's often hard to accept it emotionally—especially if you're the kind of person who wants to invest yourself wholeheartedly in anything you do and be rewarded commensurate with that investment. Your family made play fulfilling; school made learning fulfilling; college made higher learning fulfilling; why shouldn't your employer do the same? And you have a point. Work *should* be fulfilling. Life is better when you can be wholehearted about it.

But if you're not careful, this yearning for a wholehearted work opportunity can pull you directly into the trap of "Core Group envy": continual covetousness of the Core Group relationship you don't have and may never have, resentment of those who have it, and a keen sense of betrayal by your organization and your peers. I have known people who spent their entire careers mourning the attention or recognition they feel they deserved from the larger organization, and responding in petty, passive-aggressive ways: for instance, scheduling meetings for Core Group members that will be obvious wastes of time, but that no one can exit without enormous loss of face. There is much more power and dignity available to you in embracing the options that you have as an employee of mutual consent.

To be sure, being an employee of mutual consent requires some toughness that a Core Group member doesn't need. Betty Lehan Harragan was probably the first management writer to spell this out, in her classic 1976 book for women entering the corporate world, *Games Mother Never Taught You.* The basic premise of the book was forged during Harragan's twenty years as a copywriter at J. Walter Thompson and a moonlighting copywriter/speechwriter for a series of industry associations. Men, she realized, understood (in part from all their years playing team sports) the innate "mutual consent" nature (she called it "detachment") of corporate culture. Women, just entering the workforce for the first time en masse, did not get this, and women's naiveté thus allowed the men to take advantage of them.

In the 1970s, Harragan counseled scores of underpaid women in staff positions who hadn't been given raises in years and were afraid to ask for them. "There was a recession," she later recalled. (Interviewed in her Manhattan apartment, she had an acerbic wit and hearty laugh that reminded me of Phyllis Diller.) Women were shunted into "nice little staff jobs that were a total dead end." Or they were treated as glorified secretaries, even though they were in managerial posts. In those jobs, she said, "You'd do all the work for someone else, who got all the credit. You'd see people hired at twice the money, and promoted way ahead of you, who didn't know how to run the place. And if you knew how, you'd be told, 'Go help him.' "

Something crystallized for her around 1974, during a shared car ride from New York to Detroit. She was heading, with three other professional women, to a National Organization of Women convention in support of the Equal Rights Amendment. The women began talking about their jobs, the ways in which they were taken advantage of, and the promises that their employers had made to treat them better in the future. In Michigan, too, a group of male state legislators had promised to vote for ratifying the amendment, and Harragan suddenly realized that they were going to break their promise. "We're going to lose this amendment," she said. "Because we don't understand the way the system works." She went on to explain that it was terribly naive to expect anyone in organizations to "do the right thing" just because they espoused it. Of course, she was right about the ERA; it was voted down across the country by many of the legislators who had promised to defend it.

By the time it failed, Harragan was back in New York, teaching a course called "Corporate Politics" at a new independent program called Womanskool. Because her students were so discomfited by the term "corporate politics," she changed the course title to "Things Mother Never Taught You." A publisher heard about the course by word of mouth and approached her about writing a book, on the condition that she change the title from "Things" to "Games."

In her book, Harragan describes how to bargain for advantage, approaching the organization not as a community with your interests at heart, but as a different kind of game whose rules had to be learned. Consider, for instance, her advice on asking for a raise:

> One inviolate rule of management is to never give away money, which is understandable when money is the lifeblood of the organism. Players have to trick [the organization] out of it, so the game is eternal between em-

ployer and employee. The overriding rule for all players is
get as much as you can because that's the objective of the
game and it's taken for granted that all players know it.

If you've never tried approaching an organization asking for as
much as you can (or at least as much as you deserve), you should
experiment with it, perhaps during your next raise request. Asking
for "as much as you can" feels disloyal and contentious, especially
if you're the kind of person who has always expected organizations
to take care of you. But it is remarkably liberating when you try it,
and better for the organization as well. You may get turned down,
or bargained down to a lower position, but you will not get penalized. In a transactional relationship, you've simply demonstrated
that you understand the rules of the game, and you'll be appreciated for being savvy about them.

In addition, for employees of mutual consent, it is a natural way
to demonstrate your worth to the organization. A single employee
who bargains hard, and delivers, is far more useful to the organization in the long run than an office full of employees who wait for
approval and nurturance, and compensate with passive-aggressive
resentment when they don't get it. Harragan's book is full of this
kind of tough, unsentimental awareness. Underlying it all is the
basic premise that, although the organizations we work for are
powerful, as employees of mutual consent, we remain responsible
for our own fates within them.

This premise was most shocking of all to Betty Harragan's early
audiences. Inevitably, someone in her class would ask: "But aren't
you giving in to the system? Don't we want to try to change it?"
Harragan's voice (as she later mimicked it to me, at least) took on a
pitying tone, and she would ask: "But what do you want to change
it to?" And there was never any answer. (Personally, I think there
are some answers. There just weren't enough good examples in the
mid-1970s. But now there are. See Chapter 12, "The Expanded-
Core-Group Organization.")

It was only after publishing her book in 1976 that Harragan discovered she had an audience of male readers as well. "The takeover thing," she told me in the early 1990s, "has made a lot of men see that they don't know how these games are played. They can work so hard all of their lives, give their all to a company, and then have someone decide to sell them out—and be out of a job through no fault of their own."

In other words, corporations had learned through the 1980s that they could thrive, in the short term at least, by treating their employees of mutual consent as disposable entities. Onlookers interpreted this to mean that corporate loyalty was "dead," when in fact the transactional nature of employee status was simply coming to the fore. Corporate loyalty was still alive wherever Core Group members recognized that they would benefit from it in the long term.

In 1997 Tom *(In Search of Excellence)* Peters announced a new strategy for employees of mutual consent, the "brand called 'You.'" Good riddance to company loyalty, he said. It had always been a kind of indentured servitude anyway, a vestigial piece of baggage left over from the days of hidebound bureaucracies. Instead, he exhorted his audiences to package on-the-job personae for themselves—to find those attributes that, with a little buffing up, could comprise their own unique selling proposition, and then accentuate those qualities into a continuous presence that people want to buy. "Make it useful," he said, "stick to it, and go where you get the best deals."

It sounds like the best strategy for an employee of mutual consent, doesn't it? But, unfortunately, the strategy doesn't work for most of us. Maintaining a *personal* brand is all-consuming; it means applying the same rigorous, locked-in discipline to your life that Coca-Cola applies to its secret formula and bottle shape. In a person, we call this kind of obsessive behavior "shameless self-promotion." It's no coincidence that notable "brand-called-me"–style personalities—Martha Stewart, Donald Trump, Oprah Winfrey, Lee Iacocca, Geraldo Rivera, and Tom Peters himself—morph so easily into caricatures of themselves.

Furthermore, as brand-called-me people proliferate in organizations, they face competition from each other. A few early adopters will find terrific niches, inside or outside their companies, to dominate. For everybody else, the brand-called-you will be a ticket not to fame, but to obscurity—going from one work situation to another, never able to feel at home anywhere.

There is a much better approach for employees of mutual consent: a strategy not of blind loyalty to the organization, but genuine friendship with it. Like all friendships, this is a stance of mutual admiration, respect, enjoyment of each others' presence, and a modicum of care for each others' welfare. You can be friends with an organization if you genuinely believe that, because it exists, your life is better, and so is the world around it. But friendships cannot be entered into out of need or dependency. The organization and you can be friends only if you are on an equal footing. Exactly what that means, and how to achieve it, is the subject of Part 4 of this book.

But first, let's consider the challenge faced by people within the Core Group. There, too, the channels of power and authority are not quite what they seem to be.

Part 2

Leading
the Core
Group

CHAPTER 7

A Core Group
Way of Knowledge

I f behind every great organization there is a great Core Group, then what makes great Core Groups great? What can the people at the heart of an organization, or at the top of its hierarchical structure, do to foster greatness? Is there something that the best organizations crave and demand from their Core Groups, something that only a healthy Core Group can provide?

There is, in every case, an essential form of knowledge held by the Core Group. The Core Group members themselves may not actually possess this knowledge as individuals. But they set the context that establishes this knowledge as significant. There are two parts that fit together neatly: the knowledge of the problem to be solved, shared by every organization of its kind, and each organization's unique way of solving that problem, which constitutes its own distinctive edge.

For example: Winemakers must develop an enormous base of knowledge about the problems to be solved: Grapes must be cultivated and harvested, varieties must be chosen and blended, the wine must be pressed, fermented, bottled, packaged, and marketed. Staff must be chosen and cultivated, land must be financed and tended, the winery's reputation must be overseen, and taxes must be paid. All wineries face these challenges. But French and American wineries, as anthropologist Mary Douglas points out, solve them in characteristically different ways, requiring very different kinds of knowledge.

The French winemaking guilds have developed their knowledge over centuries. Each chateau specializes in one or two grapes, submitting their vintages to tasting by a local community of experts, grounded deeply in the tradition of place. California wineries, by contrast, began to rival the French only in the 1970s. They never learned to duplicate the depth of French viticulture, but they learned ways to produce and market diverse types of wine under one label, in a way that the French never matched. The Americans solved the winemaking problem so differently than the French had that it changed the classification of wines themselves: from regional (Bordeaux, Burgundy, Loire, and Rhine) to varietal, by type of grape (Zinfandel, Gamay, and Sauvignon).

In every organization, the Core Group symbolizes power and influence. But in a great company, the Core Group also symbolizes knowledge—the unique knowledge held by each company or organization, distinct from all others. French winery Core Groups each embody a traditional core of knowledge descended through generations, each regionally distinct. American winery Core Groups each embody a core of knowledge established through innovation and marketing, each distinctly tied to the predispositions of the Core Group members.

The importance of this latter organization-specific kind of knowledge has often been noted by management writers and thinkers. Peter Drucker refers to the comparative advantage of making knowledge workers productive; Gary Hamel and C. K. Prahalad write of "core competence." The preeminent historian Alfred D. Chandler, Jr., surveying the full complement of modern organizations from the railroads to biotechnology, argues that the most successful are those with a solid and impregnable "integrated learning base," which is the term I prefer. Some of this knowledge is tacit (held only in people's ingrained habits and assumptions); some is explicit (written down in manuals and passed on from one employee to the next).

The part that many writers overlook, however, is the symbolic importance of a Core Group that maintains the significance of the knowledge and its link with the organization. Even if there are whole aspects of the integrated learning base that the Core Group members know very little about as individuals, they are ultimately responsible for it. There will always be some people in the organization who embrace knowledge for its own sake, but the prevailing body of organizational members can take it seriously only when they see the Core Group paying attention to it.

Why, for example, do only a handful of Coca-Cola executives have access to the Atlanta bank safe-deposit box where the original Coke formula is kept? Why is it limited to the crème de la Core Group? It's not just to keep people from stealing it. (I mean, could the formula be *that* hard to reverse-engineer? And if someone *did* steal it, how could they possibly market it in any sustainable way?) As long as the formula is sacrosanct, people who work for Coca-Cola (including the bottlers and distributors) know that the unique knowledge about Coke's taste, knowledge that no other soft drink company can claim, is still held closely by the Core Group. And so, therefore, is all the other critical knowledge about Coke's solutions to its business challenges.

Pepsi, meanwhile, has its own integrated learning base—its skill at marketing to young adults and other demographic segments, for example—that Coca-Cola can't match, because Coca-Cola never learned how to do things the same way. Similarly, if there is room for both Toyota and Ford in the automobile industry, it's because each has its own form of innovation and savoir faire that the other cannot match. Ford, which is struggling to rebuild its quality and reliability practices as I write this, will probably do so, but it will never, no matter how hard it tries, match Toyota's methods for mass-producing high-quality cars to order quickly, methods that have been developed through years of collaborative learning by production and marketing people. On the other hand, Toyota will probably never match Ford's ability, honed through the years, of pulling an archetypally mythic new model out from seemingly nowhere: the Model T, the Thunderbird, the Mustang, the Taurus, the Lincoln Town Car, the Explorer. Why is Toyota focused one way and Ford another? Because of the preoccupations of both company's Core Groups.

When the Core Group fails to embrace some form of knowledge wholeheartedly, the company as a whole never really learns it. In his book *Inventing the Electronic Century*, Alfred Chandler describes how Philips and Sony essentially invented the compact disk together, and reaped enormous profits. Then the Dutch electronics company Philips, whose "integrated learning base" (as Chandler calls it) was highly grounded in technical engineering, invested billions in the Digital Video Disk Interactive, an ingenious but superfluous device for playing games and showing pictures on home television sets. They just couldn't seem to stop pouring money in; their Core Group, while paying lip service to the need to develop a market, was visibly far more interested in the technology for its own sake. If they built it, the market would come.

But it didn't. Philips ultimately wrote off $6 billion in DVD-i investment. In the mid-1990s, drained of cash, the company had to license its manufacturing to Matsushita and Toshiba—a very bad move. Manufacturing new technologies is a high-learning endeavor: Companies gain expertise, especially in the first few years of a new production process, that gives them a dramatic edge over competitors. Now Philips' rivals had that edge—which they promptly used to lower the costs of CDs and DVDs and undercut Philips' existing manufacturing position. Philips' consumer electronics business, which had once seemed like it would dominate the industry, dwindled in the 1990s to almost nothing.

"It's extraordinary," says Professor Chandler, who knows a good business epic when he sees one. "It's just a wonderful story." Wonderful, that is, if you're not a Philips executive or shareholder.

An integrated learning base does not merely include secret technical formulas, or patents and trade secrets for that matter, but an embedded awareness of the market, the partnerships, the regulations, the aspirations, and the management techniques, so ingrained and deep that it becomes second nature to the people of the organization. It also includes deep sensitivity to the patterns of decision-making and relationship within an organization. A great

Core Group, as Roger Saillant (the CEO of Plug Power) has noted, is tuned in to the professional ambience of the organization in the same way that a good conductor can listen to a symphony orchestra and hear that the piccolo is coming in just a little too soon or the violin is a little too loud.

That's why you can't transplant a manager like, say, John Sculley from Pepsi-Cola to Apple Computer and expect competence in selling sugar water to translate into competence in selling computers. The executive may understand the language; he or she may even be able to publish a successful book about the transition, or engineer a coup that removes the founder. Sculley did both. But he or she had better be humble, because there's an enormous learning curve ahead.

Nonprofits have integrated learning bases, too. The World Wildlife Fund excels at funding conservation projects, almost like venture capitalists. Greenpeace is highly skilled at pulling off bold and interesting stunts and then following through with negotiation and organizing. The Environmental Defense Fund is a group of savvy deal-makers who know how to find leverage behind the scenes.

I didn't fully understand the importance of an integrated learning base until midway through writing this book, when I saw the consequences of a breakdown firsthand—as a customer. For years, I've flown Delta Air Lines regularly, in part because of the remarkable quality of service on the part of their ticket agents. A passenger's feeling of comfort and safety depends as much on the ticket agents as on anyone in the air; it's often on the ground, when you're struggling to make a connection or switch a flight, that you *really* need a home away from home. Every airline has its own on-the-ground personality, which stems directly from the ways they recruit and train their staff, and the design of the computer systems and management approaches that support them. Hospitality on the ground has been a key part of Delta's integrated learning base, as you might expect from a corporation with roots in the southern United States and a long tradition of close-knit employee-management relationships.

In summer 2002, however, amidst a complex trip involving a

family emergency, my wife and two of our three preschool-age daughters got caught in traffic on the way to the airport. They reached the ticket counter a few minutes too late to catch their flight. Delta's ticket agents were abrupt and dismissive to my wife; worse still, they failed to tell her about another Delta flight which would have been almost as good. Needing to get home quickly, she switched to a Continental flight. Two days later, when I flew home with our third daughter, Delta's agents failed to tell me about a critical connection; I also flew Continental home. These two unnecessary Continental flights cost us almost five thousand dollars.

"Why do you keep flying with those people?" my wife said to me, and I didn't have a good answer.

I only found out the full extent of what had happened when I began to ask around among Delta's own staff people and contacts in the company. "You have every right to be upset," one mid-level Delta supervisor told me. "It's been happening more and more." Like most American airlines, Delta had laid off thousands of people after the World Trade Center attack on September 11, 2001; many were experienced ticket agents and supervisors who took early retirement. Unfortunately, these were the people who carried the institutional memory of the enterprise—they knew how to help customers navigate difficult hurdles, for instance. The new hires, who were paid less than their counterparts at the security checkpoints, were being put in place hurriedly after very little training. It was all they could do to get people checked in.

Something similar had happened once before to Delta in the mid-1990s, when customer service suffered after a severe bout of downsizing; the company's board had ultimately forced CEO Ronald W. Allen to quit. Now it was happening again, and apparently I wasn't the only long-term customer waiting, with bated breath, to find out how they'd handle the challenge this time.

All of this, of course, is taking place within the context of the collapse of the conventional airline hub-and-spoke system, and new price and service competition from no-frills carriers like Southwest Airlines and JetBlue. The only way out for airlines like

Delta is by building on their distinctive knowledge base. To some extent, Delta's managers realize this; they are promoting kiosk-based check-ins, a highly improved website, and an expanded form of code-sharing and booking-sharing with other airlines.

But suppose they took the cost-cutting challenge as a way to fully tackle the customer service conundrum. Suppose, for instance, they assumed that anyone with a full-fare ticket should get business-class-like on-ground service. They might redesign the entire check-in process so that, instead of waiting in lines at all, patrons sat in a check-in lounge sipping drinks (bought from Delta's concierge) while ticket agents roved among them with portable computer scanners. Suppose they reconfigured their computer system to simplify the codes so that they could allow flight changes without hassle or penalty. Gate agents, staring at their screens, would seem less like harried computer-system-fighters and more like confident web-surfers. They might add wireless Internet service for frequent flyer members, so anyone with a Delta relationship could log on to the Web (or check e-mail) while waiting for flights or on the plane. In short, they would reconceive the atmosphere of privilege and on-the-ground comfort that is currently extended to high-mileage frequent fliers; it would now be extended to anyone who flew Delta instead of another airline. In effect, this would represent a redesign of Delta as (in part) a premium airline for savvy travelers. If they organized it right, the costs would more than be made up for in people switching from other airlines, particularly if they were allowed to book connections on competitors' flights, but with their own on-the-ground service.

This is one thing that Delta can do that Southwest and JetBlue cannot; those airlines know how to turn a plane around in twenty minutes, but not how to provide an atmosphere of privilege for experienced businesspeople. Because many on-the-ground irritations stem from airport infrastructure that is beyond the control of any one airline, they'd have to think about them unconventionally. Which, in turn, would further deepen the airline's integrated learning base.

And there would be other advantages as well. As airplane manufacturing costs fall and air traffic control systems get more powerful, airlines as we know them are evolving into far more flexible "air taxi" services with smaller planes deployed at will. Airlines won't just match passengers to flight schedules; they'll schedule flights to match passenger requests. It could happen as early as, say, 2005. Full-fledged carriers will probably resist this at first, in the same way that the recording industry resisted Napster, Kazaa, and other vehicles for downloading music on the Internet. But the airlines will come around. An airline with a truly great ticket agent–oriented integrated learning base will have a tremendous advantage for embracing that flexibility.

The Core Group need not feel obliged to invent all of this creative new approach—or any of it—by themselves. The Core Group's role is to demonstrate, by where it pays attention, which forms of knowledge creation are significant. Once it consistently embraces a particular form of creativity in a wholehearted enough manner, then others will jump in and creative miracles will ensue. This is not a pipe dream; we're all using products today that were developed this way, including both Apple and Microsoft computer systems.

The late management researcher Elliott Jaques suggested that the critical factor for senior executives is a long-term view: the ability to deal with enough cognitive complexity to make plans and follow through on a twenty, thirty, or fifty-year time frame. Perhaps, in the end, that is the most critical component of a Core Group way of knowledge. It is necessary, but not sufficient, to understand something that no other organization's Core Group understands. One must also understand the significance of that knowledge heading out into the future—the ways that it might influence the world. For in a creative enterprise with the power of an organization, the Core Group's knowledge has an impact and influence that will last for decades.

Diagnostic Exercise 4

What Does the Organization Know?

- What is the "integrated learning base" of this organization: The distinctive competence in knowledge that exists here and nowhere else?
- What difference does that knowledge make? What does it allow this organization to do?
- Who in the Core Group is identified with that knowledge?
- Who in the organization holds that knowledge?
- What kind of knowledge could the organization develop to move into its next phase of activity?
- Who in the Core Group is aware of this? How do you know?

CHAPTER 8

Guesswork

The king had been betrayed. Henry II, twelfth-century ruler of England, had arranged for his bosom friend, fellow *bon vivant*, and military partner, the archdeacon Thomas à Becket, to become Archbishop of Canterbury. Henry assumed that, this way, he could better control the Church. But the new Archbishop suddenly got religion and shifted allegiance; he broke contact with the King, gave up his palace and rich clothing, and refused to agree to Henry's demand to have clergy tried in the royal courts. When Becket excommunicated some of the bishops who were loyal to the King, they went to Henry to complain. At dinner one evening in 1169, the King was overheard grumbling, "Shall a man who has eaten my bread [meaning Becket] insult me and all the kingdom, and not one of the lazy servants whom I nourish at my table [meaning his knights and courtiers] help me fix this affront?"

Four of the knights took Henry's remark as a command. They slipped out, rode to Canterbury, and killed the Archbishop. This murder, which the King apparently never intended, cost him nearly everything he valued: his former friend (with whom he had hoped to reconcile, and whom he missed terribly); his standing with the Church (he was immediately excommunicated); the love of the people of England (despite humbling himself in his own pilgrimage to Canterbury); the political concessions Becket had

74

spent years demanding from him (which he now granted with no further argument); and the respect of his own sons, who fought him in a series of wars that lasted the rest of his life. (And the hapless knights? Henry imprisoned them.)

Organizational theorist Charles Hampden-Turner calls this kind of phenomenon *"amplification."* When you are a Core Group member, your remarks are automatically amplified; people hear them as louder, stronger, and more commandlike than they seemed to you when you uttered them. Casually mention a product you'd like to develop someday, and discover three weeks later that someone has spent a million dollars introducing it. Wrinkle your nose when talking to a new hire, and discover, a year later, that they have been systematically steered away from attending any more meetings with you. Remark in passing, "Wouldn't it be nice if we had more open office space, so we could be more flexible?" Suddenly, contractors appear to tear down walls and soft couches get moved in. Then show up and muse, casually, "This looks awfully flaky. How do people get any work done?" The walls go back up; the furniture is sold off (or perhaps put in storage until your next casual change of heart).

Why does this happen? Because nobody knows exactly what you want. They assume it is part of their job to guess. They may be too intimidated by your Core Group status and the legitimacy you've acquired in their minds to ask. Or they may be so remotely placed from you in the hierarchy that even though they'd like to ask you, there is no clear channel for posing the question. (Sometimes the best they can do is ask someone who is perceived to be close to you, like your secretary or assistant, for clues—in which case that person develops an enormous amount of influence over the direction of your group.) You may give the impression of being too busy to approach, or you may have the mien of an inaccessible snarler. Even if you are reasonably open and even-tempered, you probably discourage inquiry, in subtle (or not-so-subtle) ways. ("I promoted you because I believed we thought alike. I guess I was wrong.") It probably takes tremendous strength of character to deliver bad news to you, because even the tiniest amount of irritation you show, even if it's not aimed at the messenger, has disproportionate impact.

Even if you are that rare kind of boss who is visibly eager to be asked for clarification, your subordinates will *still* tend to guess instead of ask. You would do the same. (Back when you were in their place, you probably gathered in the hall yourself, like your subordinates do now, and asked, "What did the boss mean by that?") They want you to experience them as trusted protectors of your interests and fixers of your problems—especially the interests and problems that you didn't know you had.

Alas, they often guess wrong—or partially wrong. Or they hedge their bets by making so many half-hearted, contradictory decisions that they might as well be wrong. Why? Because guesswork tends to pick up coarse signals—the craven, unsubtle, and cruel signals—that represent only a fraction of the actual intentions of the human beings in the Core Group. "I can talk about problems with the defense industry as a strategic challenge," said Jack Welch in an interview years ago. "Meaning that we've got to be the lowest-cost player because there are fewer contracts. And the people in the room will say, as they leave the room, 'Jack Welch hates the defense business.' Or, 'He's given up on defense as a place for us to be.' "

People's guesses, after all, are based on what *they* would want if *they* were in the Core Group, or on what they imagine the signals from the Core Group might mean. They probably have only a fraction of the information available to you, and even if they had it all, through some "knowledge management" computer system, they still wouldn't have your judgment and experience.

Meanwhile, *you* probably have only a fraction of the information available to *them*. Perhaps your last conversation with them showed that you didn't have the patience or interest to explore their perspective. Instead, you asked the kind of seemingly innocuous but cutting questions that make people feel particularly stupid: "Why doesn't this take into account what they're doing in Eastern Australia?" You may be genuinely intent on the answer; you may be trying to teach and develop them; you may be trying to bolster your authority by showing how much you know; or you may be one of those malign people who deliberately try to demoralize the people who report to you. In any case, the effect is the same: After you go back to your office, thinking little of it, the presenters huddle themselves in the corridor for another two hours, asking each other how serious you were, which *part* of Eastern Australia you want information about, and what got you interested in Eastern Australia in the first place. Most important, what should they put in the presentation next time that would induce you to give them the go-ahead they're looking for, while allowing everyone to save face?

The consequence of guesswork? Sometimes it's simply wasted effort and miscued performance. "When I worked at *Newsweek* in the late 1980s," wrote journalist/weblogger Mickey Kaus, "our ultimate boss was Katharine Graham [owner of the Washington Post Company]. Worry about what Mrs. G would think was a constant low-frequency subtext of editorial meetings. At the time, she was intensely interested in the international debt crisis (not a newsstand winner). The result of this worry was probably more coverage of the debt crisis than would have occurred if Mrs. G had actually been present at the meetings."

Sometimes it's waste of talent. A member of the Core Group is embarrassed when there is no aide to provide a key number in a presentation. Subordinates guess that this must never, never happen again, so they create a new position for an aide, and hire someone to fill it. But there is nothing for her to do. She is assigned at random to people in the department, without any direction or explanation. She ends up sitting at an empty desk. She wonders: What am I doing here?

Sometimes it's just funny. I once met a software engineer whose company gave all its mid-level managers copies of *The One Minute Manager*. "One of [author Ken] Blanchard's tenets is that you deliver praise to an employee, then touch them—hand on the shoulder, handshakes, something like that. My dry cleaning bill went through the roof for the three months after they got that damn book."

And sometimes guesswork can ruin people's lives and hamstring the organization's future.

Suppose that you, as a member of the Core Group, are forty years old. You head up a division, and I'm an employee on your staff. There are layoffs, and you've given me the assignment of deciding who must be cut. (Thanks, Boss.) Working in the division are a group of older managers, a few years from retirement: Clint Eastwood, Tommy Lee Jones, James Garner, and Donald Sutherland might play them in the movie version of your division's life story. And there are some young managers without much experience, but with some potential to learn: Tom Hanks, Bill Paxton, Kevin Bacon, and Gary Sinise might play *them.* All are competent, and the most logical decision might be to lay off, say, Sinise, Bacon, Garner, and Sutherland, and pair the others up so that the remaining younger managers can, in effect, apprentice to the older ones.

But if I'm the aspiring executive with this assignment, it is not my job to use logic. Instead, I imagine what it must feel like to be in the Core Group, in your shoes, giving orders to those fifty- and sixty-year-old men. I visualize the expressions on their faces, the deference they would feign. I feel a twinge of shame on your behalf. In some unspoken corner of my mind, younger people are not supposed to give orders to older people. And I can't help but imagine that you would feel the same. It is my job to spare you this discomfort.

Then I imagine the bright-eyed enthusiasm and energy of the younger people in the room, unfettered by caution, and the genuine leadership you would demonstrate for them. The mentoring! The heady quality of creative flow in the conference rooms! The racquetball games! By the time I get this far in my imagination, I'm already writing out the pink slips for the elders. And the level of experience and awareness slips a notch or two for the entire division, because the elders carried the lion's share of knowledge, judgment, and perspective. I rationalize all this on your behalf by saying that we need to invest in the organization's future; the younger guys might be with us thirty more years, while Eastwood and Jones will be gone in ten.

Paradoxically, you may well reward me for my decision. No one will see its debilitating effects. But those who live by guesswork die by it as well. I make bolder and bolder guesses on your behalf, until the day inevitably comes when I guess wrong. Perhaps I volunteer to set up a new information technology system for the department. You casually mention some terrific security feature that your brother-in-law at CitiCorp told you about. I authorize purchase of the only product I can find with that feature—a cumbersome, overpriced white elephant that continually crashes and that accidentally erases some of your most vital e-mail.

Well. A couple of episodes like that, and I'll never take initiative again—and neither will anyone who works nearby. (Nor, I'd guess, did any of Henry II's knights after that Becket episode, which probably explains why the rest of his military campaigns went so poorly.) From now on, I'll wait for you to spell out assignments completely, volunteering nothing, because I've lost confidence in my ability to guess your needs. Over time you will come to believe that no one who works for you is capable of thinking for themselves. I will come to believe that you are self-centered, arbitrary, and oblivious.

If we didn't know better, we might almost assume that this whole guesswork phenomenon was put in place to keep you members of the Core Group unconscious and unaware. As your employee, I'm so busy "managing upward" to keep you happy and get what I want, that I have no time left to find out your true purpose. But I follow the rules. I give you no problems without solutions. I avoid surprises. I'm the nail that doesn't stick up too far, so I don't get hammered down. And both of us get used to living this way, until neither of us can imagine how it might ever be different. In fact, if I do things in your name because I think this is what you want, you may well feel such pressure to back me up, out of a sense of loyalty (or a need for future loyalty), that you will endorse actions that you would never have chosen in the first place. In other words, you would go far beyond where Henry II went: "I now realize it was important to assassinate the Archbishop after all."

Core Group members, particularly executives, tend to wake up from the guesswork cycle as if waking up from a long narcotic-induced dream. They shake their heads, look around, and realize: *Everybody's trying to make me comfortable, but nobody is giving me the performance I really want!* Some Core Group executives, desperate to show how willing they are to endure innovation and discomfort for the sake of high performance, drag their direct reports through arduous mountain-climbing trips and desert safaris to shock them out of complacency. Subordinates come back talking about the life-changing team enrichment experience they've had. But they all infer a very different message: If you want to tell *this* guy the truth, you've got to let him drag you out to the Sahara first. Henceforth, they know what their job requires: trying to impress you by acting more like risk-takers, without taking any actual risks.

If you really want to break the guesswork cycle—for instance, if you want to keep older employees around long enough to learn from their experience—then you can't do it by convening a retreat, or even by proclaiming a new policy. A first step toward improving any organization involves reducing the level of distortion in the signals that the Core Group sends. Politicians, diplomats, and psychiatrists have long been aware that they have to be exceedingly careful with even their most casual remarks, because these can have huge effects on their listeners. Every national leader quickly learns, for example, not to make casual remarks about currency exchange rates. Few business leaders have that instinctual level of noblesse oblige. To compensate, therefore, they need to make themselves more aware of the signals they send, both intentionally and not.

You may have to set an example yourself of the new behavior you want to promote. You may even have to do your own firing, instead of delegating it to staff. Then promote an older manager or move some younger ones out of the organization. (You'll have to be clear about what you're doing and why; you won't be able, for instance, to say, casually, "Well, we have to keep Eastwood and Sutherland. We don't want any age discrimination suit.") Better yet, you could bring everyone involved in the department together and talk through the knotty problem and all its ramifications. Perhaps there's a creative solution that no one has thought of yet. Have you asked Sutherland for his perspective? Or Sinise *and* Sutherland?

Diagnostic Exercise 5
What Signals Are We Sending?

We now move from merely mapping the Core Group membership to naming the attitudes and assumptions that have become part of the organization's culture, particularly through guesswork.

This is the kind of exercise that produces very different results if you are in the Core Group than if you are observing from the outside. The ideal way to conduct this exercise is through several separate groups, some in the Core Group and some outside, all with enough support, anonymity, and protection against repercussions that they will talk openly and freely. Then compare notes.

   A. What does the Core Group say? What does it espouse in official documents and pronouncements?

   B. What does the rest of the organization hear? What are the logical inferences from the Core Group's actions—from the programs it favors, the ideas it turns down, the measures it favors, the risks it takes (and doesn't take), and the taboo subjects that can never be mentioned?

   C. For those in the Core Group: What is your intent? What signals are you trying to send the organization?

   D. And now, for everybody, upon comparing notes: Where do you see mismatches among A, B, and C?

If A and B aren't aligned, then this is probably the kind of organization that breeds cynicism about its leaders. They aren't "walking the talk," so why should anybody else?

If the Core Group itself is split on C, then there's probably room to build some bridges and open some conversations among Core Group members themselves. What do we really want to create with this organization this time?

If B and C aren't aligned, then the Core Group has a lot to gain by clarifying its messages to the organization, and especially in learning to listen to the organization more effectively.

Which means it may be time to take A in for an overhaul.

CHAPTER 9

"Doggie Treats"
(Incentives, Targets, and
Measurements)

A manager at a Fortune-500 manufacturing company asked me, "How does the Core Group theory deal with doggie treats?"

I looked at her blankly. "The people I work with," she explained patiently, "aren't thinking about the Core Group. They aren't thinking about anything except the bonuses and points they receive at the end of every quarter." And then she mimicked them. "We *could* develop a new market or innovate new products. But my bonus depends on meeting quarterly targets." Or, "We *could* create a great laboratory here. But I get bonus points only for laying people off."

Oh. "Doggie treats." Incentives and rewards, based on measured performance according to numerical targets. Of course. She went on to say that there were plenty of messages coming down from the Core Group in her company: pronouncements, memos, conferences, and reports in the press, announcing a wide variety of aspirations and ideals. But people paid attention primarily to the incentives, targets, and measurements. They didn't care about some metaphysical "needs or wants" of any Core Group; they were saving up for the down payment on a house, or a car, or their kids' college tuitions. At some companies, a big bonus in a boom year, or a chance to flip stock-option shares during a temporary spike, can be an immense onetime bonanza worth thousands of dollars to employees of mutual consent. How can any Core Group perception compete with that?

It is said that "what is measured matters." Measure something, and the organization moves to produce it—especially if you set up incentives accordingly. One of the most popular management theories of the past twenty years, the "Balanced Scorecard," is based directly on this premise. If you want to generate better results (the theory goes), then select more strategically oriented incentives, targets, and measurements. Be more attentive to the doggie treats, and you will develop an increasingly sophisticated body of employees—in the same way that a really good circus-animal trainer, armed with the right kinds of food, can develop an increasingly sophisticated cadre of performing animals.

The "Balanced Scorecard" theory (or, if you prefer, the "doggie treats" theory) is a natural evolution in the history of modern management. Organizations as we know them started with the nascent railroading enterprises of the 1840s, which gained competence by comparing the measured speed and reliability of each railroad line against the others. The scientific management of Frederick Taylor and the in-depth division management system developed by Alfred Sloan and Donaldson Brown at General Motors in the 1920s both depended on innovative uses of financial measurements, incentives, and rewards. Modern finance is, itself, a kind of magic: It allows for the instant comparison, in objective terms, of the basic worth of human beings, the future risk of their endeavors, and the potential reward—the kinds of things that, previously, could only be talked about with vague terms like *karma* and *hubris*. This power was reinforced when behavioral psychologists entered the corporate consulting world in the middle of the twentieth century, showing managers how to use rewards and punishments much more effectively. Ever since, much of the power of the modern organization has stemmed literally from the use of incentives, targets, and measurements to standardize and roll out technologies and practices. No wonder "doggie treats" work so well; they're the visible edge of the system of thought that gives organizations their power in the first place.

But when you look more closely at "doggie treats," you soon see that their real nature is not quite as tied to organizational success as this venerable history would suggest. "What is measured" does indeed matter—but only in light of the Core Group's perceived intentions and priorities. In practice, no matter how the measurements and incentives are intended to work, only what seems to matter to the Core Group will be measured.

Does anybody really think, for instance, that racing to ship product before March 31 will make a difference to any strategic goal? Incentives, targets, and measurements are relied upon because they're fast and consistent; they reach across an entire hierarchy with lightning speed. Their purpose is not to help the organization succeed. Their purpose is to help it perform well enough to make it through another day, without overtaxing the attention of the people in the Core Group, while reassuring them that the organization is under control.

A CEO of General Motors—or of Ringling Brothers, Barnum and Bailey Circus, for that matter—can't take each employee aside individually for an in-depth, trust-filled conversation. Nor can the organization rely on "cascading" that conversation down the hierarchy, because most middle-managers (who are not themselves members of the Core Group) will inevitably distort the message through self-interest and guesswork. So the Core Group members, particularly those at the top of the hierarchy, translate their goals into numerical targets and measures. These, at least, cannot be distorted. They are "objective." In fact (people tell themselves) the results will be better than they would be if the CEO *could* get to know each manager personally, because the results will be less influenced by the individual idiosyncrasies of the CEO's judgment.

In a typical incentive-and-target structure, communication between the Core Group and the rest of the organization is squeezed into an extremely narrow channel. Estimates flow up the channel from employees, through bosses, to the Core Group. Targets based on those estimates flow back down from the Core Group to the employees. Results flow back up again, and demands for better results back down again. All of these are expressed in terms of numbers alone, without any explanations of the meaning of the numbers. The numbers are sacrosanct on the page, but everyone knows how fictional they are in reality. Former MIT accounting professor (and current organizational-learning theorist) Fred Kofman puts it this way: "When the numbers take on a life of their own, they sever their associations with us. They lose the memory of the process which created them. The accounting system then becomes like the Frankenstein monster: a human construct which turns on its creators."

Kofman quotes a manager at one of the companies he worked with: "I know how fuzzy my calculations were, how wide the margin of error in my measures was, how I had to combine the data to end up with a summary statement. But once my calculation is on paper, it becomes the truth and boy oh boy, you'd better not disturb it."

In many organizations, even the Core Group will shrink from criticizing them, and for good reason. If the incentives and measurements are questioned, then the Core Group will have to step in and replace an established set of numbers with something else, something much more (God forbid) qualitative and time-consuming.

But at the same time, these numbers do not address any of the ambiguities that decision-makers must resolve to earn their doggie treats. For example: Which performance targets must be embraced wholeheartedly, and which can simply be fudged for the next quarterly review? Which "stretch targets" can be met simply by saying, "Well, we tried," and which require working all weekend and missing your kids' soccer games? To what extent must people work alone to meet targets, and if they work collectively, how will the incentives recognize this? What are the acceptable and unacceptable ways of fudging the numbers, and how can people avoid embarrassing themselves or the organization? In short, what sort of response to the incentives and measurements is acceptable around here? And what is not?

As people come up with the answers to questions like these, and act accordingly, they turn once again to their perception of the Core Group. Two things happen simultaneously.

First, people assume that they should interpret the numbers according to the Core Group. They base their behavior (for instance, their willingness to fudge numbers) on whatever signals they get from (or about) the Core Group.

For example, at an insurance company I know, officers have long been rewarded for "volume": the number and size of new policies and premiums. But several years ago, some Core Group members realized that profits depended far more on the speed, responsiveness, and efficiency with which claims were handled, because well-settled claims never went to court. Incentives and targets were adjusted to reflect profitability as well as volume. But which would matter most? Employees learned the answer in review meetings, where the first question that Core Group members asked was: "How much business do you expect to sign this year?"

Second, people assume that they should interpret the Core Group according to the numbers. If the incentives, targets, and measurements send a clear signal, then people assume that is where the Core Group wants the organization to go.

For example: during the cutbacks at AT&T in the mid-1990s, it gradually became obvious that the AT&T Bell Labs Research Group (which was, after all, a cost center) might not continue to enjoy its exalted status as a source of basic scientific research and an incubator of breakthrough technology. A high-level task force was appointed to come up with key metrics that would measure the research group's productivity. They eventually settled on the number of patents that each individual produced. ("I think it was the measure that everyone in the Core Group could agree on," said former labs researcher David Isenberg, who told me this story.) Thereafter, everyone at the Labs had "number of patents" added as part of their annual merit review. People adjusted their behavior accordingly, even though they felt it was "a clueless measure of productivity," as Isenberg put it. After all, it gave the innovators at the lab no incentive to think about potential customers or revenues.

But it did show what was important: a measurement that would impress the larger AT&T Core Group enough for them to keep supporting the Labs.

In many large companies, the measurement and control systems proliferate so wildly that they become, in themselves, a kind of robotic, machinelike Core Group. "I think control systems are one of the most important, least understood, and least examined aspects of management that we have today," says McKinsey partner Richard Foster, author of *Creative Destruction.* "If you ask companies how many control systems they have, they don't know. If you ask them how much they're spending on control, they say, 'We don't add it up like that.' If you ask them to rank their control systems from most to least cost-effective, then cut out the twenty percent at the bottom, they can't." (And this from a partner at McKinsey, the firm whose advice has launched a thousand measurement and control systems.)

What we really need around here, then, is a genuine conversation about the value of the measurements and incentives. Which ones truly matter? Why do they matter? Who put them in place, and what were they thinking of? How do they help the Core Group get what it needs? Did Core Group members ask for those particular measurements? Do we know why? How well do they serve the organization now, and how well might they serve it in the future? Do we even *need* measurements and metrics that go up the hierarchy, or should we reorient them so that the people conducting the work are the same ones who receive all the measurement reports, instead of melding them into aggregate figures that ring up on an abstract scoreboard? And, by the way, what are the appropriate incentives, targets, and measurements for Core Group members themselves? Can we construct and use the measurements to actually improve the organization, instead of just to keep score?

If we start to answer those questions effectively, then the measurements are no longer just "doggie treats." They gradually become a necessary vehicle by which the organization learns.

CHAPTER 10

Welchism

etween 1955 and 1970, America was paradise for middle managers, and General Electric was the most paradisical of companies. Everyone in the management ranks was effectively in the Core Group—virtually assured of a promotion every eighteen to twenty-four months, and taking cradle-to-grave security for granted. As Peter Block once noted, "Half a generation behind us, people were going crazy in the streets, but the workplace was stable." GE was particularly stable. Its revenues had doubled in size, on average, every eight years since 1892. Its diversification—GE made turbines, medical instruments, lightbulbs, household appliances, jet engines for military and civilian planes, sensors, and plastics—made it relatively immune to business cycle downturns.

By the late 1960s, GE had evolved into a complacent bureaucracy. It was known for its highly ritualized strategic planning sessions and review meetings (one manager called them "poker games"), in which executives questioned each other—demonstrating their intelligence, while being polite and deferential enough to protect each others' jobs. To be sure, there was a growing feeling within GE that this way of management couldn't be sustained—especially after several prominent lines of business, including computers and nuclear power plant development, became money-losing drains on the GE bottom line. But few people could imagine any way to shift the direction of the company out from under its huge, well-entrenched Core Group.

When Jack Welch was appointed the new CEO in 1981, chosen specifically because he was the only person who might turn around the situation, few GE insiders believed he'd be able to pull it off. But he did. He did it by creating one of the most widely copied management practices in history, a philosophy that will undoubtedly come to be known as Welchism. It is the deliberate streamlining of the organization by redefining the Core Group—from a large body of employees with lifelong membership to a very small group of people whose membership is permanently insecure. The net effect is like putting blinders on a horse to make it go faster.

Welch did exactly that during his first critical transition years, from 1981 to 1985. The company eliminated 112,000 jobs between 1981 and 1985, about one-fourth of its workforce. Simultaneously, GE added about 50,000 new people. All businesses were informed that they had to become either number one or number two in market share in their industries, or they would be "fixed, closed, or sold." Traditional flagship businesses (for instance, air conditioner and TV manufacturing) were sold or traded away. Some staff functions were downgraded or nearly eliminated—notably finance, strategic planning, and human resources, whose minions Welch privately called the "dinks."

Most notably, Welch put in place a performance appraisal method that he came to call the "vitality curve": Managers identified the top twenty percent ("A players"), the middle seventy percent ("B players"), and the bottom ten percent ("C players") of their top-level subordinates. The evaluations were based on two criteria: "Do they get results?" and "Do they match our values?" To match GE's values, people had to be the same kind of hard-driving, energetic, brash person that Welch himself was. The A players got stock options, promotions, and large raises; the B players got modest rewards; and the C players got laid off. This meant, by fiat, the bottom ten percent of GE managers in any group looked for new jobs elsewhere every year. A *truly* compassionate organization, argues Welch, is bold and quick at getting rid of such people, rather than letting them hang on, depressing everyone's morale and holding back its star players.

"Losing an A is a sin," Welch wrote in his autobiography. "Love 'em, hug 'em, kiss 'em, don't lose them! We conduct postmortems on every A we lose and hold management accountable for those losses."

Want to be in the Core Group at GE? Be an A. But don't expect to *stay* an A unless you stay on your toes, because you will never be allowed to coast.

The people I've met who are most bitter about Welch are not the C players who left GE during the first years of Welch's transition. They were the B players who stayed on in GE's new corporate culture, never quite reached A status, and either left or retired without feeling fulfilled. They all spoke with awe and admiration about Welch and the company he built. But they grieved for the passing of the old Core Group and were unhappy with the harshness of the new one—particularly its willingness to let people go who underperform.

For instance, I talked to an operations troubleshooter-turned-product-manager who had been laid off in the early 1990s. Like everyone else I have ever met from GE, this man (we'll call him "the troubleshooter") was fascinated with the history of Welch's temperament. "Back in his early days at GE Plastics," said the troubleshooter, "Jack was known for staying closely in touch with people. He would take them out Friday nights for a pizza and beer, saying, 'What's going on with you?,' trying to learn what they knew about the business. But after he became CEO, his vision seemed to change: 'We will be a leaner, meaner organization. We will work people to their maximum, a hundred and fifty percent. We will give them a hell of an experience and push them to their limit. Until they can't do it any more. When they burn out, we'll get rid of them. But any other company will be thrilled to have them. Plus they had a great experience with the company. They're better people because of it. Look at all the training we put them through.' "

Then his voice got bitter. "Look at the training. Look at the stress. Look at the weekend hours, the time spent on the road. Look at the alcoholism, the drugs, the sex that people turned to in order to cope, to keep their goddamn sanity. Look at what we did for them."

In other words, there was a Core Group attitude, cascading through the hierarchy, that established a general atmosphere in which employees were taken for granted and then pushed out the door. "I was very successful; I saved them millions of dollars and then created a new business for them," said the troubleshooter. "It was always implied that if I was contributing, I could stay there until I retired. But when people at GE get to be thirty-eight, thirty-nine, or forty, they start to feel like there's a bull's-eye on their back. And sure enough, I was pushed out at forty-two. Someone who wasn't familiar at all with the business I built was put in my place, and it ran into the ground. Yes, I'm still bitter about it, and there were a lot of people who felt like I did."

When I heard this, I was struck by the clash against Welch's principle of "boundarylessness": anyone who could demonstrate such a clear contribution to the company should be able to make a case to keep running the business, even if it meant going several rungs higher in the hierarchy, right?

"I raised the issues to my boss's boss," said the troubleshooter. "That was as high as I felt I could go. There was an outplacement package that I wanted to get, with a glowing replacement letter, benefits, and a bonus. If I had pissed them off, I wouldn't have gotten it. They could have terminated me for other reasons. And my name would get on the street as a troublemaker." In other words, the espoused values of Welchism couldn't compete with the genuine vulnerability in a culture where people are not innately valued.

Said another long-standing observer of the company, characterizing the GE ambience under Welch: "You're either on the team or off the team. If you're off the team, you may be able to stay if you do your job, but you'll never feel like anybody really wants you here." It is no coincidence that the nickname "Neutron Jack" ("He took out the people and left the buildings in place"), which Welch personally hated, was kept alive not by those who left GE, but by many of those who stayed.

The influence of Welchism has extended far beyond GE, to such unlikely industries as advertising. Robert Jacoby, the CEO of the Ted Bates Advertising agency during the early 1980s, reshaped it in a Welchist model—cutting waste, trimming staff, and boosting efficiency—to make it attractive for a sale. In 1985, Saatchi and Saatchi paid more than $500 million for it. More than a hundred Bates managers and staffers became millionaires, including Jacoby's secretary and driver. One of the account executives who was included in this told me that Jacoby was the greatest advertising genius he'd ever known; no one else had ever thought to extract money from the industry that way.

But Jacoby also tried to stay on as the president of the agency he had just sold. There followed an intense Core Group battle in which the Saatchis, Jacoby, other top executives, and several large clients all fought bitterly for control of the agency. As news of the dealing and battling spread, the agency could no longer preserve the illusion that its clients came first. Several long-term clients left; others (like Procter & Gamble) pressured the Saatchis to drop Bates clients who were competitors. Bates itself was ultimately folded into another Saatchi acquisition, Backer Spielvogel. The Saatchi empire, overextended, began to diminish. And Jacoby, who pocketed $100 million but lost much of his reputation in the deal, ultimately expressed regret. "Clients were partners at one time," he said. "They trusted us. They lost that somewhere along the line. And some warmth went out of the business." He didn't see the extent to which his own Core-Group-shrinking moves had created the situation he bemoaned.

Other companies which practiced Welchism (Ameritech and Owens-Corning come to mind) saw similar effects. In the late 1990s, then–Ford CEO Jacques Nasser instituted a series of hard-driving, cost-cutting measures, with University of Michigan professor Noel Tichy (a former consultant to and biographer of Jack Welch) as his chief advisor. Both Nasser and Tichy came on like tough reformers, eager to shake the company up from top to bottom, threatening to fire or exile people who didn't get on board with them. They grilled Ford executives about their financial acumen and embarrassed them by revealing that many of them couldn't recite their own company's earnings per share or cost of sales. And at first, the regimen seemed to work. The Ford share price soared from twelve dollars in 1993 to almost forty at its peak in 1999.

Then came the fatal failures: tire blowouts on the Ford Explorers and quality declines in other Ford vehicles. The stock price crashed back to fourteen or so in late 1999. Nasser was not just a convenient scapegoat, but a source of genuine resentment, for his cost-cutting and deliberate upheaval of Ford's long-standing quality management practices had led directly to these declines.

That's the Welchist pattern. The warmth, as Jacoby said, goes out of the business. What's left is a fractured and isolated Core Group that (all too often) loses its ability to inspire commitment, foster quality, and sustain business success.

This should not be read as an apology for entrenched bureaucracy. A "Welchist" redefinition—in which the Core Group shrinks from thousands of bureaucrats to a sharp, tight, lean machine in which no position is taken for granted—is not in itself a bad thing. The defining characteristic of a bureaucracy is insulation from objective measures of its performance. After a few years of that, organizations not only cease to be profitable, but they become spiritually moribund as well, and stultifying to work in. Welchism is an important antidote for all of these tendencies. Being in a Welchist company can feel like being in a dynamic, powerful team of winners—a breath of fresh air after being in a company full of sinecures.

(Even the castaways often learn to agree. The GE troubleshooter I interviewed, for instance, started his own supply business after being laid off. It gradually developed into a business that is more successful, more rewarding, and more his own than anything he did at GE. He now sees starting his own business as something he had to do to get back into a Core Group.)

But all too many Welchist efforts throw the human creativity out with the bureaucracy-water. They move foolishly and overbearingly. Welchism at these organizations is simply a vehicle for consolidating power in a new, smaller Core Group, and extracting money from the rest of the organization for the benefit of that Core Group.

The Welchist efforts that succeed in the long run are, paradoxically, intensely devoted to cultivating their people at the same time that they prune them. They don't just pay lip service to this; they relish it. Jack Welch himself was an unusually skillful Welchist. He invested time, attention, and money in building the capabilities of his Core Group at GE and in fostering their sense of responsibility for their whole enterprise. The A's, the managers who thronged into the famous GE management training center at Crotonville, New York, took part in eager give-and-take with Welch and other top managers in an auditorium called "the pit." Other senior GE executives did the same; GE's ability to invest top-level Core Group attention on its "A-team" development became a key part of its integrated learning base.

But executives at other companies often try to follow Welch's example with a fraction of the skill, initiative, or management maturity. They interpret Welchism as: "Identify the weakest twenty percent across the board—and downsize them." That's the fairest, simplest way, isn't it? (As it happens, it's also the way with the least wear and tear on the Core Group.) They assume that this is the way to keep the organization's resources from being depleted. They're partly right—it is *one* way. But it's not the *only* way. And it bears a terrible cost, not just for the people laid off, but for the organization itself.

Wayne Cascio, a University of Colorado professor who tracked the results of downsizing (and other restructuring) episodes across a ten-year period, is one of several researchers who has found that across-the-board cuts do not lead to profitability. At best, the effects of downsizing are negligible; those who slice brutally will see, a few years later, that their competitors who did nothing at all are at least as profitable. One of his most interesting findings is the addictiveness of downsizing. Some companies (Kodak was one) start with zero-layoff histories, experiment with downsizing, and then apparently get caught up in a cycle where they feel they have no other choice, even though they know, by now, that it will lead to lower profits each time. In other words, they are aware of the destructiveness, but they can't help themselves.

"I really believe that the CEOs I've spoken with informally would like to have alternatives," said Dr. Cascio. "They would like to have some other strategy that they could pursue. But on the day of the downsizing announcement, the stock price spikes up about eight percent. They get the kick from the market. Wall Street's applauding."

There *are* some other Core Group models that *do* seem to work. None of them can be imposed wholesale from outside. They all start the same way that Welch apparently started: by thinking about the kind of Core Group that we would most like to work for (or be part of), and then developing the changes that would allow that kind of Core Group to emerge.

CHAPTER 11

The CEO's Choices

A t Innovation Associates, the consulting firm founded by Charlie Kiefer and Peter Senge, a fable was sometimes told of a fast-track executive who was continually frustrated by the bureaucratic rules that kept him from getting things done. He assumed that when he got to be the big boss, he would sit down at a desk replete with levers and switches that could make things happen around the company. Then he was finally appointed CEO. On his first day, he sat down at the desk—and sure enough, there were all the controls in a row on a mahogany panel, plus a sealed note from his predecessor. "Welcome to your control panel," it said when he opened it. "None of these are connected."

Actually, they *are* all connected, sometimes in great detail, to operations throughout the organization. But they all work inconsistently. If you are a senior executive, then you have fairly broad power to give commands—for example, to promote people, lay off people, set targets, move resources into and out of projects, and authorize decisions. Those are the levers and switches of formal authority. But they are constrained by guesswork. You cannot specify how people interpret your commands, or how they interpret information. Nor, unless you are willing to micromanage the entire enterprise, can you specify how people will lead individual projects. Your greatest formal power comes from the fact that when everyone else bypasses or delegates a tough decision upward, you represent the last line of authority. But by the time you reach that "buck-stops-here" moment, the organization has already lost many other opportunities to change or improve the situation at lower levels of the hierarchy.

As CEO, you are also constrained by Core Group priorities. In every large or medium-sized organization, there will be other Core Group members besides yourself, often with conflicting goals: subdivisions with their own leaders, labor unions, key constituents (like investment groups), perhaps regulators, and (let us not forget) major customers. You have influence over these Core Group members, but not total control. (Even Jack Welch, arguably the most fully-in-charge CEO of any contemporary corporation, ruled only partly through formal controls, and primarily through what he called "values": promoting people who thought the same way he did, and setting up many opportunities for informal contact and collaboration with them. He cowed and bullied people, but he also respected and listened to them.)

In the end, you may have good reason to override the needs and priorities of other Core Group members, but whenever you take on that challenge, the way in which you do it becomes all-important. Running roughshod over them simply because you have formal power to do so—as Al Dunlap did at Sunbeam in the late 1990s, or as the majority famously does to the minority in the U.S. Congress—can have long-lasting, undesirable consequences.

In *The Fifth Discipline*, Peter Senge proposed that the executive leader functions best not as a manager, but as a "designer"—as the creator of structures and procedures that enable people to be effective. When you are aware of Core Group dynamics, the possibilities for this kind of design become much clearer. Executive leverage, in short, lies in sending signals and establishing constraints; setting an environment and context out of which a great Core Group can emerge. For example, you can affect:

- **The paths by which people are recruited, promoted, trained, rewarded, and laid off—and, most important, the assumptions about employees of mutual consent which underlie those paths.**

No one, not even the CEO, can choose *all* the members of the Core Group, because only some of them reach Core Group status through their position in the hierarchy. But the CEO and other top hierarchical leaders automatically show the kinds of people they favor at the core, through the diversity and quality of people they promote, and through the types of training and development they support. Every one of these practices is keenly scrutinized by people throughout the enterprise; every one of them sends signals, either consciously or not.

Probably the highest-leverage place to begin is training; the right kind of training initiative drives decisions made throughout the company about recruitment and promotion. Not long ago, for example, BP established a companywide training initiative for its 10,000 "first level leaders." The initiative was intended to bring trainees to the point where they could legitimately answer yes to four key questions:

1. "Do I have enough awareness of the context and direction of this organization?" In other words, am I exposed to the organization's strategic thinking?
2. "Do I have the skills and support to deal with the current challenges of my immediate business?" In other words, are they giving me what I need to do my job?
3. "If I'm a leader, do I have the skills and support to deal with the leadership challenges that I face now?" In other words, can I be the kind of person I need to be in this realm?
4. "Do I have enough support and feedback from my workplace to make the right personal choices about my life and work?" In other words, does the organization as a whole support my aspirations as well as its own?

I suspect that the hardest part of such an initiative is not recruitment, training, development, or design, but finding a way to ask the questions with enough protection and anonymity that people can tell the truth. In the late 1990s, for example, Motorola proposed a similar set of questions to its employees under the theme of "individual dignity and entitlement." Every quarter, bosses conducted conversations with their direct reports, asking questions like, "Have you had feedback in the last thirty days?" Or, "Do you know what your job is?" The stated intent was to apply the same "six sigma" approach that had worked so well in quality control for semiconductor manufacturing. Motorola set a target: less than six standard deviations from "yes" answers throughout the organization.

The result: A quiet breakdown between some employees, who tried to use the interviews to raise troublesome issues, and their mid-level bosses, whose bonuses depended on getting a high score of "yes" answers. Ultimately, the sessions were discontinued. It would have been much better to not bother asking the questions at all, but rather to open discussion among Core Group members: "What do we need to do around here to ensure that the answers *would* be yes if we asked?"

- **The visible ways in which senior executives pay attention (and some of the channels through which that attention is made obvious).**

The Core Group is like the Sun King—wherever it puts its attention, things shine. Employees take careful heed when Core Group members listen. It matters when Core Group members attend a design meeting, even if they don't say anything. It matters which prototype cars they drive longest, which computer software they experiment with, whom they talk with regularly and visibly, and especially which ideas they mention to others. If the primary repository of organizational knowledge is not in any databank or website, but in the tacit knowledge held at large by all the employees of an organization, then the Core Group's pattern of listening is like an index to that knowledge base. Everyone else uses it to learn what forms of creativity, innovation, performance, and accountability are relevant.

At Xerox in the 1970s, for instance, the Core Group effectively quarantined one of its own facilities, the immensely innovative

Xerox Palo Alto Research Center. Everyone at Xerox therefore inferred that Xerox PARC's work wasn't relevant. Only when Apple (and then Microsoft) adapted the graphic interface invented at PARC did Xerox's Core Group realize what they had lost—and suddenly, everyone at Xerox knew to appreciate the labs.

Here's a hypothesis I'd like to see tested by some management researcher sometime: When Core Group people and creative people talk easily together, the organization is innovative. When they don't, it is not. Many highly creative people are quite happy outside the Core Group, but they are keenly aware of whether the Core Group is listening to them. Moreover, the wider the base of creativity to which the Core Group pays attention, the more overall creativity the organization can muster. Finally, a Core Group that truly understands creativity will demonstrate it by bringing creative people together across boundaries to solve common problems. When that happens, creative people truly can change the world.

- **The patterns of information and communication flow.**

Core Group members have a great deal of influence over the accuracy, amount, and quality of information available to employees, and the ways in which they communicate together. It starts with the statements made by Core Group members themselves about strategic priorities and collective goals. When those statements are well-conceived, deliberate, and consistent over time, and when most of the Core Group members seem to be aligned, then Core Group messages can build, year after year, into an increasingly complex but coherent worldview that educates the entire organization together.

Social-network researchers, like Karen Stephenson, and researchers on collective intelligence, like William Isaacs, are just beginning to document what savvy managers have known all along: The *form* of talk is profoundly important. It is as palpably influential on the organization as a magnetic field is on a cluster of iron filings. If you want to change an organization, you start by changing the patterns in which people talk together, the things they talk about, the frequency of their contact, and the makeup of those who overhear them.

You can, for example, bring together your direct reports across boundary lines. You might bring together the protégés of several executives, or set up regular meetings in which business decisions from all units are discussed, or develop task forces in which the colloquy and connection is as important as the final solution. If you don't set up some kind of bridgework among people, nobody else will. The more informal and good-hearted it is, the better. If you set it up well, then you won't need to micromanage them; they'll guide each other.

- **The support given for entrepreneurialism and error.**

People who are trying new things need two types of freedoms: the freedom to say no to trivial but numbing requests, and the freedom to experiment without fear of vulnerability. These two freedoms will be extended only if it's clear that the Core Group supports them.

One organization with a Core Group that understands this is the Reticent Airplane Oil Corporation. That's a pseudonym, of course; this company, which supplies jet fuel to airports around the world, deliberately shuns publicity, because they are afraid that competitors may copy their unique system of management, with its remarkable secret ingredient: trust. (They don't really seem to understand how reluctant most organizations are to apply this ingredient.)

Operating an airline fuel business is a continual exercise in breaking into new markets, particularly during politically turbulent times, and Reticent's people are perhaps the fastest and most creative in the world at this. Every time they enter a new country or region, they carry with them this message from the Core Group: *You are more important than the deal.* "My boss told me, relax," one business developer said. "Do your best. Find out about the market, find as many opportunities as possible, and don't do a deal unless you feel comfortable. Your performance will be measured not only by the amount of deals you do, but by the quality of work and the amount we learn about the area. In fact, we chose not to enter one country, even though we had a local partner with government influence who knew the market. In my skin, I didn't feel we could trust this partner personally. And that was the right decision, because some of our competitors have been hurt there."

Said another Reticent manager: "We understand that you have to try five, ten, or fifteen things to make one thing happen successfully. Nothing is ever lost, and you build up valuable networks of relationships along the way."

Reticent is not soft on its people. People are continually grilled in no-holds-barred conversations, and pushed to make sure they believed in the stands they took. But they know that, where it matters, they will be backed up and protected. Even when they come back from a failure, colleagues gather around to learn what happened, and why, and how they could make it work better next time, without anyone being afraid of being disciplined or penalized for taking a chance.

- **The quality of your own leadership.**

I could probably develop a list of twenty more aspects of organizational design, all of which influence the caliber of Core Groups. But this would then be a far more tedious book—and it would not lead to better results. In the end, the effectiveness of organizational design depends on something far more personal: the presence and maturity with which Core Group members enact and embody them.

That presence begins with a recognition of your privileged place within the organization and the commitment that it requires. Many Core Group members have this awareness, but a surprising number, for whatever reason, underplay it or refuse to embrace it. An organization development consultant whom I know often conducts an exercise where she asks people to line up in order of their influence in the organization. "It's amazing to me," she says, "the number of leaders and managers who don't want to stand at the front of the pack. They inevitably shove a secretary or lower-level manager to the front."

Why is it hard for Core Group members (or anyone) to see themselves as privileged? Maybe they want to believe that the attention and affection they receive stems from their personal relationships with people, and not their Core Group status. Maybe they feel vulnerable when their status is on display. Maybe they are more aware of the thresholds they haven't crossed than the thresholds they have.

Or maybe they aren't quite ready to give the organization what they know, in their hearts, that it needs from them: an authentic willingness to take a stand on behalf of the organization's greatest possible future.

Diagnostic Exercise 6
What Am I Doing to Foster a Great Organization?

This diagnostic exercise is primarily for Core Group members—or people who hope to be Core Group members sometime soon.

    A. If somebody watching you from within the organization said, "Here's what he or she cares about," what would they identify? Performance? Creativity? Innovation? Customer satisfaction? Shareholder value? Resilience? Being right? Being the best? Being first? Nobility? Greatness? Something else?

    B. What would have led them to identify those particular qualities? For example, if you picked innovation, what aspects of your own behavior would imply that innovation is important? Or if you picked being first, what are the events of the past year in which being first was critical?

    C. Just for the sake of curiosity, which values are important to other Core Group members?

D. And which are prevalent in the rest of the organization, but not in the Core Group at all?

E. Here's the most critical set of questions. Please feel free to take some time to think them through: On which values does the organization's future depend? Which of these, if cultivated, would make the organization great? Or, if you prefer, what do you want people to remember you for when you leave the organization?

F. Now: Where are the discrepancies between E and A—and, for that matter, between E, C, and D? What kinds of changes would be required to shrink the gap of those discrepancies? What kinds of changes might be needed in the way that you (and other Core Group members) think and behave? And which of *those* changes, in turn, represent a choice that you would want to make?

CHAPTER 12

The Expanded-Core-Group Organization

ould there possibly be an organization where almost everyone is in the Core Group—where decision-makers take into account all of the members of the organization whenever a decision is made, where everyone works on behalf of everyone else, and where things *don't* dissolve into either bureaucratic torpor or chaotic everyone-for-themselves anarchy?

Can such organizations exist? Certainly. Many of them are famous, at least in managerial circles, for their unusual and all-encompassing styles: Scientific Applications (SAIC). Southwest Airlines. St. Luke's Advertising Agency in London. W. L. Gore. Toyota. These organizations have expanded their Core Groups without gargantuan salaries or extravagance. They've done it by establishing a design that makes it clear where people stand—and by following through on the idea that everyone's welfare and development is one of the entire organization's priorities, as important as the share price (and a key factor in keeping the share price high).

In each case, there are structural elements that allow the organization to pursue this path: Employee stock-ownership plans. Financial literacy. Nonhierarchical decision-making. In-depth training. None of these are panaceas in themselves. (The United Airlines bankruptcy proceedings should convince anyone that employee stock-ownership plans alone won't save a company.) But when they are combined together in a comprehensive and consistent design, with top managers who are deeply committed to a heartfelt, thoroughly engaged presence, then the result is often an "Expanded-Core-Group" organization with this critical feature. There aren't merely a few people looking out for the future of the whole system. There are always a few far-sighted people predisposed to do that. In this type of organization, it is easy for everyone, from the CEO on down, to take the needs and priorities of *everyone* into account when they make a decision.

It takes constant effort to create and maintain such workplaces. It requires careful attention on one hand to reporting procedures and financial controls, and on the other hand to the ways in which people learn and grow personally. In the companies that make this work, executives are preoccupied with both of these factors; they continually refine and expand the financial structures and the learning-and-development structures, trying to make both more transparent and inclusive. In the process, they automatically foster a Core Group–style attitude about the business among people throughout the organization, and they encourage people to make decisions on behalf of all employees.

The performance benefits of such organizations, while anecdotally far superior, have not been fully established in systematic research. One researcher, MIT's Diane Burton, has measured the returns from Silicon Valley organizations with varied management and recruiting styles; the companies she calls "high-commitment" score much better on financial measures in the long run. There is also a growing body of anecdotal evidence from people who have worked in such places, and who would not willingly work anyplace else, even if it meant better salary and benefits. They will do whatever they can to make sure the enterprises and operations thrive.

One of the best-known Expanded-Core-Group organizations is Springfield Remanufacturing Corporation (or more precisely, SRC International), the parent company for about twenty industrial-equipment and business-service companies, mostly in the business of remilling and rebuilding used heavy-duty engines, located in the Ozark Mountains city of Springfield, Missouri. The Springfield companies are known for a particular management design called "open-book management": They deliberately educate their employees in all the financial numbers of the company's business. This information is typically posted on mural-sized charts in the employee cafeteria. Staff members "huddle"—a word deliberately chosen to evoke game-playing strategy—at least weekly to talk about the financials and the strategies they suggest. They take the company's growth and prosperity personally, in part because they nearly all own shares in it, generally through employee stock-ownership plans (ESOPs). And they are keenly aware that their retirement incomes depend, in part, on the company's ability to thrive. At SRC, people speak seriously but lightly about the loss of a sale or the rise of a cost, as you might hear a baseball fan talk about the batting average of a favorite player.

Jack Stack, the cofounder and CEO of SRC, is also the coauthor (with Bo Burlingham) of two books on their system: *The Great Game of Business* and *A Stake in the Outcome*. Almost as a side effect, he says, his system has naturally solved some of the most entrenched problems of entrepreneurial capitalism, such as the difficult problem of finding new challenges for longtime employees and managers who get bored with their old positions but have nowhere in the company to go. Or the complacency that sets in at even the most entrepreneurial companies, blinding them to new opportunities. Or the brutality of most layoffs. In a typical business downsizing, as Stack puts it, "the laid-off worker walks out to the parking lot for the last time, wondering, 'Why didn't they tell me that the company was in trouble?'" At SRC companies, by contrast, everyone finds out about the troubles ahead of time, because the accounting statements have been demystified. In fact, open-book management makes clear what many wage earners would never otherwise understand: the reasons cost-cutting may be the right thing to do under certain circumstances (for instance, in a cash-flow crunch).

And then there's the deeper aspiration: spreading the opportunity to build wealth beyond the Core Group, to the broader population of employees at SRC and its subsidiaries. "I grew up in a lower-middle-class family that didn't have a lot of money," Stack says. "My parents worked extra jobs just to be able to fund Christmas. There was a lot of fear in my house. What we're doing here in Springfield is showing people how to get through life without fear. Once people understand what it takes to be a business person, not just a cog in the system but somebody on the brighter side of capitalism, then their lives can change forever."

Springfield Remanufacturing Corporation began life in the early 1980s as a last-ditch effort to keep alive an obscure International Harvester engine-rebuilding plant that was losing $2 million a year. Harvester had brought Stack in, in fact, to close the plant—but he and twelve other Springfield managers decided to ignore the demands and keep their people employed, even if it meant trolling for business on their own. From there it was just a natural step to offer to buy the plant from Harvester and set it up as an independent company.

Stack and his partners had very little money of their own, and it took two years to secure the financing, with Stack himself taking on the grueling but eye-opening task of wooing investors. Their task was complicated further because, to enlist the workers' commitment and help, the new managers had promised to give everyone shares in the company. Stack never forgot one venture capitalist telling him the company lacked "schmozzle"—meaning a credible story, backed up with detail, of how the company could return the investment in a reasonable time.

This was more worrisome than it might seem at first glance, because all the employees would be investors, and they'd want "schmozzle" too. But the partners were determined, and they finally raised enough money to buy and open the plant. Then, to make matters worse, they lost one of their key customers, whose revenues had been an integral, irreplaceable part of their business plan. So there they were. Burdened with an 89:1 debt-to-equity ratio ("on a par," Mr. Stack later commented, "with the government of Poland"), an enormous cash crunch even if they were profitable, and an unforgiving creditor, Mr. Stack and his twelve confederates felt they had no choice but to let everyone in the plant know exactly how bad things were.

It turned out that people appreciated the opportunity to learn and to proactively take part in saving their jobs. "We realized that we could run out of cash any moment and not make payroll," says Ron Guinn, then an hourly worker at SRC and now a senior manager at ReGen, one of the SRC companies. "Pulling together and watching our cash became a way of life. If you bought a tool, you realized what the effect of that expense would be. It finally dawned on me that I didn't have to trust those thirteen guys in management. If I learned the numbers, I could figure out the business for myself and determine if it would do for me and my family what I thought it should do."

It also helped that everyone could see managers out on the floor at the end of the month, working to ship the last bit of product. In 1988, it became clear that the company had won its workers' trust and respect when the staff at the plant voted to defer a bonus and build up the company's long-term strength instead. By that time, the stock had risen from its original dime share price to $15.60. Then it fell to $13.02 (the slump was the reason for the bonus deferral), but that still meant a rise of 13,000 percent in four years.

In 1986, the company began to diversify—first into automobile engines in 1985, after a janitor (a former stockbroker at a major Wall Street firm who had burned out and moved to Springfield for a less pressured life) stopped Mr. Stack in the hallway to remind him that truck engines were a cyclical industry. By the early 1990s, there were so many requests for paid tours of the plant that SRC formed another business, the Great Game of Business, based on packaging and selling the Game. They were now beginning to get some press attention—first in *Inc.* magazine in 1986, then in a variety of places after *The Great Game of Business* came out in 1992. But they were still seen as a small, local, ESOP-based firm, definitely not a model for the great commercial enterprises of the Fortune 500.

Besides, they were distracted by a challenge that emerged from within, once again threatening the survival of the company. One of the original twelve founders left the company in 1986. Buying back his stock cost $660,000—a huge amount of money in the SRC balance sheet in the mid-1980s. At most firms, either that figure would have been hidden, or there would have been a taboo against discussing it. But at SRC, it came up in one of the huddle meetings. An hourly worker gave it voice: What would happen when he and his peers began to retire, many of them around the same time twenty years hence? Where would the money come from to purchase back their stock? "We've got a lot of cash tied up in connecting rods," he said. "We can't eat connecting rods."

"It was absolutely the right question to be asking at that time, and I should have been proud and happy to get it," writes Jack Stack in *A Stake in the Outcome*. "That's why we were teaching and coaching; this guy 'got it,' no question. . . . [but] I was thrown for a loss. I hadn't given any thought to how we were going to cash everybody out."

This is, of course, one of the great unspoken dilemmas of entrepreneurialism, especially in places like Silicon Valley where stock options are rampant. How *do* you cash people out? The more successful the company, the larger the buybacks have to be. Many companies solve this problem by going public. This leaves the entrepreneur with no real option but to leave, raise venture capital for a new company, and start the process all over again, in a blockbuster-style syndrome that, in the long run, is probably destructive to the entrepreneurs, the markets, and the industry—and certainly to any Core Group that aspires to greatness.

At SRC, nobody wanted to relinquish control to an outside group who might misunderstand their Great Game, and its requisite investments in training and huddle time. They trusted themselves and their hard-won business sense more than they trusted anyone else, and they wanted to build a legacy business that could live longer than they would. They also disliked the option of putting cash aside for buyback time; they wanted cash available for growth when they needed it, not tied up in reserves. There had to be an alternative—a way to use the built-in entrepreneurial incentive of the SRC system to keep creating enough wealth to allow them to buy back their shares.

Then Stack found his inspiration—in a story told to him by a Missouri neighbor named Mike Ingram, a fireworks importer who had trekked into the Chinese hinterlands to visit one of his suppliers firsthand. Expecting to see a fireworks factory, Ingram had emerged over the crest of a hill to see a village spread out before him, with hundreds of little huts. The huts were the factory. If one hut exploded, the others could continue operating. "We too were protecting a village, just like the fireworks manufacturer," Mr. Stack recalled. "So we broke our village into huts as well."

The first "hut" that SRC spun off, a marketing organization, failed. But in 1986, the second new company took root. It was called Engines Plus Inc., and it remanufactured junked oil coolers, a critically important part for rebuilt engines, with SRC itself as the first customer (but not the only one).

They invested only $6,000 and underwrote a $54,000 loan, thus starting Engines Plus with a 9:1 debt-to-equity ratio (not quite like the government of Poland, but still harsh). Thus, if the new company succeeded, its share price would rise dramatically, too. And in fact, Engines Plus went from $286,000 in annual revenues to $7 million within a few years. It's now worth more than 250 times the original investment. The upshot? If SRC needed cash suddenly to buy out shareholders, it could sell this expendable subsidiary and keep the main company solvent for a while longer.

The number of SRC affiliate companies has grown at an accelerating pace ever since. None of them have been sold so far; the cash generated from the affiliates has enabled SRC to buy back the shares of retiring employee-shareholders. Since the various companies can share resources (like a collective health care fund that replaces health insurance), their overhead is also lowered.

SRC succeeds at this where other companies might fail, because of the extended experience that all employees have with financial literacy, disclosure, and shoestring frugality. Most of SRC's new businesses are pushed out into the world with one or two revenue streams set up—just enough to cover overhead and generate some cash. They are expected to amplify that by diversifying new customers and product lines as quickly as possible. If the subsidiary businesses falter, it won't take SRC workers by surprise. They'll know well in advance, because they will have been tracking the company's movement, huddle by huddle, on the wall charts. Stack and other SRC founders sit on the boards of each of these new businesses, which means that the Core Groups of the new enterprises, while distinct, also have well-defined relationships with the Core Group of the whole SRC group. Stack and one or two other people (such as Mike Carrigan, a former engineer who is now a vice president overseeing the technological businesses) are in the Core Groups of all of the companies.

The open-book process also seems to foster a sense of mutual concern. Some of the SRC senior managers are former high school dropouts who went to work at SRC as janitors and got pushed by their colleagues into going back to school so they could be promoted to management. At several open-book businesses (including some not directly connected to SRC, such as Trinity Services in Chicago), staffers have created "cookie jar" funds to help their colleagues in trouble.

Meanwhile, the Springfield area (where all the SRC businesses are located) is burgeoning; once a sleepy trucker's hub and college town, it is now a small city with more than 150,000 people. Jack Stack is now president of a business coalition that, in September, opened a new Partnership Industrial Park, designed for quality of life (for instance, the driveways are set up to avoid traffic jams at five P.M. as people leave to drive home). Stack and a group of partners have also raised $6 million in local investment money for a venture-capital fund called Quest Capital Alliance—with a deliberate strategy of long-term investment in Midwestern companies and an informal affinity for companies that play the Great Game already (and that have a willingness to instill the Game in other companies they invest in).

A more typical path for the CEO of a fast-growing $140 million company would be to move to the next level through acquisition, as Cisco Systems Inc. did, or to break out into internationally visible businesses, as Virgin Atlantic did. At the very least, Jack Stack could have easily established subsidiaries of Springfield Remanufacturing around the world, bringing open-book management to businesspeople everywhere. Instead, he has tried to maximize his influence in a specific local sphere, a place where he can still make time for his family, for bass fishing (in which he's a fierce competitor), and for casual conversations at the local bar and golf course. He still visits each of the companies about once a month or so; he still tries to know the names of as many people on the shop floor as possible. That would be much tougher to do in a production territory that spanned the country or the globe.

I've gone into so much detail about SRC to show how systematic its design is, and yet how flexible. SRC's approach encompasses all of its practices—from compensation to training to management style to new ventures—while continually expecting to be surprised (and adjusting accordingly). The same is true of all the effective Expanded-Core-Group designs that I know of. For instance, the W. L. Gore management system is well known for its democratic, cell-like structure in which teams of people make strategic decisions. The "Requisite Organization" design championed by Elliott Jaques is an elaborate hierarchical system in which each level of the hierarchy is matched to managers' cognitive capabilities, bosses are responsible for their subordinates' results, and the entire management structure is set up to systematically develop the talents of people within it. The Toyota structure is based on a sophisticated systemic approach to production, in which plants are designed so workers leave them refreshed (like leaving a gym after a workout), and each station operates at a rhythm set not by production quotas, but by the orders from the next station downstream—ultimately taking their cues in real time from the customer requests that come in.

None of these approaches can be applied piecemeal; you can't take one aspect of the Springfield system, like the employee stock-ownership plan, and get the same kind of results. Indeed, few companies are modeled directly on SRC. Although the SRC companies are remarkably open to outsiders, following their example isn't a naturally easy thing to do. Their particular qualities were designed and selected by the organization's own Core Group, after thinking seriously about the design and development of the organization as a whole.

Why then don't more companies follow the model of Toyota, Volvo, Southwest Airlines, et cetera? Because it would require most Core Group members to fundamentally change—not just what they say, but how they think, how they are paid, how they carry themselves, and how they build relationships. Almost by definition, no one has either the courage or the organizational wherewithal to propose this kind of change unless they're in the Core Group themselves. Most of us, after all, have an unconscious vested interest in keeping ourselves and our organizations going in the same pattern of basic management where they already exist. We've invested our careers, our habits, our thinking, and our feeling in an organization that maintains its current Core Group form.

CHAPTER 13

The Glass Ceilings

Toni Gregory, a former research director of the American Institute for Managing Diversity, once gave a lecture on diversity at a liberal-arts college in the Rocky Mountains (let's call it Western Slopes University). During the discussion, a student complained about the "streaking skiers," a group who had skied nude down the mountain on Easter Sunday and been arrested for indecency. Another student spoke up to defend the streakers and complain about how uncomfortable people were making them feel around the campus. And then someone else said, almost in passing, "Well, what about the people who don't ski at all?"

Silence. For at Western Slopes, the great taboo was the subtle but pervasive class system on the slopes. Nonskiers were shunned at this school. They got turned down for plum assignments and opportunities; they missed all the casual conversations about grants or fellowships that took place on the lifts or in the lodges. They endured constant questioning: "Why did you ever come here in the first place?" With the subtext: "And why don't you just leave?" (The answer: Most of the nonskiers had come from flatter, warmer places without knowing about the skiing culture, and didn't have the resources to leave once they arrived.)

Maybe coming to this school would be a god-sent opportunity for nonskiers to learn the sport. But it might also mean spending their entire careers ranked as beginners, in a community filled with experts, with their dignity subtly but pervasively denigrated all the while. They'd be expected to visibly turn their back on the parts of themselves that never chose to ski. They would stop spending time with their nonskiing friends.

And even if they did all that, without a single slipup or false thought, they *still* might not get into the Core Group, not even if they were stars on campus otherwise. ("What about putting Edwin on that committee? Well, he's a brilliant physicist, a great lecturer, and a terrifically nice guy, and he *has* taken up skiing. But you know, he still doesn't go any higher than the intermediate slope.") If people drifted away from the college, it would be natural to express regret. ("It's a shame Edwin didn't make it here.") Left unvoiced would be the sharp sense of relief that many people might feel. Had Edwin stayed, he would have been a constant reminder of the Core Group's closed nature, which no one had ever been willing to challenge, and which once again, everyone could safely sidestep.

Diversity is a Core Group issue. If conversations about diversity in an organization bypass the Core Group, then the organization hasn't dealt with diversity at all—no matter how many lawsuits have been filed or workshops conducted.

To be sure, there is a generic workplace issue involving tolerance and communication. Large corporations, in particular, throw people together from varied ethnic backgrounds, religions, sexual orientations, political points of view, economic classes, levels of education, and family backgrounds. Sometimes they find it useful to raise awareness of the misunderstandings and abuses that occur in everyday working life as people get used to working with others different from themselves.

But a thousand training courses will not address the Core Group diversity issue, unless Core Group members lead the way. No one else can do it; no one else has the wherewithal to unravel the barrier that prevents certain types of people from entering the Core Group no matter how valuable or worthy they may be.

The most evocative name for this barrier was coined in the late 1980s: the "glass ceiling." Three researchers with the Center for Creative Leadership (Ann Morrison, Randall White, and Ellen Van Velsor) had noticed a pattern. Women rose in the ranks easily to lower executive levels, but continually failed to rise higher. It was as if the entire organization were conspiring to keep them from (for example) becoming COO, CFO, or CEO. The researchers predicted that it would take until 2005 for women to break the barrier and become CEOs in any significant quantity. They didn't say so, but it was obvious that the Glass Ceiling didn't apply just to women. It applied, and still applies, to any group that, in the eyes of the organization, doesn't quite fit with the Core Group's makeup.

Whatever the particulars of the group it excludes, the Core Group sends a message that it's not just all right, but mandatory, to treat some people as innately worth more than others. (In his book *Somebodies and Nobodies,* Robert Fuller calls this attitude "rankism," and argues that it's at the heart of much of the dysfunction of modern civilization.) Over the course of time working for organizations, some people tend to internalize this attitude. They come to believe it about themselves ("We're not in the Core Group, so we're not worth as much."). They begin treating others as worth intrinsically less because of lower rank. Because this attitude is often unconscious, it pervades organizational life—which of course reinforces the hold that the existing Core Group has upon people, who go on to carry these Core Group attitudes throughout their careers.

Does it matter? In the end, why should we care when an organization's leadership is closed off from a significant number of its members—especially when it's a private organization?

Let's consider that question from two perspectives—the two sides of the conversation about diversity that the organization needs to hold. First, suppose you are a member of the Core Group. Your strength comes, at least in part, from your insularity and cohesion. You talk easily together, and you look for people to join you who will also be able to talk easily. Moreover, everybody in the organization recognizes this. Whether or not they approve of that insularity, they see the ways in which you as a group depend on it; and they assume that challenging that insularity is *not* part of the job.

And yet . . . how do you know you aren't missing something important as a result? And if others in the organization are aware of this, how do they get both the permission and the wherewithal to bring it to your attention?

In 1981, when the eighty-year-old statistician Dr. W. Edwards Deming was first becoming famous in America as the expert "who had helped the Japanese learn about quality," he was invited to help a small chemicals company in Ohio figure out a production problem involving a paint-drying solution made from organic metals. As Harold S. Haller (the quality consultant who introduced Dr. Deming there) tells the story, they were ushered into a room with the corporate staff on one side of the table and the operations staff on the other. A vice president stood at a blackboard covered with text, presenting the problem and their proposed solution. Deming paid scant attention to the board; instead, his eyes continually wandered over the faces in the room.

He asked, "How do you test your raw materials?"

The vice president gave him an extended explanation, essentially saying, "We can't test our raw materials effectively. It isn't possible." He returned to the blackboard where he'd left off, but Deming broke in again with the same question: "How do you test your raw materials?"

"Dr. Deming," said the VP, "I already told you that!" Deming let him continue a while longer, but then broke in again with the same question. It happened several more times, and the VP grew more and more anxious.

Meanwhile, a chemical engineer in the back of the room kept motioning for a chance to speak. Deming finally told the VP to sit down—"We've heard enough from you"—and invited the engineer to take the floor. "I've been telling you for the last fifteen years you're wrong," said the engineer. "You *can* test it. You just never listened to me." Suddenly, people began shouting at each other across the table. It turned out that this company had systematically kept its chemical engineers out of the Core Group, for reasons that went back many years. Consequently the engineers had long since stopped volunteering information, except to say, in effect, "I told you so." Which the people at the top never quite heard.

In the midst of the melee, Dr. Deming got up, and said, "I've got to get on my way. Thank you for inviting me. I think this man has found your problem."

Having a Core Group open to diversity is one of the keys to building an effective integrated learning base. (Not the *only* key; one of several important ones.) A Core Group needs to understand the lives of its organization's constituents—which means being willing and able to learn from them. For example: Banks with no Core Group members who grew up in inner-city neighborhoods know nothing about those neighborhoods. Their ignorance leads them to redline neighborhoods, and therefore miss opportunities. Advertising agencies with no Spanish- or Chinese-speaking members in their Core Groups tend to produce patronizing and lackluster campaigns in those languages. Companies with no women in senior management never quite seem to learn how to develop and promote their women managers and executives.

Second, consider the perspective of the people who are systematically excluded from the Core Group and blocked by the Glass Ceilings of your organization. They want to be promoted, but not at the expense of changing the way they talk, think, and act. And even if they make over their personae, what if they still can't fit in?

I've met people wrestling with this dilemma in every type of organization, from the U.S. Central Intelligence Agency to local school districts to manufacturing companies to small consulting firms. Most of them eventually make one of two choices. Some establish themselves as employees of mutual consent. Or they leave, to find or start an organization with a Core Group that they have some hope of joining. They may also take their customers with them.

No one but Core Group members can decide how inclusive your Core Group can be. (To be sure, employees can influence the makeup of the Core Group significantly. But it's almost impossible for employees to propel people into the Core Group who are otherwise systematically excluded.) So it's up to you: How open do you want to be to varied kinds of people? How much deliberate effort do you want to put into making your Core Group resemble your employees, customers, and constituents?

And when you decide that it's time to open up your Core Group to "nonskiers": Will you know how to begin?

Part 3

The
Essential
Core Group
Career Guide

CHAPTER 14

Your Inner Core Group

*I am invisible, understand, simply because people refuse to see me.
When they approach me they see only my surroundings, themselves, or figments of their imagination—indeed, everything and
anything except me.* —Ralph Ellison, *Invisible Man*

You never quite forget your first relationship with a Core
Group. I didn't quite realize this until I conducted a work-
shop on Core Group theory with a group of United
Kingdom professionals.

"This core group theory reminds me of a story," said one of the
participants, a management consultant named Grace. During her
twenties, she had been the chief administrator of a health services
agency in London dedicated to helping homeless people. After a
year or so, she found herself virtually running the agency; she was
also one of its most visible spokespeople. But inside the agency itself, she felt almost invisible. She attended internal management
meetings, but when she spoke up at them, her advice was ignored.
People often looked across the table at her or made snide comments, as if she had no real legitimacy to speak. She came to feel
that no matter how credible she might be on the outside, she would
never have any influence on the direction of the agency.

This agency, as it happened, had a very tight-knit Core Group—
a group of idealistic male medical doctors who had cofounded it together. There were probably several reasons why they kept Grace
at arm's length. She was the only woman on the staff. She was
younger. She had no medical degree. Most important, she wasn't a
founder. She hadn't gone through the experience of deciding to
start the agency and setting it up with them.

She spent five years at the job. When it became clear that she would need a postbaccalaureate degree to get the kind of Core Group role she wanted, they suggested that she enroll at a nearby university for a master's in medical administration. She was eager to go. But there was always too much to do at the agency, and they never quite got around to sending her. By the fourth year, her ambition to stay, or to make a difference there, had dwindled. "By the time I realized the score," she recalled, "I no longer wanted to play the game."

She held seven jobs during the next ten years. She would sit at her desk and ostentatiously peruse the want ads, as if to show that she was just passing through. The Core Group stayed with her long after she left the agency. And everyone else in the room had a similar story. We had internalized the Core Groups of our early careers and carried them with us, like "inner Core Groups" that shaped our expectations for the rest of our lives.

One of the people in the room, for instance, worked in human resources at a large UK company. Her job included advising the CEO, who was routinely brusque, critical, and dismissive to most of the people who reported directly to him. "I walked out of his office after an argument one day," she said, "and I noticed that I was like this"—she held up a fist like a boxer—"in a fighting stance."

This was a far cry from the energy company where she had first gone to work—a tough, performance-driven corporation, but one which also had a tradition of collegial, respectful relationships between bosses and subordinates. "The Core Group at my earlier job," she told us, "took the time to reinforce me." They had invested in her training and backed projects she initiated. Instinctively, she now realized, she was looking for that same kind of validation in her new job . . . but her new Core Group wasn't really interested.

A third person in the room was a senior executive of a small utility company. He had joined in his mid-twenties, and a few years later, the company had been acquired. "Right at the start, the new management asked our opinion in an elaborate consultation process. We gave them a well-detailed blueprint for the future. We never heard anything back from them—no thanks, no interest, and no response. And the next few years showed that none of our recommendations were adopted." He'd hung on through the frustration of the next few years, seeing some of his ideas adopted by other companies as well as his own. They became standard industry practices. After another management change, the new president saw potential in him and began grooming him as a successor. Suddenly, he was back in the Core Group, generally regarded as legitimate. Somehow, though, he couldn't quite find the confidence to conduct himself as presidential material; the old Core Group's indifference to him still lingered within.

I too had an early Core Group story to tell. In 1980, fresh out of journalism school, I went to work for the *CoEvolution Quarterly*—a far-sighted nonprofit magazine published by the *Whole Earth Catalog*. Both the quarterly and the catalog reflected their roots in the hippie subculture of the late 1960s and early 1970s; the blockbuster sales of the 1972 *Last Whole Earth Catalog* had, in effect, subsidized the magazine for a decade. But by the time I joined, the magazine was struggling, with a fiercely loyal circulation of about 30,000 people. All of our dozen or so staff members earned the same amount, ten dollars an hour. (Stewart Brand, who was founder, publisher, and editor, earned only slightly more.) Most of us worked only part-time, and we were allowed to use the office and graphics equipment for our own freelancing. We also had other unusual perks: completely flexible hours, lunch prepared by an in-house cook, and volleyball every day on a small court adjacent to the office. It was an idyllic existence—albeit one that didn't leave us quite enough money to rent our own apartments. Like many nonprofit staffers in the San Francisco Bay area, most of us settled into shared rentals with roommates.

Then Stewart signed a contract with Doubleday for $1.3 million—at the time, one of the largest trade paperback advances ever granted—to produce the *Whole Earth Software Catalog*, a consumer guide to the then-nascent personal computer industry. We also launched a computer magazine to spark the research: a full-color magazine without advertising. We soon discovered that we couldn't lure knowledgeable personal computer writers unless we paid the astronomical salaries (to our naïve eyes) of $25,000–$35,000 per year. As Whole Earth's "computer maven" of the moment, I was deemed essential to the project. When I demanded $30,000 per year, I got it. My first move: signing a lease on my own apartment.

For a year or more, I thought it was my responsibility to resolve the tension between my old CoEv colleagues (still making ten dollars an hour) and the higher-paid *Software Review* professionals. If I had known then what I know now, I wouldn't have bothered. The *Whole Earth Software Catalog* appeared during the first big downturn in the personal computer industry, the slump of 1984. (It's been since overshadowed by the bubble collapse of 2001, but it was no small matter at the time.) The book didn't sell enough copies to support a full-color magazine with no ads. At Whole Earth, all the high-priced computer editors were gone within two years, including me.

To an outsider, it might have seemed as if the higher-paid computer people were the Core Group. But the real Core Group was the lower-paid, more "authentic" staff. They had the more viable business; the *Whole Earth Review*, through many financial and editorial vicissitudes, is publishing and vibrant still. In retrospect, had we foreseen our potential contribution more clearly, we could have set up a much more frugal computer publication, on cheap paper with lots of advertising. It could have become a cash cow for the other, more idealistic publications and enterprises that we wanted to fund. (Almost certainly it would have evolved into a magazine like today's *PC World* and *MacWorld*, which have similar computer-hippie roots.) We could also have set up ways for the computer editorial people to learn more from the CoEv Core Group, who were eager for respect and opportunities to collaborate. Had we pulled it off, we could have raised *everyone's* salaries and integrated the two publications together into one organization.

We didn't pull it off. But I emerged from that experience with an instinctive view of Core Groups as people below the top of the hierarchy. They aren't necessarily the highest-paid, but the entrenched keepers of the spirit of the enterprise. I intuitively expect such people to be power centers, and it took a long time for me to learn that Whole Earth is *not* typical—that few other organizations have the same kind of Core Group.

In all of these stories, people mistakenly assume that a pattern set long ago, by some other Core Group in some other organization, will be universal. We carry with us the Core Group members who have supported us or rejected us in the past, in a kind of Inner Core Group—and we try (usually unsuccessfully) to recreate the nature of that Inner Core Group in the organizations of the moment. Perhaps this happens because people respond to authority so viscerally, with (as writer Diana Guilbert puts it) "a mixture of fear and longing, secret fantasies of ecstatic union or deep vengeful resistance." Perhaps we're playing out a pattern of response to authority that we learned from our own parents, or from some other form of transference set into our psyches long ago. Even if those emotions have lain dormant for years, our early Core Group experiences seem to bring them back to prominence within us.

It's easy to say, "This inner Core Group is all in your mind," or "Don't act like a victim." But breaking this kind of cycle is far more difficult than it may seem at first glance. The Inner Core Group is invisible when you are consciously at your best. It manifests itself in high-stress moments—arguments with the boss, sudden deadlines, decisions to quit—when you don't have much perspective and it's particularly hard to change old habits. And in low-stress moments, when there's lots of time to reflect, it doesn't seem quite so important or difficult to deal with.

Some people find that they can break the cycle by "rehearsing" alternative approaches. Write down some dialogue, as you remember it, from the recurring patterns that have frustrated you in dealing with Core Groups. Then look at them in light of other Core Groups you have known in the past. Consider how you could respond to the provocations differently. During your dispassionate, reflective moments, "rehearse" those new ways of acting by literally role-playing the things you could do or say differently. Then, when the stakes get high and stress mounts, try to bring yourself back to the mind-set you had in your rehearsals. Gradually, in this way, build your own ability to break the pattern. Do it with a fair amount of charity toward yourself, recognizing that it may take a while to see real progress. (See Diagnostic Exercise 7, page 131.)

When you conduct intensive reflection of this nature, you're doing something that very few people do: You're creating an alternative Core Group within yourself. Henceforth, you will be carrying a consciously created mental image of the people who are truly important to you, on whose behalf you will be making decisions. That can't be done simply through intellectual cogitation; it requires practice, because it means reframing habits that have built themselves up through years of employment (and probably through childhood before that).

I have learned much of the significance of "inner core groups" through work on dialogue—a practice of collective thought and in-depth conversation. One leading dialogue practitioner, William Isaacs, reminded me not long ago that there is a kind of innate authority that develops within each of us as we cultivate our Inner Core Group. Ironically, that's probably the best way to get into the *external* Core Group of an organization worth working for. Such organizations are naturally attracted to people with the kind of maturity that stems from long-standing intensive reflection.

"You think you're in a Core Group or you're not," says Isaacs, "because of some external factor. You go to school, for instance, because you think the degree will get you into the Core Group. You wonder, 'How come this person got in and that person did not? How do I get to be part of it?' And all along, you're bypassing the critical question: 'Are you at the Core of your own life? Are you making decisions on behalf of your deepest unfolding potential?'"

Diagnostic Exercise 7
My Life Among the Core Groups
(Developed with Peter Garrett, Jane Ball, and Kelvy Bird)

Recall an organizational turning point where you were either in a Core Group, or in relationship to a Core Group and felt you were not being heard or understood.

1. What happened? (Write out some of the critical dialogue that took place during this episode.)
2. What did you do?
3. How did it affect you?
4. What could have been done differently?
5. What kinds of Core Groups are you attracted to today?
6. What kinds of Core Groups put you off?
7. How do you behave with the Core Group in your current organization?
8. What aspects of this behavior are inherited from other organizations?
9. How could you act differently now? (And what would happen if you rehearsed it during some relatively low-stress time? Would that make it easier to act differently during, say, an argument with your boss?)

CHAPTER 15

Core Group Enablers

W hat do these stories have in common (besides all being true)?

- In a small West Coast town, the most popular high school teacher has been there thirty years. He teaches advanced placement courses and coaches many teams, including some girls' teams. He is active in the teachers' union. All the faculty look up to him, and so do the students. But twice or three times a semester, a teenage girl appears with her parents at the office of the superintendent. The teacher, she says, made inappropriate remarks or touched her, or in one case, tried to kiss her. Each time, the superintendent, who is a sincere and harried woman with only a few years in residence, says something like this: "That's a very serious charge, and, you know, you're the only one who has brought it up. Are you sure you want to go all the way and make it public?" Rather than make a communitywide example of themselves, the parents end up sending their daughters to the only other high school available to them—an hour's bus ride each way.
- In a staff meeting at a small professional services firm, everyone complains about the behavior of Fred, the firm's founder and leading rainmaker. Breezing through the office between appointments, with a thousand details to coordinate in a couple of

hours, he has been brusque, abrupt, dismissive, critical, and un-
communicative, and feelings are rubbed raw. "I just don't see the
point in walking an extra mile around here," one staffer says.
"The one person who matters doesn't think I can do anything
decent anyway." Suddenly, an associate named Joyce is so upset
that she can contain herself no longer. "It makes me feel terribly slighted," she says, "to hear that Fred is the 'one person who
matters.' For weeks, I've been making an extra effort to compensate for him—to show everyone the respect they deserve, and
tell them what a terrific job they're doing. And now you're saying all that effort was wasted." People nod at her. That effort
was wasted. And yet they know, and she knows, that she's going
to try even harder next time, because if she doesn't try to make
things better, who will?

- The director of nursing in a private hospital reaches her one-
  year anniversary on the job, but she feels perpetually frustrated.
  Decisions that affect overall budgets and schedules are made in
  meetings to which she is not invited. She has no say in the
  salaries or compensation packages that she can offer her staff.
  Hers is a lonely voice of protest against staff cuts that will mean
  a drop in the quality of care (medical treatment won't be affected, but the intangibles of comfort, attentiveness, and nurturance will definitely be affected). And then, the hospital's
  financial officer decides to experiment with the staffing structure of one of the busiest units. Many nursing tasks are shifted
  over to lower-paid, less-educated orderlies. The director of nursing spends the weekend juggling schedules, so that the shift will
  do as little damage as possible. Her predecessor lasted fifteen
  months. Will she make it that long?

- A human resources executive at a major energy corporation lets
  down his guard one day and pours his heart out to a consultant.
  "I've been a patsy," he said. "A stooge. And everyone knows it."
  He had reported directly to a division head who had used him as
  a hatchet man during four years of downsizing. The HR executive had handled the job well: not just laying people off, but

chastising, demoting, and exiling them to far-flung outposts when they displeased the boss. Then his protector, the division head, retired. He himself had ten years to go before he could retire with a pension. Everyone throughout the company knew his record. No one respected him. Where could he exile himself?

- Overheard on an eleven P.M. weekday commuter train leaving New York City, a young woman talking on a cell phone: "I worked sixty-eight hours so far this week." Pause. "Sixty-*eight* hours." Then in a softer voice, "What they don't seem to understand is, I don't want the pity and the cab ride. I want them to appreciate what I do by *paying* me for it." Pause. "My sixty-eight hours got them to meet a $5 million contract. And I know it's all about profit margins, but . . . they're not starving." Then: "I know architects are notorious for not getting paid. But I'm not an architect." Later: "We went down to the wire and it might not make the bid and it looks like hell . . . all because *they're* disorganized."

All of these people are Core Group enablers. They have all adopted, down to their core, attitudes that they know are wrong, but that keep a dysfunctional Core Group in place. They may not be literally addicted, but they are all dependent on deeply held theories about the way the world works—theories that, upon examination, are deeply destructive to both their careers and their inner integrity.

The West Coast school superintendent has chosen to deny the facts about her abusive teacher. Joyce, the professional services firm, has bought the idea that if she doesn't make people feel better about working in that firm, it will fall apart. The director of nursing is going along with a premise she knows is wrong: that lowering costs means reducing the quality of care. The head of HR has spent his career assuming that his job means pleasing the boss, no matter what. And the woman on the train believes that she, and only she, can save this organization, and that sooner or later they will appreciate her.

All of them think that they are simply doing their job.

Moreover, all of them are sacrificing their own futures in the process. For example, the days of that "touchy-feely" high school teacher are numbered. Inevitably, he will be forced to resign. The superintendent who shelters him, because she feels she has no choice, will be forced out with him. (It happened a year after the visit I made in which I learned about that story.)

Many people who get caught up in this dynamic recognize the resonance with codependency, enabling, and addiction. "I'm just like the wife of an alcoholic," an internal consultant said to me, "except the alcoholics are the whole executive team. And I can't get away." After a while, if we're Core Group enablers, we start to exhibit some of the classic forms of codependent behavior in an abusive situation. We deny that the organization is exploiting us. ("No, this is a *great* place to work, and they're really looking out for me.") We see ourselves as unselfish and essential to the operation of the place. ("I have to stay; they'd fall apart without me.") We assume that our problems with the place stem from not being good enough. ("If I were really executive material, they'd have given me that raise.") We hide the organization's secrets from the outside world. ("If the SEC only knew what I know . . .") We compromise our own values and integrity, for the sake of loyalty. ("I wouldn't do this for anyone else, but Joe is my boss.") And we become resentful when we sense that the organization doesn't need us. ("They'll be sorry when they find out how indispensable I really am.")

In most of these cases, we strike an implicit bargain with the organization, a bargain that is neither heard nor honored by anyone but ourselves. "If I do good things for you, you'll take care of me when the time comes." Then, we keep a mental (or more likely, emotional) tally of the "good things" we've done, and we interpret dozens of random signals—from promises of promotions to invitations to make presentations to performance evaluations—as evidence of the organization keeping up its side of the bargain. These signals don't come very often, but they are enough to keep us hanging on, doing more than we're expected to do, continually hoping to be treated with respect but continually taken for granted, and defending the treatment we get. Every now and again the frustration is too much for us, and we express it in some passive-aggressive way: For instance, we perform some task in a way that will embarrass our boss, just enough to let us feel a little better.

It's not that the organization is deliberately trying to exploit us, or hold us back. It's just that most of its members don't see us. They only see the Core Group. They don't recognize our openness, engagement, and curiosity. If we want to give more, they'll happily take it, but they won't value it. Only the openness, engagement, and curiosity of the Core Group is valued.

What a waste of our time. What a waste, for the organization, of our potential.

It's also a waste of our perspective. Core Group enablers generally become what systems expert David Kantor calls "disabled bystanders." We see a terrible dysfunction, but we agree not to call attention to it; not to make waves. This is smart; we are poorly positioned to talk about these dysfunctions effectively. That's one reason why we became Core Group enablers in the first place. But by continuing down this path, we are reinforcing our powerlessness; we are making it easier for ourselves to continue our disabled, enabling, codependent role.

Nor can we expect the organization or the Core Group to do anything to help us; that's how we got into the situation in the first place. We'll have to extricate ourselves from this one on our own. We can only do that by thinking seriously about our "equity": the portfolio of resources and talents that we bring to the organization when we walk through its doors.

CHAPTER 16

A Portfolio
of Equity

Several years ago, at a medium-sized manufacturing firm, a young electronics engineer named Frederick was assigned to lead a team to develop and launch a new piece of high-tech equipment. Idealistic and thoughtful, Frederick saw his assignment as an opportunity to set an example for the whole company. Many projects came in after deadline and over budget, in a manic, round-the-clock final stretch accompanied by browbeating from senior management and desperate pleading from customers. This time, they would use state-of-the-art "team management" methods to change all that. They would "own" their project, organizing their own work processes, setting and tracking their goals and targets collaboratively. Frederick's bosses agreed, and the young team leader went to work.

But then, a few months after the project began, Frederick took a week's vacation. While he was gone, his boss stepped in and "tinkered a bit," changing the schedule and undoing a deal that the team had made with a supplier. When Frederick came back, he felt as if his legitimacy had been eroded. What was the point of team management if a higher authority could override it at any moment? Discouraged, Frederick quit his management role and dropped back to being an engineer again. Within a year, he dropped out of the company entirely, leaving his profession to become a sculptor.

"I wasn't treated like a person," he said. "They treated me like a commodity."

Three years later, he still spoke of the company with bitterness. And it wasn't just his loss. The product team forged ahead without him, pulling in his old boss as project manager on top of his other duties. Everyone reverted to the old way of operating: browbeating, missed deadlines, and high-stress panic. Eventually, they produced the new device—two years late and a million dollars over budget, amidst a grueling lawsuit with one of their suppliers. Had Frederick stayed on the scene, by all accounts, he probably would have prevented all that.

People like Frederick are everywhere, of course, in large organizations—both in good times and bad. And they always seem to fall into the same type of story. Smart and committed, they know a better way to operate. And then, smash! They come up against the organization's immune system. They go from being the organization's best hope to being seen as a kind of alien invader. And they never seem to recover their equilibrium.

Had he been more conscious when his new team approach was approved, Frederick would have realized that he didn't have the support he needed to make it work. Even though Frederick's new approach was formally approved, people all around him just assumed that, when push came to shove, the Core Group would reject it. Naturally, feeling that way, they had to tinker; they *had* to make Frederick feel like a commodity. They *had* to destroy the project in order to save it.

Imagine that you are someone in Frederick's position—someone who sees a new way of operating or a new strategy, and yearns to make it work in your company. You recognize that the organization, simply by its nature, cares more about the perceived priorities of the Core Group than it does about committed, creative junior people like yourself. How then can you gain any leverage at all? At first glance, the circumstances might seem to call for cynicism; in the working world, you might think, idealists like yourself will always come to nothing. But there is another way of looking at it that can be highly liberating, one which allows people at every level of an organization to act with integrity and intelligence to pursue what they most want and what they believe is best for the organization. In this view, Frederick suffered not because he lacked integrity or intelligence, but because he lacked organizational equity—the kind of equity that you can create yourself, which increases your influence in your organization, and helps you fulfill your own dreams.

You may ordinarily think of equity as the assets, transformed into stock, that shareholders own. And this is of course a valuable form of equity for employees—whether purchased through options, awarded in grants, or bought through 401(k)-style investments. One could call this "ownership equity." Paradoxically, its greatest value comes before it's cashed in: as a visible sign of your commitment to the performance of the whole. It aligns your fate and the company's fate together in a tangible way. But if it's the only form of equity you own, as many employee-shareholders have seen since 2001, it makes you all too tangibly vulnerable.

In the end, our conventional definition of equity is far too narrow. Equity is any share of accumulated wealth, including such intangible forms of "social capital" as relationships and reputation. There are dozens of types of equity that an individual can accumulate, including these:

- **Fungible financial equity:** Can you accumulate, through savings or other means, enough money to be able to walk away from an organization if you can't live with the Core Group? Can you accumulate enough to invest in your own development, even if your employer doesn't? Having this amount actually makes it easier to live with the organization, which will sense that you are staying with it through genuine interest, not financial dependence.
- **Rainmaking equity:** The ability to raise money or business is a form of capital. It depends, in part, on your contacts in the outside world, and even more on your ability to approach them. If you

are not in the Core Group, you can still command respect for this skill, especially in some nonprofit organizations.

- **Credential equity:** Once you have held a position, or acquired a credential, it remains with you for a lifetime. Those who have been presidents of companies can become presidents of companies again. Those with degrees in a field, from engineering to education, are qualified for life for employment in those fields. Most corporations are relatively stalwart meritocracies outside the Core Group; credentials are an indispensable form of equity within them. They're so invaluable that nontenured academics at some universities (such as Cambridge University in England) sometimes pay for the privilege of maintaining an office there, for the credential of association that goes with it.

- **Reputation equity:** People who live by their wits, like lawyers, doctors, consultants, and writers, have always known the value of managing this kind of equity. "Any general statement is like a cheque drawn on a bank," wrote poet Ezra Pound. "Its value depends on what is there to meet it. If Marconi says something about ultra-short waves it *means* something." I know several innovative managers who have protected their right to innovate by continually writing for outside publication and speaking in outside conferences—thereby demonstrating that *someone,* at least, honors their ideas.

- **Relationship equity:** Some people never have a problem meeting new people or making trusted friends. People seek *them* out. As Malcolm Gladwell noted in *The Tipping Point,* Paul Revere was able to roust the farmers of Middlesex because he was a natural convivialist, a frequenter of bars, and a member of social groups, including the budding groups of revolutionaries then emerging. In corporate America, such relationship equity (particularly the ability to know the Core Group) can save people from losing their jobs, even though they challenge the top.

Journalist Dominick Dunne's memoir/novel of the O. J. Simpson trial, *Another City, Not My Own,* is a textbook on relationship equity and how to cultivate it. Though he was an unabashed partisan who repeatedly proclaimed his belief that O.J.

was guilty (the courtroom TV camera focused on his shocked ex-
pression when the verdict of innocence was announced), he got
to know people on all sides of the story, including celebrities,
prosecutors, lawyers, quiet noncelebrity bystanders, those who
were estranged from each other, and Simpson's mother and sister. In one of the book's most compelling scenes, Dunne's narra-
tor brings an elaborate present to Simpson's sisters from the
designer Carolina Herrera, who (like most socialites) is con-
vinced Simpson is guilty. Yet the encounter is suffused with gra-
ciousness and with the awareness that, despite everything, there
is something human common to everyone, something closely
tied to the motions of everyday life, that must be acknowledged
even in the most extraordinary of circumstances.

- **Capability equity:** Perhaps the form of equity that does the most for
you is your ability to gain new capabilities and skills—because
these accelerate your accumulation of all the other forms of equity.
Most organizational-learning literature, emotional-intelligence
literature, all forms of how-to literature, is about building
capabilities.
- Health, fitness, family, love, awareness, sensitivity, spirit—these,
too, are forms of equity that either grow larger or smaller with
time, depending on how we cultivate and pay attention to them.

Some forms of equity are measurable while others are not, but
all of them have two key features in common.

First, they give you leverage in an organization (and in life in
general).

Second, they accrue exponentially, with the same compound-
interest emotional dynamics as a savings account.

When you first consider building a nest egg (say, in your twenties), it seems impossible that your amounts will ever amount to
anything of significance. But suppose you stick with it. You even
pick up the pace of savings as your income increases, eventually
crossing a threshold of confidence; the recognition of your own
ability to acquire a significant stake. In other words, you've demonstrated your ability to save. Moreover, in the process, you've learned

something about making money and investing it. You're probably earning more, so your savings represent a smaller proportion of your discretionary income. (This is one of the key themes of such bestsellers as *Rich Dad, Poor Dad,* which stress building financial equity not primarily as money saved but as knowledge of business and of one small realm of investment where your expertise will catapult you into confidence.)

Sometime in your forties or fifties, your account crosses another threshold—the threshold of sustainability. It is large enough to generate a significant income just from the interest. You have created what economists call capital: a resource that replenishes itself. For example: With enough capital to generate, say, $15,000 per year in interest, you could find a part of the world where you could live cheaply, peel off the interest, keep the principal intact, and never have to work again. You could devote your time and energy to the things you'd always wanted to do: creating a business, writing a novel, starting a new kind of agency, or saving the world. (This is the basic theme of the sustainable-life money guide, *Your*

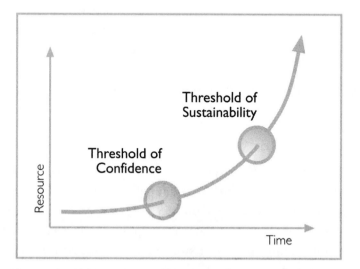

Two thresholds in building any kind of resource: the threshold of confidence (where you start to grasp, emotionally, the power of your accumulation) and the threshold of sustainability (where your equity generates enough to replenish itself without effort).

Money or Your Life, which posits financial independence as a goal for anyone on any income level.)

Other forms of equity can also become self-sustaining. People with a sufficient number of friends and acquaintances find it easy to make more; relationships breed more relationships. Similarly, people who already have significant reputations automatically attract opportunities to build their reputations further, through speaking, writing, teaching, and sometimes television appearances.

All forms of equity involve the same two thresholds: confidence and sustainability. Most coming-of-age stories have to do with crossing the threshold of confidence: Harry Potter learns to play quidditch (skill equity); E. B. White's Wilbur the Pig establishes a form of notoriety that saves his life (reputation equity) through his ability to befriend others (relationship equity); the J. D. Salinger heroine Franny Glass in his classic novel *Franny and Zooey* develops a kind of emotional and spiritual depth (capability equity). The message of these stories to the listener is: "You can do it, too."

Stories about sustainability usually take the form of tales of long-lived dynasties—the Rothschilds, the Kennedys, the Rockefellers—who continually build on their holdings. And, of course, there are many cautionary tales about ne'er-do-wells or hapless types who lose their sustainable position. Just as a family fortune can be dissipated, "shirtsleeves to shirtsleeves in three generations," nonfinancial equity will erode if it is not well managed. Once it is drawn down past the threshold of sustainability, it no longer can replenish itself, and it can vanish with unexpected speed.

Although all equity growth is compounded, different forms of equity have different rhythms for growth. Money accumulates gradually, with a smooth exponential curve of steady, mathematical advancement. Skills and capabilities accumulate through a kind of punctuated equilibrium; the innovative organizational psychologist Elliott Jaques demonstrated that the human ability to deal with complexity crosses a cognitive threshold every fifteen years. (Have you ever had the experience of suddenly realizing that you're routinely doing the kinds of complex tasks that flummoxed you a few years ago? That's what it feels like to cross a cognitive threshold.) Reputation's curve seems to advance on accelerated momentum and then come to sudden stops, with no clear cue about when it will start up again. Only seizing the moment when opportunity strikes develops rainmaking equity.

Our organizations *should* be helping us accumulate a variety of forms of equity, just as they help us accumulate stock, and for the same reasons: to cement loyalty, align people with the purpose of the enterprise, and build the strength of the whole system. In the absence of that help, at least we can build equity for ourselves, and lead a rich, rewarding life in the workplace, whether or not we are part of the Core Group.

In retrospect, the reason Frederick, the young electronics engineer, got into so much trouble was this: *He didn't have enough different kinds of equity to match the complexity of the job he had taken on.* People like him often are invited to take on roles and projects that look like one-way tickets to the top. But they are actually tickets to failure, granted thoughtlessly and irresponsibly by managers who think they are being benificent. Before too long, inevitable roadblocks are raised; people come in and micromanage; rumors of incompetence spread. The only way to deal with this is to have accumulated enough equity, of various sorts, that you can protect yourself.

Consider Frederick's story in terms of the equity he had—and didn't have:

Type of equity	Applicable to this situation	Available to Frederick
Fungible financial equity	Frederick was not being asked to invest money in this project; he would need financial equity only as leverage, in case he decided to walk away from the company.	Ultimately, he *did* walk away. Had he not had enough financial equity to begin his sculpting career, he would have been stuck in an untenable situation.

Rainmaking equity	The budget was set from above, so ostensibly there was no need for more; in reality, however, the ability to raise more money would have greatly increased Frederick's options (and the team's).	Frederick had almost no rainmaking equity, and suffered accordingly.
Ownership equity (stock in company)	Stock in the company was not critical for Frederick's success. Significant stock or options would, however, have made it clear that he was potential Core Group material.	There was no plausible way at his level for Frederick to hold enough stock in this company to make a difference here.
Reputation equity	Any new team leader trying a massive experiment in new approaches needs a highly competent and creative reputation.	Frederick lacked the reputation he needed. At minimum, a presentation of the rationale for his approach would have made a difference. Even if people at the top didn't attend, the presentation might have made them aware of Frederick's contribution and foresight.
Relationship equity	Frederick needed a great deal of strategic power to maneuver through the infighting among his various bosses, to get sponsorship for his new approach, and to provide "air cover" for his team so they would be let alone.	Frederick had excellent relationships on a peer level and with suppliers. But his lack of good relationships up the hierarchy was a crippling factor. There was no one he could go to for candid counsel or perspective; there was no one who would give him "air cover" without raising eyebrows or concern about the project.

Credential equity	Once you are a team mana-ger, you will always be a team manager.	This was Frederick's first time as team manager. He had only partially built the credentials he needed for credibility in this bold step.
Capability equity	Significant capabilities are needed to manage a team that must work together in new ways.	Frederick, despite the training he had undergone in "team dynamics," lacked the facilitation and project management skills that he needed. He was trying to build them through "on-the-job train-ing," which meant that he had some capital, but had not yet crossed the sec-ond threshold to have a sustainable set of skills.

Anyone, no matter how downtrodden (or how excluded from the Core Group), can build some kind of equity. But there is no one-size-fits-all strategy for building a portfolio of organizational equity. Your choice depends on what is easy for you, and what kinds of equity your organization and its Core Group value. Most impor-tant, your choice depends on the kind of life you are trying to cre-ate. Because you cannot tell in advance which will be most useful to you, accruing many forms of equity helps contribute to a well-rounded life. Having a reputation for being trustworthy and capa-ble, and having an extensive network of competent, trustworthy people who take your calls, is a better hedge than a lot of money invested in an unbalanced portfolio of stocks. A lifelong strategy of building equity also means that we don't have to wait for someone else to bestow something on us—whether it's stock options, jobs, or membership in the Core Group.

Each of us has a head start in some forms of equity, but not in all of them. Some people who have no money but who have, from a very young age, been gifted in relationship equity, don't really *need* a lot of money to be secure. They will always find a network of people to rely on. They probably grew up in a house with people passing through all the time and intuitively understood how to cultivate relationships.

One final bit of encouragement: Building any of these forms of equity is easier than it seems. It always starts off slow and agonizing until you cross the threshold of confidence. By the time you cross the threshold of sustainability, it's hard to remember that you ever had a problem.

When taking on a new assignment or pushing your job to a new level, ask yourself: What kinds of equity does this challenge require? How much of that equity will I need ahead of time, and how much can I build on the job? And if I don't have it, what do I do to develop it, and how long will that take?

Diagnostic Exercise 8
My Own Portfolio of Equity

Without any blame or harsh judgment, maybe it's time to take an inventory of your own portfolio of equity.

For each of the following, ask yourself: Where am I? Am I past the threshold of confidence? Am I past the threshold of sustainability? And what would be a good indicator that I have crossed the next threshold?

For instance, if you're in financial debt (welcome to the club), you're probably not past the threshold of confidence with fungible financial equity. How much money would you need to accumulate, and how liquid would it have to be, to gain confidence in your ability to preserve that kind of wealth? Or, if you have confidence in your reputation, what would be a sign that your reputation was, in fact, generating more interest on its own?

- *Fungible financial equity*
- *Rainmaking equity*
- *Ownership equity (stock or other ownership in the organizations where you work)*
- *Reputation equity*

- *Relationship equity*
- *Credential equity*
- *Capability equity*
- *Health and fitness*
- *Family and love*
- *Awareness, sensitivity, and spirit*

Suppose now that you could focus your attention on only one of these at a time. Which is the greatest "toothache"—in other words, the gap in equity that screams so much for your attention that it is hard to focus on anything else?

And which is the greatest leverage—in other words, if you crossed a threshold here, would it help you cross thresholds of others?

Finally, if you were willing to ignore the "toothache" equity long enough to focus on the "leverage" equity, if only for a little while, how would you begin?

Part 4

Core Group

Stories

CHAPTER 17

Parasitic Core Groups

The parasites of the business world who garnered so much attention in 2002, such as the Core Group members of Enron, Worldcom, Tyco, and other prominent mendaciously bankrupt enterprises, are relative amateurs.

The most successful parasites don't get caught. They bleed their organizations dry, build up the stock price, flip the company to someone else, and walk away rich. One could argue that this is the easiest way to get rich in the United States—if you don't mind doing so at the expense of employees, shareholders, and customers. There is only one prerequisite: to be willing and able to use your power as a Core Group member to reframe the purpose of an organization. You do this by sending a consistent message, day after day: The organization exists to extract money from its businesses. It is willing to starve and potentially to die, so that the parasitic Core Group may live well.

A parasite, as Arie de Geus puts it, is any part of a company that "serves its own self-interest at the expense of the natural functions of the host organization." Any parasite can damage its host, but a parasitic Core Group is particularly devastating, because its priorities are so loudly amplified throughout the organization. One shouldn't assume that any particular type of organization has a monopoly on parasitic Core Groups. Some of the most prominent dot-com bubble Core Groups, like the management teams at

Amazon.com and eBay, aren't parasitic at all. There are parasitic Core Groups in small-scale, nonprofit, and government organizations as well as in large corporations.

Alas, it's not easy to detect the presence of a parasitic Core Group while there is still time to stop it. Some of the most open-seeming and collegial Core Groups have turned out to be the most exploitive in the end. The best-known example is still Enron. As late as the summer of 2001, Enron's Core Group was seen as one of the most energetic, employee-enabling leadership teams in corporate America. I knew relatively high-level executives at other oil companies who asked themselves, that year, "Why can't we be more like Enron?"

From inside Enron, it was easy to believe that *everyone* was in the Core Group, or at least everyone who "ranked" relatively well. The company's dramatically-rising equity, in which most employees felt they had a share, wasn't the only factor that kept them motivated to show up at six A.M. and leave at seven P.M., day after day. There was the excitement people felt: "You walked in the door," one employee recalled in the *Houston Chronicle,* "and got energized. You worked with the best, the most brilliant." Merely making it through the "rank and yank" performance system, in which the top ten percent were lionized and the bottom ten percent were jettisoned, made you part of an elite. There was a continual feeling of being in touch: George W. Bush, during his presidential campaign, was often seen in the building. And while there was a perpetual *Animal House* atmosphere (complete with CEO Ken Lay in the Tim Matheson role as the charmer who beguiled outsiders), there was the sense that they could do good for the world like no one else could. In the days after September 11, 2001, Enron provided shuttle buses so employees could donate blood.

They also did well for their employees. When floods struck Houston early in 2001, Enron immediately gave $1,000 to all employees who needed emergency cash. Everyone could feel the company continually trying, as a whole, to give them what they wanted. In some departments, employees received a cell phone, pager, personal data assistant, and laptop; people often flew around the country first-class on company business. In the e-commerce group, they got free pastries, communal dinners during late-night assignments, foosball games, and big-screen TVs in the company lounges. Ironically, this was one reason why Enron got into trouble in the first place. There were simply too many people acting as if their apparent Core Group status gave them free rein over the company's resources. They were drawing too much money in bonuses, and making too many bad deals as a vehicle for their own rewards; it would have taken a few dozen California energy crises to provide the cash flow to sustain all that.

Then came the collapse. Suddenly, employees were stalled when they tried to sell their stock or confirm their severance package. They were dismissed summarily, sometimes in floor meetings where they were told to pack up their belongings in a half hour, sometimes by e-mail or voicemail, often without any explanation or comment about their future. Some employees learned of the insolvency of their pensions from newspaper reporters. And then came the published news that $55 million in last-minute bonuses had been divided among 500 key employees.

"As a young child of ten years of age, I witnessed the fall of Vietnam," wrote one Enron employee to the *Chronicle*. "Last Monday, Dec. 2, 2001, those memories came flooding back. There were plenty of rumors and unofficial information, but not one word of communication from upper management. By around noon, we were all told to go home and evacuate the building immediately. We did not know what to do with our badge, our parking card, or if we were officially severed from the company. Security guards walked around the floors and watched people while they packed, as if they were potential thieves."

By now, it has all become clear—not just how paltry the Enron business model was, but exactly how small and corrupt the true Enron Core Group was. The dividing line between this Core Group and the rest of the organization was not the availability of stock options (most everyone had *those*), but the knowledge of when to sell the stock, the ability to do so legally, and the awareness of the meaning of the hidden partnerships and other secret deals. Only some Enron insiders knew that a falling stock price would rapidly drain the company of cash, because it had used the stock to guarantee loans to its off-balance-sheet entities. Deals like these were the company equivalent to the Coca-Cola formula, and Enron's specialized knowledge (its "integrated learning base") included the ability to create them. But when the stock price fell, the deals could no longer be sustained.

A few Enron employees escaped the crisis. They were the ones who never bought the story that they were part of Enron's Core Group. Instead, despite all the camaraderie and perks, they recognized their true status as employees of mutual consent. They took the stock they were granted, sold when the price was reasonably high, and diversified. Some of them saw the fall coming but, for reasons of their own, chose not to escape. The head of research at Enron, for instance, has been acknowledged by some as a principled individual who refused to resign because he felt he had to protect the people who worked for his department.

What might you look for, to recognize in advance the presence of a parasitic Core Group? A veil of secrecy at top levels. Great levels of debt, and immense pressure to keep it hidden. Inherent conflicts of interest. A lack of strong governance—for instance, when the CEO either serves as chairman of the board or handpicks most of the board members. A large gap between the salaries of the highest- and lowest-paid employees. A culture of profligacy, especially compared to others in similar industries (money for perks and bonuses must be coming from somewhere). Lack of response when insiders ask difficult questions (as many insiders apparently did). A discrepancy between the hyped performance and real performance—for instance, even at its height of glory, Enron earned only one-half of one percent on its sales.

And maybe you'd also have noticed an arrogant, self-satisfied culture; as a letter writer to the *Houston Chronicle* put it, "the employee mentality was always, 'How can I get a piece?' " Another wrote, "Upper management of Enron was filled with very young, mostly early thirties and forties men and women who were promoted faster than they could move to their new office. As their income grew, so did their heads and their selfishness." There are stories of Enron's traders buying all the lines leading to a competitor's new natural gas production plant, shutting off the valves, and effectively holding the plant hostage until another deal they wanted from that competitor came through. In March 2001, according to a California state attorney general, Enron's staff responded to a document subpoena by sending 940 file cartons full of discarded Kleenexes, old pizza boxes, and other garbage. It's hard to imagine a company capable of generating this behavior unless the Core Group was parasitical and arrogant.

Unfortunately, however, these factors also describe a lot of companies with Core Groups that aren't *quite* as parasitical as Enron's. They aren't parasitical enough to self-implode, only to make life miserable for their employees by exploiting them.

There's another Houston oil company, for example, which has weathered the Enron storm quite effectively. Arrogance and selfishness are at least as much in evidence, but they take a different form. A vice president at this company regularly makes visits to field offices where the local executives—who are Core Group members of the local outposts—suddenly become his handservants. They know that he needs a certain brand of bottled water, a particular type of hotel room, a preferred cigar after his meal. If the details aren't carried out to the letter, their jobs will be affected. After the meal and the cigar, there inevitably comes a presentation at which people throw themselves at his feet, offering an explanation of their last half-year's performance in an elaborately choreographed slideshow-and-booklet presentation, with every detail in place. He routinely interrupts to belittle them, making jokes at their expense. When you factor in the wasted time and stress-related side effects, somewhere between one-quarter and one-half of the administrative budget of every local office goes to stroking the egos of this vice president and other Core Group members.

Most parasitic leaders don't start out fraudulent. They're simply self-indulgent. They're like antiheroes of a film noir, starting out with one or two expedient moves and gradually getting drawn into a web of perfidy, almost despite themselves. Gradually, they become the organizational equivalent of gigolos: taking advantage of their organization's infatuation with them, and pretending to return the same level of affection.

What do we do about parasitic Core Groups? As an Enron alumnus (one who emerged relatively unscathed) wrote me: "Once criminal behavior sets in, the only realistic choice, if you see it, is to leave. Even Core Group members who wouldn't go along had to leave; they couldn't influence change from within."

But in the wake of the scandals of 2002, "freedom to leave" is not enough of a disincentive for parasitism. There is now a movement to set up far more stringent laws and policing practices. Over the next few years, the debate over policing corporations will rage, and ultimately it will lead to a new set of legal restrictions, along with some new zeal for enforcing the old ones.

I personally believe that formal policing, in itself, won't suffice. If policing is left to formal entities alone (regulators, the board, and the hierarchy) then Core Group parasites, who are deeply embedded in the organization's informal networks, will find ways to circumvent them. The Core Groups themselves have to be involved in the prevention. They have to realize that the survival of the enterprise depends in the long run on their willingness to engage others around them. Which in turn means they have to be transparent and open.

If we're serious about cutting back parasitic behavior in organizations (and I'm not sure we are), then we need some way to pick up the small indicators of parasitic behavior that set the stage for larger-scale parasitism to develop. In other words, there's an organizational analogy to the "broken windows" theory of criminality. Small environmental factors—graffiti, building upkeep, tolerance for small violations like subway toll jumping—send a collective signal about the level of crime that is permitted in that community. Similarly, an organization's small-scale parasitic behaviors—reluctance to reconsider exploitive accounting practices, administrative staff who are treated like servants, an obsessive attention to parking spots and pecking orders, the willingness to "do whatever it takes" to get some new star on board—may send a collective signal about the ultimate levels of parasitism that this Core Group could embrace.

When it's hard to make contact with a Core Group—when its members don't return legitimate calls, or don't explain their rationales clearly, or insist on drawing clear boundaries of inaccessibility between themselves and the rest of the organization—that isn't automatically a sign that you have a parasitic Core Group on your hands. But in the wake of the parasites of 2001–2002, it's clearly a worrisome signal. It would be nice if the best employees and investors began to recognize this, and started putting their time and money into those organizations that respond openly to them. Such organizations may not perform best on every measure, but they are the least likely to turn out to be parasites. That almost certainly makes them, as a whole, the best performers in the long run.

CHAPTER 18

Core Group Feuds and Maladaptive Companies

When she first came to Hewlett-Packard as CEO in 1999, Carly Fiorina was a great symbol of hope. Not only was she the only female CEO in the Fortune 200; in her first year, revenues and earnings jumped higher and so did the corporate atmosphere. Barbara Waugh, who was the worldwide change manager at HP Labs (and whose book *The Soul in the Computer* is a powerful guide to being an effective change agent from within), described Fiorina as "a CEO who cares about her company's soul." Fiorina was an early and eager champion of such farsighted projects as the "E-inclusion" strategy, in which HP set up partnerships with microlenders to create Internet access, new markets, and other services for entrepreneurs in impoverished areas around the world. Fiorina's tag line, "invent," seemed to capture the HP ethos to many people inside the company.

But then came the profit slide, the failed attempt to purchase Price-Waterhouse Coopers, a round of layoffs, the announcement of a proposed merger with Compaq, the opposition from "Bill and Dave's" children, the proxy battle with Walter Hewlett (son of founder Bill), the angry ads in the newspapers, the leaked arrangement that Fiorina and other top executives would receive multimillion-dollar bonuses upon completing the merger, the official renunciation of those bonuses, the booting of Hewlett from the HP board, and the announcement of a second round of 15,000 layoffs. It soon became clear that Fiorina was trying to accomplish what so many companies had done successfully during the 1980s and 1990s: a Welchist redefinition of the Core Group from "everyone in the company" to a "few select insiders."

But HP was not a typical company. It was a highly networked company founded on personal relationships. William Hewlett and David Packard had been friends who wanted to work together, and had designed the company accordingly. For instance, they flipped a coin to decide which initial would come first. *The HP Way*, their 1957 management credo, was written in part to inoculate the company against the destructive temptations of short-term investment financing. It put forward employee welfare, intellectual contribution, inventiveness, entrepreneurship, and community values as the goals of the company, and said that profits were important only as a means to those goals. The "HP Way" mind-set had led directly to some of Hewlett-Packard's most famous practices: "Management by walking around" (Tom Peters gleaned the practice and the phrase at HP), informal gatherings on Friday afternoons, free donuts, and the Open Door policy—symbolized by literally "open doors" in the founders' offices.

To be sure, there were also a lot of problems at HP. It was a company of fiercely competitive people. (Michael Maccoby's concept of the organizational "gamesman," for whom winning is everything, was conceived during a study of HP managers.) Its top leaders, each with their own functional fiefdoms, quarreled bitterly and sometimes tacitly sabotaged lucrative opportunities that would have required them to cooperate. Barbara Waugh once gave a speech in which she recounted how a veteran HP manager told her, "Stick around and look deep. You'll find that HP is an ocean. The senior management cruises around in battleships on the surface, shooting at each other, declaring victories and suffering losses. About two feet down and for all the miles below are the rest of us, swimming around doing the business of the ocean. We try to make sure that what's going on up there doesn't affect us too much. We just dive a little deeper into the work when the turbulence threatens to touch us."

Many companies endure such turbulence as a matter of course.

They manage to keep going, despite having fragmented Core Groups. But the fracas over the Compaq merger transcended business as usual. When Walter Hewlett decided to initiate a shareholders' revolt against the merger, and then a lawsuit, he visibly broke away from both the management and the board. The company's Core Group split down the middle. On the Fiorina side was the CEO and most of the board; on the Hewlett side, some key leaders inside the company and the representatives of the two founders' families. By early 2002, HP had fallen into one of the most destructive circumstances an organization can face: a feud within the Core Group.

To be sure, most Core Groups are somewhat diverse—and should be. Too little dissension in a Core Group is unhealthy; it suggests not just groupthink, but insular domination by one or two people. By contrast, healthy companies often have established and even ritualized forms of conflict, in which executives and other members can bring up the most vicious disagreements in a thoroughly impersonal way, without breaking their relationships. This becomes a healthy model for everyone in the enterprise.

But when a Core Group splits into Hatfields and McCoys whose attention is focused (or perceived to be focused) on beating the other half, then it puts the organization into a terrible cognitive double bind. Since the Core Group's signals get amplified so loudly, the organization will start to embody the prevailing message from both sides: that it's safe to assume the worst about everyone. The decision-makers can't choose one side or the other. They can't talk about the dilemma they face. And they can't talk about the fact that they can't talk about it. That, after all, would be complaining.

This is the same dynamic that psychologists have attributed as one cause of "maladaptive behavior"—behavior that causes undue discomfort to oneself or to others. When people respond to stress with uncontrollable anger (paranoia), by laughing off problems unconvincingly (hebephrenia), or by withdrawing (catatonia), there may be a variety of reasons, but one accepted explanation for many of these cases is that they have been trapped in a cognitive double bind that they can't talk about openly. In their frustration, they learn inappropriate ways of responding—ways that are very difficult to unlearn.

If you had a Core Group feud at your company, then you might well see the same kinds of symptoms rampant. Some people would be visibly, viscerally angry: "Those bastards!" Others would laugh it off unconvincingly: "There's no problem." And others would withdraw and try to ignore everything going on at higher levels: "Just go away and let me clean off my desk." No one would be comfortable talking about the reasons for their shift of behavior; people would feel vulnerable in any form of open discussion. Underneath it all, there would be a fundamental question about the makeup of the Core Group. Who is at the heart of the company? Who are we supposed to be loyal to? Whose image do we carry around in our minds? (All of these symptoms were evident at HP.)

In a circumstance like that, the first order of business is to end the feud. Because Core Groups are judged by the way they act, this articulation, of a "whole greater than the sum of its parts," has to be grounded in action. To heal a maladaptive system, there needs to be a deliberate series of small but symbolically significant actions that are consistent with each other and that build momentum gradually, so that word of mouth spreads: There is now one set of leaders again. We don't have to worry about which one will "win."

It's too soon to tell how the newly unified, newly Welchist, post-Compaq Fiorina-era Hewlett-Packard will fare. Many observers are still skeptical, but maybe the aftermath of the great HP Core Group feud will be a resolution, once and for all, of the old fiefdoms that fragmented the company at the top. And maybe, just maybe, there's another bright side to living through a Core Group feud (as long as it doesn't drag on too long). It reminds us that organizations have more significant purposes than any one Core Group faction can encompass.

Barbara Waugh puts it this way in her book: "Remember Who

you work for." (The capitalization is hers.) In other words, you may report to a boss, but your true employer is a principle larger than any boss: "It might be ending poverty, God, a sustainable planet, or whatever is big enough to be worth your life. If you can hold that stance, you'll stand in a place that gives you much better options than simply standing inside the teeny little problem of the moment, trying to figure out what to do for the boss on the organization chart. And incidentally, you'll do better by the boss on the org chart, too."

Diagnostic Exercise 9
Where Are the Feuds in the Core Group?

Starting with the diagram you produced for Diagnostic Exercise 1, overlay another drawing of the key interrelationships among Core Group members.

Which members of the Core Group are generally aligned with each other, operating to common aims? Draw dotted lines among them.

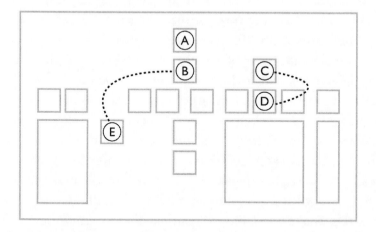

Now group the various Core Group members according to the affinities you have identified. You may find some people with ties to more than one camp, but in general, group people according to which are pursuing the same basic goals and aims:

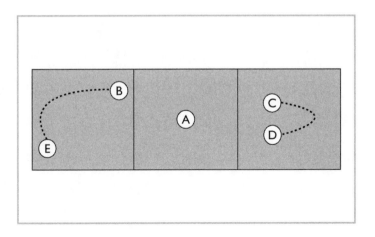

What does each of these groups stand for? What goal is it perceived to represent or pursue?

Which of these groups are actively feuding with each other? Which of these feuds are perceived by the organization to be important?

What is the effect on the organization of each of these feuds? How are they amplified through "guesswork" or other means?

Which of these feuds are irreversible and unhealable? Which of these feuds could be dealt with, a bit, by bringing people together to talk them through?

Where would be an appropriate place (if any) to start?

Which Core Group member or members would sponsor such an endeavor?

How might it begin?

CHAPTER 19

Government Agencies

N ow that we understand about Core Groups, what are we going to do about government agencies?

We may well be at a historic choice point. For the past century or more, economists and politicians have fiercely debated the most effective way to run an economy or a government: with relatively free markets, or with relatively strong governments. But now a recognition is sinking in that the argument itself is irrelevant. It doesn't matter whether the market or the state is in charge. (In fact, a competent public sector and a competent private sector can actually reinforce each others' competence if they're willing to work in partnership.) Indeed, the boundaries among government agencies, nonprofit organizations, and for-profit entities have been blurring for decades, and are destined to keep blurring.

What matters most is the quality of the Core Group. Competent organizations with high-quality leadership are likely to produce the most effective infrastructure and services—public *or* private. All the blame and finger-pointing about corrupt plutocrats and entrenched bureaucrats is simply a distraction from the most essential question: How can government agencies be set up to foster high-quality Core Groups?

This is also the conclusion reached ten years ago by the most authoritative and comprehensive study of government agencies that I know of: *Bureaucracy* by James Q. Wilson. Wilson opens this masterwork by describing three government organizations that produced dramatically effective results compared to their peers: the German army at the start of World War II (when it invaded France), the Texas state prison system in the late 1970s (in which prisons were orderly and clean, the level of violence went down, the cost-efficiency was high, and inmate education seemed to be effective), and the George Washington Carver High School in Atlanta (whose quality underwent a dramatic improvement despite no turnover in staff). In all three cases, the effectiveness stemmed from the ability of a particular leadership team—a Core Group, though Wilson doesn't call it that—to take charge of an operation and make it work.

There are more examples: "The Army Corps of Engineers, the Social Security Administration, the Marine Corps, the Forest Service, the FBI," writes Wilson. "For many years after they were created, and in many instances still today, these agencies, along with a few others that could be mentioned, were a kind of elite service that stood as a living refutation of the proposition that 'all bureaucrats are dim-witted paper-shufflers.' And these are only the federal examples; at the local level one can find many school systems and police departments that have acquired a praiseworthy organizational character." He might have found still more examples by looking outside the United States, to (for example) the Netherlands, Singapore, Australia, Canada, or Chile. These are all countries where public service is seen as a viable career path for the "best and brightest," and where the phrase "great government agency" doesn't sound like an oxymoron.

If great government agencies are rare in the U.S., it's not because government people lack dedication or intelligence. James Q. Wilson identifies several factors, but they all seem to come down to the mandates, rules, and oversight with which agencies are established—and which continually change with the political winds. Every time a legislature (or an executive) feels the pull of a new priority, it gets added to the agency's charter, often without much regard for other priorities. A police force is founded to provide an atmosphere of public safety; then, reasonably enough, it is charged with maintaining equitable treatment of all citizens; it is supposed to reflect the ethnic makeup of the communities it patrols; it must process all arrests quickly and efficiently; it must maintain comprehensive records that will allow overseers to track potential abuses of power; it must maintain "neighborhood watch"–style programs that build good community relations; it must focus on violent crimes; it must focus on "lifestyle" crimes like drugs and prostitution; it must focus on protection against terrorism.

How does any individual decision-maker—in this case, a cop on the street—balance all these priorities? In the best police forces, the Core Group members themselves embody that balance; they visibly make tough choices in a way that gets amplified through the rest of the agency. Rules and regulations are relatively few; people relax them when needed, but understand and obey their intent. In the worst police forces, by contrast, there tend to be a vast number of rules and regulations that look complete and comprehensive on paper, but that are far too complex to carry out with any consistency. Different members of the Core Group, loyal to different priorities, interpret the rules accordingly and end up feuding with each other.

An agency with a weak or feuding Core Group can do enormous damage—not just to the government, but to the economic and social sphere of that region or country. Perhaps the most egregious example in the United States in recent years has been the Federal Communications Commission, charged with regulating the broadcast spectrum, telecommunications industries, and satellite bands. The long-term FCC staff is composed of entrenched career civil servants, divided among separate "bureaus" that include long-distance and local telephone, broadcast, cable, and international (including satellite). Each bureau has its own internal Core Group, and each has its own friends in corporate places—telecommunications or broadcast companies who have lobbied so well, and so long, that they are in the FCC's Core Group as well. Then there are various public-interest organizations, and the congressional members they cultivate. And then there are key Congress members with an interest in telecommunications, the political parties looking to place key members in sinecure jobs, the key decision-makers in other executive branch departments (such as, for example, the secretaries of commerce and defense, both with an interest in telecommunications), the key agencies (like the National Security Agency) with the ability to stop certain types of initiatives, and key journalists who cover the industry that the FCC regulates. The FCC Core Group members, who include (but aren't limited to) the commissioners, cope with all these imperatives by picking sides: choosing which interests they will represent.

Thus, in any significant decision, the agency must make decisions on behalf of Core Group members who are not just divided, not just disrupted, but fundamentally opposed to each other. As Peter Schwartz, who has conducted extensive scenario work with the FCC, described it in his recent book *Inevitable Surprises:* "It's a system tailor-made to produce regulatory gridlock, which is arguably what many of the lobbyists want." For example, High Definition Television is not available over cable television in the United States, because the organization in charge of standards for television sets (the broadcast bureau) has different Core Group loyalties than the organization in charge of cable television standards (the cable bureau). Each group is doing its best to protect their Core Group members from taking any risks. Each is struggling to keep their own bailiwicks separate, because even though merging them would mean a stronger, more potent FCC, it would diminish the power of the Core Group fragments.

Arguably, FCC Core Group feuding was the single biggest factor in the crash of 2000 and the ensuing recession. If there had been a cohesive FCC Core Group, it might have been enthusiastic about broadband to the home. And with an energetic broadband push (instead of one undermined by the existing local phone companies trying to protect their existing investments), then the broad audience for Internet commerce would have emerged in time to meet the projections of some of the more sober dot-com business plans. A great FCC would have taken a stand on behalf of a coherent, high-powered Internet infrastructure—one which would have fulfilled the Internet's promise of universal, high-quality, democratic, innovative connectivity, with ninety percent of the homes in America wired through fiber-optic cable at reasonable rates.

What, then, does it take to set up a system where great Core Groups can more easily arise in government agencies?

"To do better," writes James Q. Wilson, "we have to deregulate the government." Agencies would have to be established with a clear, simple set of criteria for success, based on reasonable objectives. They would need the authority to choose their own operations methods and to hire their own staff. They would need rewards commensurate with results (including not just financial reward, but recognition, information, and access). They would need the appropriate amount of help, with as little micromanagement and day-by-day oversight as feasible. Finally, they would need an exit strategy so that this Core Group can leave the scene and allow others to enter and flourish, after the appropriate amount of time—which might be thirty to fifty years. Otherwise, agencies would end up with Core Group figures like J. Edgar Hoover, whose influence hangs on long past its time.

There will always be figures like J. Edgar Hoover and Robert Moses, who reshape agencies in their own image and wield disproportionate influence accordingly. There will continue to be a host of forces trying to weaken, overtake, or corrupt government agencies and organizations from all sides. In that environment, it's tempting to believe that great government Core Groups cannot exist. But on the other hand, government cannot be ignored, or wished out of existence, not even by devotees of Ayn Rand. Representative, democratic government, with an active role in providing services, is an integral part of the infrastructure that makes civilization run. To make that kind of infrastructure work is going to require a lot of design work. We may not know yet how to consistently create powerful, responsive, and corruption-free government-based Core Groups amidst a multifaceted, divided political superstructure like that of the United States. But we'll have to learn sometime soon. Otherwise, a government of crippled agencies, by crippled agencies, and for crippled agencies, shall not perish from this Earth.

CHAPTER 20

Labor Unions

When the Quality Movement came to the United States in the 1980s, one of its basic tenets was the idea that management is responsible for poor quality. It can't be blamed on workers. By 1990, sophisticated managers throughout American industry understood this, and the quality of American products improved dramatically.

Yet on some deep emotional level, the lesson never sank in. In the early 1990s, I attended an electrical industry manufacturing conference on quality. At lunch, the conversation at my table turned to the problems we'd all had with American cars. I admit I started it; I told a story of a trip I'd made to visit the General Motors headquarters when I lived near Detroit. Afraid of being seen rolling up in my Toyota, I'd rented a Chevrolet. Alas, when I slammed the door, the mirror fell off—in GM's own parking lot.

Suddenly, everyone at the table couldn't wait to tell *their* American car disaster story. It was as if I'd punctured a high-pressure steam pipe. Transmission problems, brake failures, sun-roofs that never quite kept the rain out.

"It's the idiots on the line," one manager said.

Another agreed. "Most of them don't know what they're doing and don't care. We have all our new plants built in the Philippines, where people really know how to work."

And then, in rapid furious succession, people began talking about how overpaid and undermotivated American workers are;

and how the root of the problem was labor unions, with their rules, their corruption, and their short-sighted protection of slackard, destructive employees. It was as if we had tapped into an elemental underground reservoir of antiunion hatred, with both pressure and bitterness far out of proportion to any real threat that labor unions could have presented. And I've had enough conversations with managers since then to realize that the hatred of labor unions, in both unionized and nonunionized companies, runs deeper than logic or expediency; it's intense and ingrained.

Why do managers hate unions so much? Only one answer makes sense to me. Union members have collective-bargained their way into the Core Group while many managers have not.

To be sure, union workers are paid a fraction of what senior executives make. But the organization is still attentive to them, in a Core Group fashion—because it has to be. Managers can be fired at the whim of their bosses. But unionized employees can be fired only if there is a justifiable grievance, a hearing, and an opportunity to appeal. Managers can be undermined and undercut at will by their superiors. But try (as I once did) to move a table to get ready for a seminar at the Ford Motor Company, and you'll be stopped in your tracks: "You can't do that! That's a union job!" Managers may be routinely ignored and invisible, but no policy is put in place at a unionized company without wondering how the labor union leaders, and the rank and file, will respond. They're in the Core Group.

Of course, they're almost never in the Core Group by open invitation. They muscled their way in. Thus, nearly every unionized company is prone to Core Group feuds. Unions were first organized as counters to the abuses of early corporate management, which responded to them by calling in private police to break up strikes. The resulting history of labor-management relations, tempestuous and often violent, still guarantees that Union and Management will be bitter foes at times. So does the fact that most managers are college-educated, while most labor leaders are not; the fact that they often (not always) come from different socioeconomic classes; and most of all, the labor tradition of solidarity.

Unions negotiate from the premise that workers should be rewarded only as members of a group; no one should be singled out as individually worthy, for that will make all the others vulnerable. They fundamentally mistrust any distinctions that managers propose that separate people from each other. And they regard managers as hypocrites: Don't managers themselves enjoy membership in a class of people that get a free ride?

Meanwhile, management, from the era of Frederick Taylor to the era of Jack Welch, has internalized the principle that some people are worthy and some are not. The unworthy should either be retrained or (more likely) removed. (Welchists articulate this principle as "Coach, Coach, Change": If people don't perform well, or they don't fit our way of working, then they need to be coached. Coach 'em once. Coach 'em twice. If they still don't work, change 'em out.) Managers fundamentally mistrust solidarity as a system that allows the weak to coast on the efforts of the strong. And they regard labor unions as hypocrites or, worse still, criminals who hide behind the "solidarity" shield.

Labor leaders tend to blame the external political environment for their distress, and in a sense, they're right. "In high school," writes yuppie-turned-labor-lawyer-turned-writer Thomas Geoghegan, "we all learned in American history that in the 1930s workers won the right to organize. . . . But over the years, the right has become illusory. . . . The main reason is, employers can [legally] pick out and fire all the hard-core pro-union workers [with] no legal sanction for it, except maybe, *possibly*, having to cough up some sliver of back pay, some $2,000 or $3,000 a body: and this is much later, three or four years from now, long after the drive is over and the union is in ashes." In short, because of the current structure of labor laws and the ways they are enforced, it's so difficult to start *new* unions, at least in the private sector, that labor has focused on the battles it can win: perpetuating existing unions and starting unions in the public sector.

But labor leaders (like all Core Group members) also have themselves to blame for their predicaments. Aside from the obvious problems with many unions—startling levels of corruption, for instance—there is the ongoing mutual problem created by the inherent Core Group feuding in unionized companies. Both sides have learned through bitter experience that they can't trust the other. Each side assumes the worst of the other, and sees enough in the other's behavior to justify it. The more adversarially that unions behave, the better their constituents like them. Tough, ornery negotiators get reelected, just as tough, punishing managers get promoted into spots dealing with the union; both sides assume it's the only way to keep their enemies under control.

Thus, even when the union members *own* much of the company—like the pilots and mechanics of United Airlines—they will tend to vote themselves pay increases (for instance) at the expense of the longevity of the company. And even when management groups are interested in reconciliation and effective production, they still instinctively move to humiliate and browbeat their labor representatives—even down to such petty moves as scheduling meetings at inconvenient times or inconvenient places. I think it's because they've internalized the Core Group feud between labor and management, and therefore assume it's part of their job to push relentlessly for every advantage. It's no coincidence that the central motto of Ken Kesey's epic labor-union-dilemma novel, *Sometimes A Great Notion*, is the slogan of the managerial family, the Stampers: "Never Give An Inch."

The net result: Except for a very few labor leaders (like Irving Bluestone and Don Ephelin of the United Auto Workers, for instance), union leaders lose sight of the company's integrated learning base, and the fact that they are contributors to it. They cling to their own integrated learning base: the ability to win concessions and negotiations. Meanwhile, managerial Core Group members have lost sight of the potential value of the union to them. The union leader, as CEO Roger Saillant of Plug Power notes, is the only individual in a corporation whom people have chosen to lead them in a free election. He or she has a unique form of legitimacy, and organizations ignore that legitimacy at their peril.

Not long ago, I saw the principal of an American public school describe a labor-management dilemma he had gotten into. The union had been seriously weakened in the previous local election, where it had mortgaged its headquarters to raise money for the losing candidate. There was a potential innovation on the table, which both the administrators and the teachers wanted, but it would require changes in teacher scheduling, and that contractually meant the districtwide union had to approve it. The school's Core Group, in other words, included not just local union members, but the district's union; its opinion had to be considered. And these district leaders, feeling some pressure to show that they could still be a viable force for their members, chose that moment to resist with every means they could. They stonewalled the principal: They didn't read the documentation he sent them, came late to meetings, and did everything possible to provoke an overreaction. And this provocation backfired; support for the union steadily dwindled among the teachers. Nonetheless, without the union's support, it was clear the innovation would fail.

The principal believed that the union leaders were too strong; after all, look at the trouble they were giving him. But it was clear, in listening to the story unfold, that the basic problem was the opposite. The union was too *weak*. Being weak, its leaders had no choice but to move in petty, noncreative ways. If the principal really wanted to improve his ability to innovate, then, counterintuitively enough, he would have to invest in helping the union become stronger without making himself weaker. The stronger it became, the more that teachers could use it to protect their interests during the changes to come, instead of having to confront the administration over every detail. And this, in turn, would make his job easier.

The same is true, incidentally, when management is weak. They aren't strong enough to generate profits from good decision-making, so they take it out on the union. A labor leader's greatest point of leverage is to make the company more profitable and the management stronger—provided this can be done in a way that doesn't make the union weaker.

A strong union, in short, is strong precisely because it is a member of the Core Group, and it's time for both labor and management to realize this. Its unique status ensures a role for the union as a presence in the Core Group that is loyal to something other than the management hierarchy; it is protected enough to speak openly and freely; it is in touch with the attitudes of the mass of consumers and knows what it's like to struggle to make a living; and it can speak articulately on behalf of all of these people. Given all of these factors, a strong union should be a vehicle for the Core Group to learn what its unionized employees know.

In some parallel utopian universe, labor leaders and management both see this. Labor leaders have embraced education for their members, and they've gotten rid of the corruption and links to organized crime that have hobbled them. Management, in response, has dropped their underhanded union-busting activities and allowed their workers to organize themselves. They've actually seen union leaders as a Core Group asset. The U.S. Congress, under pressure from both sides, has instituted basic reforms to existing labor laws, that (for example) provide more open union elections and grievance processes. And the Core Groups are accordingly richer and more capable.

'Course, none of that could ever happen here. Why even bother to think about it? Let's just stay mired in the current system, and wait for the next high-pressure steam-pipe explosion, wherever it occurs. Or the gradually eroding economic base that occurs when manufacturing in a country declines and mirrors fall off car doors.

CHAPTER 2 1

Management Consultants

Only someone who has worked as a consultant could have come up with the Core Group theory. It is grounded, after all, in the single skill at which all great consultants excel: the ability to develop close relationships with Core Group members at client companies. No matter what their specialty or practice, in other words, all established management consultants are keenly attuned to the difference between Core Group and non–Core Group members.

And the same is true in reverse. Core Group members in client organizations may not be able to recognize their own Core Group structure well (in part because employees keep it hidden from them), but they are sharply aware of the Core Group status (or lack of it) among the consultants they hire.

Several years ago, I cofounded a small consulting firm called Reflection Learning Associates with an MIT research faculty member named George Roth. RLA's primary product was a method for conducting organizational oral histories ("learning histories") that seemed to help companies learn from their past mistakes. We claimed that we were interested in developing projects for the half dozen "learning historians" who worked with us occasionally. But clients seemed interested only in projects involving George and myself, even though some of the others who worked for us were at least as experienced (one was a University of Michigan business professor, and another was a leader in her research field). The reason only gradually dawned on me: Core Group members were interested in hiring only Core Group members. Sure, associates could tackle some of the ancillary tasks, but they would largely be treated as a group of indistinct, busy, eager "worker bees," and not as thinkers in their own right.

Here we have the source of one of the perennial frustrations that management consultants experience: the constant pressure they are under to go on the road and solve client problems themselves. The consulting firm typically argues that its methods and concepts are its primary source of value. Therefore, the physical presence of the principals is not essential for the client's success. Lesser-paid minions can travel to client sites, while the partners settle back to collect the profits.

But clients have a name for this presumption. They call it "bait-and-switch." Except for particular services in particular areas, like information technology consulting, they don't want the consultant's *knowledge*, per se; they want a thinking partner with a perspective broader than their own. They know (instinctively or explicitly) that only a Core Group member will be prepared to meet them with the directness, candor, and uncomplicated loyalty that they need. Junior consultants inevitably betray the insecurity in their status. They must perpetually check their moves with the senior consultant. They cannot "pass" as Core Group members. So only the Core Group consultant will do. He or she must hop on the plane. Only routine work—such as interviewing non–Core Group employees—can be delegated to non–Core Group consultants.

If clients are wary of bait-and-switch, then consultants have their own innate wariness. Heiner Kopperman, of the German consulting firm ChangeWorks, explicitly distinguishes between two groups of people at his client companies: the "green team" and the "red team." The green team is his phrase for the Core Group: the people with companywide legitimacy. "The green team behaves like a network," he says. "Its members include power players who share similar values and those of the company."

The red team is a group with a limited budget and a serious problem for which they need help, but no serious support from the Core Group for the changes they want to create. Their problem may well concern their frustration with the green team. As a consultant, says Kopperman, if you contract only with the red team, you will sooner or later be stopped. They can't sustain any genuine initiative, because they don't have Core Group status. (Not coincidentally, they also can't pay the bills for any sustained long-term change effort, especially if they're the only ones who see why that effort is needed.) Seasoned consultants know that their livelihoods depend on becoming indispensable to the green team: the Core Group. That indispensability will be amplified throughout the organization.

Consultants often feel genuine compassion and friendship for the red team. Lacking Core Group status, those team members have learned to use charm, openness, and intrigue as methods to get people to help them. But nothing can go forward without some green team participation. And chances are, the consultants will have a lot more leverage—not just with the green team, but with everyone else—if they don't associate you with the red team. So consultants who start with a red team engagement often find themselves in a dilemma: How to leap to the green team and still keep the red team from shutting down.

An outside consultant with access to both the green and red teams has an enviable role as the only safe antidote to guesswork. He or she can show up at a mid-level manager's office door and say, in effect, "What the Core Group *really* wants from you is this." If insiders did the same thing, no matter how well-plugged-in they were, they would be immediately suspected of hidden ulterior motives, and their messages would be discounted.

Once a consultant reaches this level of standing, there is only one thing that he or she can do to threaten it, and it happens all the time: Core Group Envy. It's easy for consultants to get so involved in helping set the strategic direction of the client company that they start to believe *they* are the direction-setters, and that the client company would collapse without them. Then they start to believe that everyone else believes it too. When they speak of the Core Group members, they use the first person plural: "Here's where we're going to take this company next year." They start to ask for perks that Core Group members get. They relocate their offices to be near the client, and spend as much time within the client's offices as anywhere else. They come to see themselves as vital to the client company, maybe more important than the CEO.

Then, one day, all this presumption becomes visible in a way that the Core Group members who hired them cannot ignore. Like sleepers awakening from a dream, they look around at their subordinates and see how much of their legitimacy has been drained by the perception that some external consultant has been calling the shots, no matter how well. And that situation cannot endure. The contract is canceled.

Why should the rest of us care about the fate of management consultants? Only because, in an organization-driven world, these people have a unique role to play. In many organizations, they are needed to help the Core Group function more effectively. "You are the leaders," the outsider says to the Core Group. "You might as well get good at it." Then the outsider becomes, in effect, a developer of Core Group talent, helping them to develop their latent integrated learning base and to establish a relationship of mutual respect with employees of mutual consent throughout the organization.

In my moods of relative optimism about human nature, I prefer to think that this form of management consultation is a temporary, transitional phenomenon, unique to this moment in history. After all, there are many examples of remarkable Core Group members who become great leaders on their own, inside hierarchies, without outside help. But there are also many examples of hierarchical leaders who, in one way or another, find themselves placed at the top of an organization where managing upward, producing consistent performance results, impressing others, and taking just the right amount of initiative (without too much risk) are common forms of behavior. These leaders see that they are called upon to become the living embodiment of the unfulfilled greatness of their organization. Nothing in their glowing careers has prepared them for this task. Can they handle it? It's not a matter of building skills, or even of developing equity, except in the deepest sense. They must find the resources deep within themselves. If they need help at this moment in history, for better or worse, many such organizational leaders have no one but management consultants to turn to.

CHAPTER 22

Schools and
the "Hidden Curriculum"

P ublic schools, in the United States at least, are among the most complex of Core Group environments. The Core Group of a typical school system is divided among politicians (who set standards from afar), active parents, school board members and local politicians (each with their own ideologies or priorities), energetic superintendents (who typically stay less than three years), long-standing tenured faculty (who have good reason to be skeptical of the energetic superintendents' ideas), local realtors (whose lobbying is a tremendous force in many suburban districts), and a few critical administrators (like the person who sets the school bus schedules and therefore ensures that teenagers will have to disrupt their hormone-induced sleep cycles to get up at seven A.M. for school).

No wonder schools get blamed for poor performance. Meanwhile, the biggest single factor at most schools in improving student performance is not class size or school budget size, but the quality of teachers. A high-quality teaching staff (as measured by their own credentials and experience) can even overcome such "ingrained" factors as parents who don't speak English or lower economic status. But when idealistic teachers feel treated as pawns by the feuding Core Groups and disregarded as professionals, they leave. The well-known teacher shortage in the United States would not exist, except for the fact that almost fifty percent of the teachers hired for public schools leave their jobs within the first five years—not for lack of salaries, but for lack of legitimacy.

In such an environment, it's reasonable to ask: What *are* students learning? Arguably one of the subjects they learn best isn't on the official curriculum. They learn first from their teachers, and then from their own social structure, how to compromise with a Core Group environment. They learn that people are basically powerless against authority, that legitimacy comes from sources over which there is no control, that conformity is desired, and that Core Groups are both unforgiving and arbitrary. In many schools, they learn this lesson more harshly than they would learn it from any other institution, because it represents the overall unintentional impact of an unusually harsh and fragmented Core Group. And they carry that lesson on into adolescence, when they set up Core Group structures of their own.

I learned this vividly when I met a trio of high school students in a small college town in Ohio. Nathan, Rick, and Nolan told me how they had decided during a sleepover one night to map the social networks of their school. They fit all the members of their senior and junior classes into a circle of cliques: "Preps," "Freaks," "Hicks," and "Gangstas." (In this rural Midwestern school, even the "Gangstas" were white; they were the kids who listened to hip-hop music.) Nathan, Rick, and Nolan called this social milieu "The Great Game of High School," and they said it occupied six-and-a-half out of the seven hours of every school day: "trying to find a girlfriend or boyfriend, flirting, dispelling rumors about yourself, starting rumors about other people, and all the other things you do to survive." The pressure to fit in, they said, was overwhelming: "You don't join a group because of the way you look. You look the way you look because of the group you join. Resistance is not necessarily futile, but there are consequences." For example, those who do not join in will not have a conventional love life.

The trio said that after mapping the school's groups, they showed some of the classmates the diagram. Everyone agreed with the basic concept; yes, the student body could be laid out in giant

polarized circles. Everyone agreed that the Preps were the unofficial Core Group of the school: unconsciously favored with money
for school clubs, permission for trips, attention from teachers, and
(most important) preferential treatment from the guidance coun-
selors who recommended students for college.

Or, as Nathan, Rick, and Nolan put it: "To a degree that very few
parents, teachers, or administrators admit, the game determines
your success at school. Parents, teachers, and administrators may
claim that every student has the same opportunities, is accorded
the same respect, or plays by the same rules, but we aren't, and
don't. Adults may think they're stressing academics, but they're
not. Instead, the adults of the system have colluded to set up its
hidden rules, and its practices mirror the game that they play out
in the 'real world.'"

It was particularly telling that some of the people labeled
"Preps," while they agreed that the Preps were dominant, insisted
that they didn't belong there. "That's not me," they said. They literally could not see themselves as special to the system. But anyone
standing a bit outside the circle could clearly see their influence.

This phenomenon is known to social psychologists as the "hidden curriculum": in most institutions (and particularly in schools),
there is an unspoken message that one group of people fits in better than anyone else. Many, many stories of adolescence—from
Cinderella to S. E. Hinton's *The Outsiders* to *Grease* to the Harry
Potter novels—are grounded in the struggle to come to terms with
the hidden curriculum. There is certainly an economic component:
The Preps are those who dress better, who act more genteel, or who
have better family connections. But the primary factor that sepa-
rates the favored from the unfavored in the hidden curriculum is
knowledge—knowledge of the subtle forms of behavior that signal your membership in the elite. That's the kind of knowledge so
important and difficult that it takes six or seven hours a day to
learn.

The phrase "hidden curriculum" was coined in the early 1960s
by Benson R. Snyder, a Massachusetts Institute of Technology pro-

fessor who later became dean for Institute Relations. Concerned that some intelligent students were dropping out, he began to explore why. He found that in MIT's highly competitive atmosphere, both students and faculty simply couldn't do everything that was officially required of them. Students used war metaphors to describe their progress; they talked about having friends "shot down" or "going AWOL." The only people who could succeed were those who learned how to play the game: who had figured out which dean wanted to see them wearing a tie and which classwork they could skip with equanimity. *That* was the hidden curriculum at MIT: learning how to "read" the culture, to distinguish important from unimportant rules, and to adapt their own survival strategies accordingly.

Snyder also conducted research at Wellesley, the exclusive women's college just south of Boston. Wellesley had been designed as a kind of garden of human development, where students were "cultivated" and "bad seeds" were dismissed. While MIT students expected to be ignored in 300-to-400-person lecture halls, Wellesley students knew faculty members would take a direct, personal interest in them—and they were expected not to chafe at the attention.

In both cases, he concluded, the real purpose of school was to teach students to adapt to an overarching culture. Sociologists have found the same is true of all sorts of schools. For instance, in her ethnographic study of an inner-city high school in Detroit, anthropologist Penelope Eckert argued that the "jocks" (upper-middle-class students) were routinely groomed for success (or as Eckert called it, a sense of being "in control"), while the "burnouts" (working-class students) were subtly guided toward failure (or being "in the wrong"). Jocks took part in school activities, built close relationships with teacher mentors, and jealously guarded personal property (along with information about their family troubles that might be used against them). Burnouts stayed clear of adults (often including their parents), spent their free time outside school, and shared continuously—cigarettes were not just a regular form of currency but a continuously shared resource. Students in both groups learned to orient themselves to Core Groups: paying close attention to the people "who really mattered," both among the teachers and students. That was, arguably, the single most important thing they learned.

You could make a case that schools shouldn't play favorites this way; they shouldn't have Core Groups among either faculty or students. But it's inevitable that they will, for schools are organizations. It may not be human nature to gravitate to Core Groups, but it's certainly organizational nature.

What we all thus need, in learning-oriented organizations like schools, are better Core Groups: Core Groups diverse enough that every student can see him- or herself reflected somewhere in one or more of them, and thus see examples of how powerful he or she could become. This might mean, for instance, inviting local business owners (including owners of working-class businesses like garages and beauty shops) to teach—not so that others will follow their example, but so that students will have examples to transcend.

That would require a willingness to teach students how to build equity. And that, in turn, might require schools to operate under open-book or transparency principles. "In every school I've worked in," says public-school educator and writer James Evers, "the budget is secret. The teachers will negotiate what they think is a piece of a limited pie. They hear: 'there isn't funds for that.' About priorities that seem to be important. And then they find out that there *are* funds for the superintendent to go off on a trip or for a few favored teachers or administrators to take a workshop. There's no clear, open sense of which parts of the budget are discretionary and which are open to discussion."

Imagine if instead of teaching students to blindly accept the harshness of Core Groups, schools became places where students learned how to build a competent, fulfilling life in a world of Core Groups. There is so much to learn: How to respect authority without debasing oneself to it. How to approach a Core Group to learn about it, without challenging it unproductively. How to conduct oneself. How to cultivate all kinds of equity, from relationships to reputation to financial, with the purpose of creating a better life within or without organizations. How to look at systems, not as a victim, but as a learner. And, in the end, how to develop, design, and situate one's own Core Groups and one's own organizations.

Most schools pick out a few students (usually Preps) with "leadership potential" and let them learn about Core Group dynamics through osmosis and a bit of practice. But schools could teach all their students how to start organizations and lead them. They could give all students the chance to create a Core Group experience for themselves. Some might not use that chance, but everyone would have it. And that in itself—the knowledge that an educator, once upon a time, trusted each person to create a Core Group for themselves—could make all the difference.

Part 5

Making

a Better

World

CHAPTER 23

The Shadow Core Group

A re you aware how dangerous it is to talk about this?"
The speaker was a Dutch corporate executive, a member of an audience at a talk I gave in Maastricht. He had put his finger on the heart of the Core Group dilemma. In most organizations, open conversation about the Core Group is taboo, and for good reason. It triggers deeply emotional feelings about privilege, power, and rank.

And yet, having become aware of the Core Group's impact, how can you ignore it? People seriously trying to influence an organization can be effective only if they understand how the Core Group's priorities are perceived, and how those perceptions differ from the Core Group's actual intentions. That means raising awareness of "who really matters" dispassionately, without triggering a backlash of resentment, mistrust, vulnerability, or fear, either from Core Group members or from others on their behalf. How on Earth are we supposed to accomplish *that?*

There *are* ways to do it, even when you're not in the Core Group yourself. It takes a certain finesse, a fair amount of relationship and reputation equity, a willingness to experiment, and an awareness of the limits of appropriate experimentation. Most of all, it takes the kind of time and commitment that people generally do not invest in organizations unless they see their future bound up with them. That combination—dispassion plus time plus commitment—is so counterintuitive that those who intervene to change organizations, whether from the inside or outside, have to learn to generate it practically from scratch.

Here, then, before anything else, is a list of what *not* to do, based on the unfortunate experiences of those who have followed their intuition as a guide:

- Do *not* try to bully the organization's Core Group into improvement. For example, do not loudly and angrily go to your bosses and say: "Aren't you ashamed of the way this organization excludes some people? Why haven't you done anything about this?" They would probably just look at you, shake their heads in disbelief, and make a note never to let you into their offices again.

- Do not adopt a passive-aggressive campaign. Do not talk behind the Core Group's back about the abuses they engender, or try to "punish" them in subtle or indirect ways. For instance, don't say anything about the Core Group to others unless you would also say it to them directly. Some people do this kind of thing, almost despite themselves, as a way of maintaining their self-respect. But it has the effect of not just insulting the Core Group, but yourself and everyone else in the organization as well.

- Do not put yourself down as a way to curry favor or influence with the Core Group—or with the rest of the organization. At best, this turns you into a Core Group enabler, and sets you up to be exploited by the organization. At worst, it marks you as a mediocre courtier in a democratic civilization. Flattery and sycophancy are games that have been honed through centuries of play in monarchies and empires; playing them well requires a level of skill and experience that (with any luck) is beyond the typical twenty-first-century individual except, perhaps, Stanley Bing.

- Do *not* put your hopes on a "Skunk Works" or other innovative operation buried within the organization and shielded from above. Conventional wisdom says that if you want to innovate

from within, "don't ask permission—ask forgiveness." But Core
Groups don't work that way. Every organization has its share of
wonderfully innovative projects that achieved remarkable results, and in some cases saved the company, but failed to influence the rest of the company *or* to provide sufficient recognition
or reward for the people involved (at least by their standards).
Three prominent examples: The Ford Taurus, whose launch
leader, Lew Veraldi, was repudiated by his bosses at Ford. The
innovative Topeka dog food factory, whose organizers Lyman
Ketchum and Ed Dulworth were pushed out of the parent company General Foods. And the Apple Macintosh, whose creator,
Steve Jobs, was forced out of the company he had founded in the
1980s. Only Jobs has recouped, and that was after watching
Apple fail without him and creating dramatic success elsewhere
(with Pixar).

There is usually an unspoken understanding that the strange,
heretical practices of the Skunk Works won't leak out to con-
taminate the rest of the organization. Trouble ensues when the
countercultural leaders of the Skunk Works start to believe the
stories of their own success. They convince themselves that
their terrific results and innovative methods will allow them to
transcend the implicit agreement they made; and if not, then
the rest of the organization obviously just doesn't "get it."
When the Skunk Works leaders find themselves frozen without
support by Core Group members, or locked out of advancement
or promotion elsewhere, their bitterness and frustration can
poison the rest of their careers—and the Skunk Works' future
as well.

- Don't start a revolution. You may be wondering: Why not just
  replace the Core Group wholesale? That's what incoming CEOs
  sometimes do. I suppose it's possible that another group could do
  it as well, perhaps through a stock repurchase. But a revolution,
  besides being immeasurably disruptive to ongoing business,
  merely substitutes one Core Group for another. It won't change
  the structure of the organization, and maybe not even the Core

Group dynamics, unless it also seriously changes the thinking of the Core Group members and the people around them.

What then *do* you do? You establish proficiency as a deliberate intervenor. Intervention in a complex system is a kind of art form in itself: the art of crafting legitimacy for a set of new ideas.

Before you even begin: Who is intervening with you, and for what purpose are you all taking this trouble? Why do you want to change the organization in the first place? If you succeed, what will that get you? What difference will it make—to you, the organization, and the rest of the world? How will you know when you're getting close? And what will it look like, in your imagination, when you're done?

Without at least preliminary, heartfelt answers to those questions, it's hardly worth starting. For this is a significant undertaking. It involves a campaign on the organizational level, an intensive set of mutual explorations on the team level, and courageous internal efforts to reach a level of maturity within yourself. It is intensely personal, but it cannot be done alone; ultimately, it will involve many people in the organization. It will take time and concentration, but you will have to "do your job" at the same time, and you may never get rewarded or even recognized for this. The payoff is in the changes that it produces within yourself.

Furthermore, there's no recipe for conducting this kind of intervention. On one hand you'll probably want to build up some equity, in the quality of your reputation and relationships and skills, before embarking. On the other hand, conducting this kind of work, with as much presence of mind as you can muster, is as good a way as any to begin building equity. Your strategy depends on the quality of the organization, and the quality of your own persona and the team you are working with. It's not something to tackle lightly. And yet it should be tackled with high spirits. Once you get started intervening in something larger than yourself or your own career, your fear will be tempered by fascination.

Probably the best way to begin is to convene an informal team of compatriots who feel the same way you do—a shadow Core Group for the organization. I use the word "shadow" here not in the Jungian sense—to imply the repressed, subterranean impulses that are painful or discomfiting—but in the sense of an alternative group without real power, going everywhere that the real Core Group goes, one step behind. The name comes from politics, where people talk about "shadow governments": the apparatus set up by the party voted out of power in an election, in which they appoint people to "shadow" each of the key posts in the other party's government, and to be prepared with their own opinions and proposals. This keeps them, more or less, in practice as governing entities for the next time they are elected, and a shadow Core Group does the same thing for you and its other members. It helps prepare you all for the time when your ideas become more formally adopted (if they ever do), for the time when you enter the Core Group on a full-fledged basis, or for the dealings that you may ultimately have with the organization in a more authoritative role.

The purpose of your shadow Core Group is to raise consciousness—to build a new awareness of the purpose and potential of the organization among Core Group members, decision-makers throughout the organization, and (most important of all) yourselves. Because the purpose of the organization is intimately linked with the image that people have of the Core Group and its priorities, that image will have to change as well. Even if the *membership* of the Core Group remains the same, the way they are perceived by the organization will have to change. That's a tall order, and it can't be done by command or fiat, not even by the command or fiat of the Core Group. It has to be approached from the inside out, with each individual who joins the cause choosing to see things in the new way, and to make decisions accordingly, until the whole organization "tips" over to a new way of doing things.

Since legitimacy is granted by the organization as a whole, at first your shadow Core Group will possess only the legitimacy that other people grant them as individuals. If you and your fellow shadow Core Group members are not in the real Core Group, you may have very little legitimacy to start with in the eyes of the organization. You build that legitimacy by developing a consistent, credible story about the unfolding potential of the organization and what it is being called to do in the world at large, and then embodying the sorts of changes and awareness that would be needed by the organization as a whole.

I've seen shadow Core Groups as small as three people and as large as a hundred. People in the shadow Core Group meet, often informally, to talk about the measures they would take if they were leaders of the organization, and the ways in which they might intervene without provoking a backlash. They think about the issues of the moment, not in terms of their own bailiwick or part of the operation, but with an organizational leader's perspective of the whole system. They provide each other with the company, counterpoint, support, and encouragement that individuals cannot provide for themselves; indeed, the work of changing organizations should not be done by an individual, because it is too easy to lose perspective and to become vulnerable. Finally, the shadow Core Group brings its own sense of priorities and greatness—an awareness that the actual Core Group probably does not have. As individuals, you do not have to be in the Core Group yourselves. You might even be outside activists trying to influence the organization's direction. But you have to be willing to develop the same level of care and commitment for the organization as if you were in the Core Group.

If you start or join this kind of shadow Core Group, you will find (to your surprise, and possibly to your chagrin) that it takes on many of the characteristics of the organization's real Core Group. Your shadow Core Group is naturally empathetic because of the quality of attention that you, as its members, pay to both the Core Group and the organization. If the real Core Group feuds, your shadow Core Group will find itself almost irresistibly tending toward fractiousness. If the real Core Group is lethargic and bureaucratic, then your shadow Core Group will seem as if it can hardly get anything done. You can even "take the temperature" of the mood of the real orga-

nization by observing changes in your shadow Core Group—if
there's a shift in openness or frustration, you can expect the same
thing to happen accordingly in the larger world. This "microcosm
effect" also works in the opposite direction. If you can heal some
kind of breach or fracture in your shadow Core Group—for instance, a labor-management clash or an argument among special-
ists—then, remarkably enough, you may observe that fracture
healing a little bit in the organization at large.

At the risk of oversimplifying the ineffably complex task of intervention, here are some ideas for what the shadow Core Group
can do:

- **Move deliberately to widen the shadow Core Group to embrace and include
real Core Group members.** "Conversations that don't include the Core
Group are *about* change," says Peter Garrett of Dialogue
Associates. "Conversations that include the Core Group *are*
change."

  If you don't have Core Group members in your shadow Core
Group, in other words, sooner or later you will need them—either as compatriots with you, or as supporters. Like everyone
else, they can join your cause only through choice. If they see
what you have discovered, in a form that they can recognize,
then you won't have to recruit them; they will choose you.

- **Understand how the Core Group defines success and frame your project as a
method or milestone for accomplishing their success.** You might approach a Core Group member in a one-on-one intensive meeting. Give them a short introduction, tailored to their interests, of
your idea and the value you think it would have—and then say,
"We're trying this on a small scale. Before we begin, in your
view, what would constitute success?"

  And then listen. If you engage them well, three things will
happen. First, you will learn some things from what they say.
Second, they will have a chance to become intrigued, which
means they'll talk about it to others, which amplifies your ideas,
which means you may end up with allies you don't expect right

now. And third, when the time comes to move another step, you won't be introducing it to them cold. They will already have thought about your success. It will, in part, belong to them. And because they are in the Core Group, that means it will belong to everyone.

- **Wait for the right moment before you ask for formal certification.** There is a time at which you need a budget approved, a check written, a contract signed, or an agreement made in writing. Don't rush that moment. Do as much as you can before that moment, primarily to demonstrate your own capability.

For example, before asking for a budget, demonstrate what you can accomplish without one. You may be able to hold the same kind of initial program, for instance, in a self-supporting way. You will learn a lot more this way. Then when you get the budget, apply the same resourcefulness.

- **Learn how to hold high-quality conversations.** Pay careful attention to the "space" in which the conversation takes place: the amount of time, the rhythm of interaction, the quality of acoustics and atmosphere, the thoughtfulness of the invitation, the presence you bring to it, the context you have set. Conversations that touch on Core Group issues need the kind of "space" that reduces tension and accentuates aspiration. People need to feel relaxed enough to recognize how much they trust others, and to become more trustworthy themselves. Most of all, they need to meet in the kind of space that makes them more aware of their visibility (the ways in which others perceive them), the stands they want to take, and the ends to which they want to make a commitment.

- **Get the whole system in the room.** The Core Group is probably larger than you think it is. And even if it isn't, have you consulted with the other key constituents? The Core Groups of critical subsystems? The symbolic people? All of these people have something to tell you that will be critically important—and if you overlook it, you will end up clashing with their worldviews later. Of course, before you get them all into *one* room, you'll probably need to approach each group separately—maybe more than once—until they're ready to meet together.

- **"Amplify positive deviance."** Some people like to "speak truth to power" by telling the Core Group what they've done wrong, and they're startled when the Core Group doesn't want to hear it. "Don't they want to learn?" Barbara Waugh, in her book *Soul of the Computer*, describes a much more effective maneuver, which she calls "amplifying positive deviance." You find the people in the Core Group who "deviate from the norm by doing the kinds of things you think are significant moves in the right direction. Then "shine the light on them, get articles about them published in the company newsletter, talk them up to everyone you meet, get them together for a conference, give them resources." And, oh yes, find something to appreciate in the individuals who are blocking you, and draw attention to *that.*

- **Articulate misperceptions.** Show people the difference between what the Core Group truly wants and needs and what they think it wants and needs. Or help Core Group members articulate this better.

- **Practice.** Learning to do all this takes time and skill. Don't expect to master it at once. Set up places where you can try to intervene without tremendous risk either to your career or to the organization. After every new intervention, reflect: What worked? What didn't? What problems did I bring with me? And how might I do it differently next time?

While there is more to read on the subject—much more—writers have only scratched the surface of what there is to reveal. In moving down this path, you'll be creating your own unprecedented story. It's not for everyone. But if you truly want to make a better world, it may be the most highly effective way to proceed. If you make a better Core Group, you may engender a better organization—and that, in the end, may be the only way, these days, to make a better world.

Diagnostic Exercise 10
How Does the Core Group Affect Your Own Team Dynamics?

This diagnostic exercise was written and designed with Dialogos associate Kelvy Bird.

First, draw a diagram of a recurring pattern in your workplace where people seem to fall into the same interpersonal traps time and time again. Here is a simple map of a typical dynamic in a large high-tech organization we know. It portrays a team producing high-quality documents under tight deadline pressure:

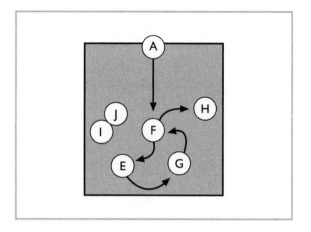

Andy, the outside executive who oversees the department, asks Fiona, the manager with the greatest reputation for quality, to produce a document. Fiona, who is busy with other deadlines, passes it on to Ernest, with a reminder of the high level of quality that Andy ordinarily expects. But Ernest is the sort of individual who habitually agrees. Rather than go back to Fiona with questions, Ernest asks Gwen, a very junior individual, to finish the job. It doesn't meet Fiona's standards, but she turns it in to Andy anyway.

That turns out to be a mistake. Andy sends it back with a reprimand. Fiona, now under great pressure and feeling some resentment toward Ernest, outsources the job to Helios, a local contracting firm. Because of the tight deadline, Helios charges almost double their normal rates. Andy, hearing about the expense, groans, "This always happens! Can't you all get your priorities straight?"

On the surface, this sounds like a story about Ernest's incompetence and Fiona's dilemma. But consider the Core Group influences:

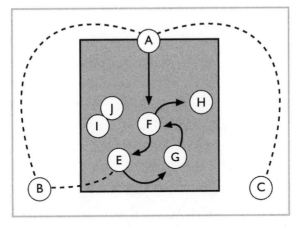

Another Core Group member, Beth, has always insisted that they should sacrifice production value for the sake of efficiency and cost. "We should just get it done," she says. "Life's too short." And she has a particularly direct influence on Ernest.

When we brought the local group together and showed them the diagram, it became clear that the tension between Fiona and Ernest was (in large part) an unconscious reflection of the tension between Andy and Beth. The end result: High-quality work was jobbed out to Helios, costs rose, and nobody ever talked about it. The diagram became a starting point for figuring out how to slow down some jobs, speed up others, and keep them all in house.

Corporate Governance

If you had to pick a single date for the birth of the middle class in modern industrial America, you might pick January 12, 1914. Henry Ford raised his auto workers' minimum daily wage to five dollars on that day. But even as other businesses began to follow Ford's example, his shareholders rebelled. Two of them, the machinist brothers John and Horace Dodge, sued him in 1916 for breach of fiduciary responsibility. He was paying his people too much and expanding his plant, they complained, rather than releasing dividends to them.

When Ford took the witness stand, the Dodge brothers' lawyer pressed him hard. Hadn't he said publicly that he had as much money as he needed? Yes, he admitted; he was one of the wealthiest men in the country. Then what, asked the lawyer, was he trying to do? Act, in effect, as a philanthropist? Employ as many men as he could, give them high wages, and provide the public the benefit of a low-priced car?

That's right, replied Ford. "And incidentally make money," he added.

"*Incidentally?*" echoed the lawyer.

"Business is a service, not a bonanza," Ford replied. And then: "If you give all that, the money will fall into your hands; you can't get out of it."

These remarks added to Ford's public luster. And they were prescient; the Dodge brothers struggled, and ultimately sold out their business to Chrysler, while Ford became one of the big-three Detroit automakers. But the remarks also lost Ford's case for him. Making shareholders wealthy, ruled the judge in effect, should not be *incidental* to making everyone else wealthy. Shareholders should come first.

Ever since then, the debate on corporate governance has raged between two rival camps. One camp could be called the "Dodge-ites": its thesis is more commonly known as the fiduciary model of corporate governance. In this model, shareholders come first. Dodge-ites argue that shareholders, as the owners of the assets of a company (if they were to be sold off), hold full authority over it, and the organization exists to serve their interests—specifically, their financial interests.

The other camp (which shouldn't be called the "Ford-ites," because Ford would probably have hated most of them) starts from the premise that "money falls into your hands" when you take all your constituents seriously. (Or even if the money doesn't come, you still owe all your constituents something.) This is often known as the stakeholder model of corporate governance. Evolved over the years from a variety of sources, this model starts from the premise that corporations are contracts chartered by the state to serve multiple interests: shareholders, employees, neighbors, suppliers, customers, managers, and the citizens of their community. All of these groups have a legitimate claim on the decision-making of management.

Both views were more or less equally influential until the 1970s, when the fiduciary model moved far into the lead. This happened in part because of some changes in finance law, in part because of the prominence of fiduciary rhetoric in conservative political circles, and in part because of a genuine recognition of the leverage of capital: The takeovers of the 1980s and 1990s showed that an executive team without fiscal support was vulnerable. It seemed for a while like the fiduciary Dodge-ites had permanently wiped out the opposition. But then came the bubble crash of 2000, the ongoing boardroom scandals of 2001–2002, and a new current of critique of the fiduciary mind-set. The stakeholder model has a whole new set of advocates these days.

Unfortunately, both models of corporate governance have serious problems. Neither one describes reality.

Consider, for example, the stakeholder model. Look at any real business story and ask yourself, "Is this organization trying to please all its stakeholders?" If the answer is yes, then you will see a moribund and paralyzed enterprise. Managers need to make decisions fast; they can't afford to be constantly aware of the dizzying complexity of all of their constituents, most of whom oppose and mistrust each other. It's no coincidence that most of the advocates of the stakeholder view are academics; managers abhor it because it's unworkable.

We can see the impact of the stakeholder view in some government agencies and nonprofits. More susceptible to stakeholder pressures, they easily become paralyzed unless they learn to resist them judiciously. (Lobbyists and influence-peddlers are merely professional "stakeholders.") "We are expected to balance all stakeholder needs," a former Coast Guard manager wrote me, "even at the expense of efficiency and effectiveness."

There is now a movement, spearheaded by *Business Ethics* editor Marjorie Kelly and writers Paul Hawken and David Korten, to "take back the charter": to issue corporate charters for limited time periods and revoke them if the company hasn't lived up to its environmental and social responsibility. I sympathize, personally, with the intent of this movement. As a proposal, it is helping to open up debate about what constitutes corporate responsibility (and, more important, who should judge infractions). But as a regulation, it would probably become a stultifying variation of the stakeholder approach. It would cripple the source of energy and capability at the heart of every great company. It could make it harder for there to be great Core Groups.

The fiduciary view has been more popular, in part, because on the surface it seems to make more sense. In its purest form it simply acknowledges the importance of capital as a limit to organizational action; even nonprofits and government agencies have burn rates. The power structure of a corporation depends quite often on the leverage that creditors and preferred shareholders can muster—the kinds of machinations that you read about in Wall Street publications like *Grant's Interest Rate Observer* or in chronicles of leveraged buyouts. Moreover, shareholders can theoretically sue corporate executives, just as the Dodge Brothers sued Henry Ford, if they perceive management to be cavalier about the shareholders' financial interests. (Corporate governance expert Margaret Blair points out that courts have not tended to enforce this "fiduciary responsibility" very much. Still and all, it serves as a powerful Core Group deterrent.)

All of this can be summed up in a single sentence: "If you have them by the balls, you can get into the Core Group." When something must be done for the shareholders urgently, and it overtakes all other priorities, then that probably means that somewhere, somehow, some Kirk Kerkorian–style or Ross Perot–style figure has managed to use debt and equity to grip an organization tightly in a way that cannot be ignored.

The fiduciary principle also accurately acknowledges the importance of employee-shareholders to an enterprise's vitality. I remember entering an elevator at Ford in the mid-1990s with a group of in-house "heretics"—people who had visibly questioned some of the company's prevailing harshness about people, for instance. All eyes turned to the monitors, hung near the ceiling on the elevator wall, that continually flashed the company's share price. "How are we doing?" said one individual. "It's above twelve again," said another. All of them, it turned out, held some Ford stock, in part because the company had a matching plan. All of them naturally identified with the share price and felt proud to be part of a company whose price was rising. The company was *their* fiduciary; they came to work, in part, to make money, and they wanted to work for a company that acknowledged this imperative.

Of course, since those days, the Ford stock has gone up above forty—and then down below eight. The rise to forty was not a predictor of future glory—it came just before Ford's quality and safety problems, and the forced resignation of CEO Jacques Nasser. Nor, I suspect, is the fall below eight a predictor of Ford's future performance. Stock prices in themselves rarely predict future performance for particular corporations.

And that's the great weakness of the fiduciary view: its claim to represent a road map to decisions for a better future. Paradoxically, as soon as the fiduciary view takes hold in an organization, the organization tends to become *less* responsive to shareholders in any meaningful way. This happens because of Core Group dynamics. The Core Group members decide that the organization's main job is to keep up the stock price. The easiest way to do that is to make quarterly earnings predictions that fall just a little bit below the expected annual results, but are still high enough to be impressive (to people who don't look at them too closely). In other words, the people at the top of the hierarchy feel an irresistible temptation to do to the stock analysts exactly what their own subordinates are doing to them: manage upward. They provide only estimates that will make them look good. Inevitably, these targets get amplified through the company through guesswork and incentives, so that people throughout the organization come to believe the idea that "great short-term financial results and shareholder returns" are the two things that the Core Group members want most. (Except for a few exceptions: exorbitant salaries, corporate jets, and other perks favored by the Core Group.) People throughout the company feel compelled to engage in a variety of short-term abuses: "end-of-month channel stuffing, the creation of noneconomic special-purpose entities, overly creative vendor financing arrangements, and all kinds of other balance sheet gymnastics that detract, rather than add to, long-term corporate value." (That list comes from a *Wall Street Journal* op-ed piece by Morgan Stanley's chief market strategist, Steve Galbraith.) There are also longer-term costs: cancerous growth, endemic fraud, and tragic waste—not just of employees and their shared visions, but their careers. The fiduciary view erodes both the "natural capital" (as Paul Hawken puts it) of Earth's biosphere, and the "social capital" of human communities.

And it doesn't serve shareholders either. Sometimes an organization needs to turn its back on short-term shareholder returns to build a dynamic business for the long run (as, for example, Microsoft did in the mid-1980s, while it was investing in developing early versions of Windows). Conversely, business strategies that seem like hard-nosed, realistic efforts to make money often turn out to be unwitting experiments in fiduciary fantasy. In 1996, the board of directors of the Sunbeam Corporation picked "Chainsaw" Al Dunlap as CEO, in part because of his flamboyant way of trumpeting the fiduciary view. They didn't know that they were testing a theory: that mature, cash-poor companies (like Sunbeam) are full of wasteful and self-indulgent practices, and that a brutally tough, unsentimental, and self-aggrandizing outsider CEO would expose these practices in the hope of making the company profitable. The experiment yielded results: a decimated organization, a glutted distribution channel, a deceptive set of accounting books, a demoralized workforce, a despairing executive team, a diminishing product line, and ultimately a devastated stock price. The board fired Dunlap when the results came in; unfortunately, the company went bankrupt in the process.

In short, if corporations were really run for the sake of return on investment to shareholders, more of them would be better at it.

We need a third model of corporate governance: one that recognizes the primacy of Core Groups while constraining them from abuses of power. This theory would start by recognizing that companies survive and thrive when the purpose of the Core Group is aligned with the long-term needs of the organization—whether they're fiduciary needs, stakeholder needs, or something else. Ford thrives not when it tries to make cars at the expense of money, or money at the expense of cars, but both in complement to each other. Xerox thrives when it tries to make both copiers *and* money; Disney thrives when it tries to make both entertainment *and* money. Even financial institutions thrive when they follow not just the money, but their own particular creative imperative as well.

Thus, under some circumstances, there would be no better strat-

egy for a corporation to pursue than returning investment to shareholders. And under other circumstances, there would be no surer
way to calamity. The way to distinguish these circumstances would
be by looking at the priorities of each corporation's Core Group,
the way those priorities are perceived by everyone else, the outside
forces affecting them at this moment, and the capacity of the organization to fulfill them. Descriptions of the Core Group's attitudes, strategies, succession plans, and investment decisions should
become a kind of report card on a corporation's well-being.
(Similar report cards would ideally exist for nonprofits and government agencies as well.)

No one picks an organizational Core Group all at once. It
evolves, emerging like a living system. But most of the time there
is a high degree of leverage in the one part of the organization that
is picked—the board. Currently, most corporate board members
are nominated by a committee of existing board members, and
then voted on by shareholders (often in highly restricted elections
where "renegades" who are nominated by outside shareholders
have a very difficult time campaigning). The net result is typically
a handpicked set of board members whose job is to show up and
ratify whatever the CEO demands. (Shareholder activists Robert
Monks and Nell Minow once famously lampooned this by placing
a full-page ad in the *Wall Street Journal,* with silhouettes of the
Sears, Roebuck board members and a headline reading NON-
PERFORMING ASSETS.)

Governance depends on the board, but the boards of most companies—and most organizations—are systematically eliminated
from the Core Group. Employees are probably unaware of the
board members and their priorities. There are exceptions, like
General Motors' long-term board member Leon Sullivan (who developed the Sullivan principles for divestment from apartheid-era
South Africa). But all too many board members have no priorities
(except those of the CEO, who secures their loyalty with doggie
treats, including lavish salaries, rides on corporate jets, and endowed university chairs in their names).

It's time to find ways to elect and select board members who care not just about the share price but the reputation, integrity, and knowledge of the organization. The critical issue is trust: The greatest way for shareholders to protect themselves is by establishing new ways, probably varying from corporation to corporation, to engender more trust in the system. This probably includes the much-suggested approach of breaking the chairman of the board and CEO into separate positions, but it also includes new and varied ways of selecting board members to represent the varied constituents of the corporation—and, more important, investing in training board members to build the kind of trust and candor with each other that will become a microcosm for the organization as a whole. As the board becomes more conscious, so does the Core Group, and as the Core Group becomes more conscious, awareness ripples out into the organization.

How would such board members get chosen? Probably in a variety of ways. In an ideal universe, some would be chosen by the shareholders, in a vote, with open campaigning and ready access to information about candidates (Nell Minow and Robert Monks advocate that all board members be chosen this way). Some might be chosen by major shareholders who control blocs of stock, as already happens in start-ups. These board members might be the equivalent of senators in the U.S. Congress—people representing blocs of interests (originally the states), who are there presumably to look out for the long-term health of the enterprise. Some board members might be chosen by the CEO or senior executive—again, as happens now, but in a more transparent form. Some would be chosen by employees in a vote. Others might be chosen by labor unions or other critical interest groups, including suppliers, dealers, bottlers, franchise holders, distributors, and key customers—anyone with a direct interest in the health of the organization's brand names. (Margaret Blair and Michael Porter have suggested this.) Some might be chosen through an essay contest: "What I would bring to the board of this organization." Presumably there might be ways to choose board members through merit. And some would be chosen by the founding family.

The ways in which each board member was selected, and the

purpose of that selection, could be written into the organization's charter, along with its rationale and provisions for changing the mechanism as the environment of the organization changes. The precise methods would vary from organization to organization. There would be no single formula for success. A field of study would emerge, devoted to the care and nurturing of great boards—and great Core Groups, for that matter.

For as soon as there is a great board in place, the makeup of that organization's Core Group will take a dramatic shift. It would now be easier for a diverse and open Core Group to emerge (in part because board members might now mentor some people). This Core Group, in turn, would now become a more powerful part of the checks and balances of the organization: keeping track of deceptive accounting practices, excessive stock options and salaries, and self-defeating strategies.

This might sound naive, but it can't be any worse than the way most corporations are governed now. Controlling organizational malfeasance through legislative control, no matter how well written, will go only so far. If we want great organizations, then we need structures that promote greatness—in the board, the Core Group, and everywhere.

CHAPTER 25

The Cycle of
Noble Purpose

uppose it is 1953, and you are the chief executive of, say, a major tobacco company. Research has just crossed your desk linking cigarettes to both cancer and addiction. While not completely conclusive (it is based on research with laboratory rats), the connection is too strong to ignore. After reflection you realize you have essentially two choices ahead of you.

Plan A would be to embrace the truth. Recognizing the health stakes, you go public with the information you have, and adopt a stance of seeking a more open exchange of knowledge. After fulfilling that moral obligation, you then have to preserve your business somehow. You might design and market cigarettes for smoking in moderation, say two or three per day, and price them accordingly. You would then become the producer of a carefully regulated but much-admired drug that engenders conviviality, slimness, and an enviable high. Or perhaps you can find another strategy for making and selling this addictive, carcinogenic consumer product.

Alternatively you can choose Plan B: deny, market, obfuscate, conceal, and fight. Promote alternatives, like filtered cigarettes, that imply safety but represent nothing more substantial than wishful thinking. Maybe you'll buy enough time to invent a safe cigarette. But if that gamble doesn't pay off, then this strategy will inevitably lead you into a "Masada" stance—you against the world. You will spend your entire corporate career under the threat of lawsuits that could wipe out your company. You'll end up spending as much on legal fees as you do on marketing or R&D. Even if you're enormously profitable, you'll end up with a legacy as a merchant of death. (And just wait until the global middle class adopts the American middle-class attitude about, say, secondhand smoke.)

Of course, you may not realize the full consequences of Plan B. It is 1953, after all. And even if you personally feel some trepidation, there is a Core Group at the company whose interests you must consider. It is not your job to think through the moral implications over a fifty-year time frame.

Hence, you probably take the course that the tobacco industry *did* take. The entire industry worked overtime to discredit independent research, to make false health claims, and to cover up their own internal reports. In the short term, this was the winning solution, and it allowed the companies to maintain high profit levels and immunity from lawsuits through the 1990s. But it also meant that, in the mid-1970s, when prototypes of safer cigarettes had been developed, the executives of all five major American tobacco companies decided separately not to produce or market them. For legal liability reasons, they could not allow their companies to admit, even tacitly, that they had knowingly produced a hazardous product in the past. They let those prototype products die. And today, they are becoming regulated companies; Philip Morris just signed a consent decree agreeing to phase out of the cigarette business entirely and to place ads about the hazards of their product. Thirty years from now, people may look back on cigarettes and wonder how anyone could have smoked them, just as we look back on nineteenth-century patent medicines like laudanum today.

Now imagine that it is 2003 and you are the chief executive of a major mobile telephone company—like Vodaphone, the world's largest cellular operator. Or Nokia. Or AT&T. A series of studies have come out, announcing that cell phones damage neurons in laboratory rats. They may well do the same in children. Other studies have linked cell-phone use to rare forms of brain cancer. The research crosses your desk. You have the example of the cigarette industry as a predecessor.

We can guess what your Plan B would be. What's a viable Plan A?

I asked this question of Mark Anderson, the computer and communications gadfly expert who publishes the prescient web newsletter *Strategic News Service* (which is where I learned of much of this research). Anderson, who knows the cell-phone business well, suggested that a viable Plan A would start with a proactive stance:

"Make sure your engineers and designers are the most exposed, aware group in the industry. . . . Design cell phones for health first, in all segments. Guess what: If you can position your company on this high ground before anyone else, two things happen: First, you get lots of business, and second, all your competitors look bad and lose share. It is a win/lose, and you win. . . . Make sure that *all* cell phones are sold, in the box, with earmikes. Make them easy to use and ergonomically appealing. Make them easy to replace if they break. Since your lawyers won't let you say why you are including them, just say that smart users use them. . . . Sell kids' cell phones that will operate only with an earmike attached. Include extra earmikes in the box. . . . None of this bad news is going to go away, but the first one to become proactive might take serious market share away from the other hundred companies still in complete denial. . . . Let's see if someone does it. They will have to, as Shakespeare once recommended, first kill all the(ir) lawyers."

And in the end, that might not be enough. It might be necessary to first invest much more in researching the health impact of non-ionizing cell-phone radiation at these frequencies. And then it might be necessary to redesign or reconfigure the technological underpinnings of the cell-phone medium—a tremendous expense and nuisance. Yet if there is a serious danger (and it looks like there is, especially for people who hold cell phones up to their ears for long intervals), then the company that takes the lead will be a visionary, well-rewarded enterprise.

Various companies have been in similar places before, and paid varying degrees of attention. In the early 1990s, while researching a story about corporate environmentalism at the Dow Chemical

Company, I interviewed an environmental regulatory official named Larry Fink, who battled Dow often over the years at the U.S. Environmental Protection Agency and the Michigan Department of Natural Resources. Dow was working hard at the time to convince journalists like me that this company, once known for napalm, Agent Orange, dioxin, and obfuscation, was now becoming an environmentally conscious organization. I had spent enough time there, both with Dow's managers and its opponents, to think that there was, in fact, some real change of heart and practice at Dow. It had pioneered a variety of groundbreaking measures in pollution prevention, and it had covered every inch of ground in its enormous hometown chemical plant in Midland, Michigan, with a plastic sheath, so that no chemicals would enter the Tittibawassee River flowing nearby. Fink was still skeptical, so I asked him what the company would have to do for him to take them seriously.

He replied by describing a particular measure that any major chemical producer could take, but that none have. Much research on chemical hazards is contested, because it's based on animal studies. Industry lobbyists claim that cancer in a laboratory rat means nothing; humans may react to the same chemical very differently. But the only alternative, epidemiology, has been undermined by chemical companies, including Dow, which have standard nondisclosure clauses in their legal settlements.

"If Dow wanted to show they were up front," Fink said, "they would put that information, without individuals' names, into a public database on patterns of toxicity." Such a data bank might include exposure records from old lawsuits, Dow's studies of its own workers, independent surveys on communities with Dow plants, and statistics from the National Cancer Institute. Researchers could use that information to come up with a far more sophisticated understanding of the relationship between chemicals and health hazards. Though no company could be trusted to produce this data on its own, any toxicological survey compiled *without* Dow's full-hearted participation (and that of other chemical companies) would be inconclusive.

The world is waiting for a chemical company with Dow's

stature, reach, and influence to make such a move. Yes, it would involve legal, competitive, and epidemiological complications—but a way could be found to protect the company from liability. Yes, it would involve short-term costs in reducing or eliminating wastes. It might force Dow Chemical to clean up areas like the Lower Tittibawassee Basin, which (according to USEPA reports) still manifests higher-than-normal dioxin levels. But in the long run, the benefits for the company could be immense, because breakthroughs in biochemistry, physics, and genetic engineering have placed humanity (as Mehmet Sarikaya, professor at the University of Washington, puts it) "on the brink of a materials revolution that will be on a par with the Iron Age and the Industrial Revolution." The first company to develop an open epidemiology practice will learn not just about which compounds are dangerous, but which compounds are safe and how to improve their safety and usefulness further.

Cigarette companies being open about health hazards, decades before they have to be. Cell-phone companies designing in protections, again before the need is proven. And chemical companies participating wholeheartedly in epidemiological openness. All three of these potential strategic directions have three things in common. First, they are extremely difficult to see from within, especially from within the Core Group. Second, they represent obvious benefits in the long run; a company that took them on would probably outlive its competitors. Third, they are immensely risky in the short run.

Such is the nature of the noble purpose in any organization.

A noble purpose is nothing more or less than the organizational equivalent to the question, "What do I want to be when I grow up?" Many individuals sense, early in life, that there is some potential destiny that they might fulfill, beyond simply leading a comfortable life. Choosing that destiny is not like selecting from a menu of options. It is a matter of developing an awareness, an attunement to a reality greater than ourselves. We sense that some purposes fit us; other purposes don't. In the end, the purpose chooses us; life selects a role for us to play. The same is true for organizations.

The noble purpose is not simply the Core Group's vision for the organization. It is the unfulfilled possibility that the organization could rise to meet, if it acted as wholeheartedly as possible to serve the world and the future. When a noble purpose comes to fruition, it's because it has been sparked in the imagination of some members of the Core Group. You can tell a noble purpose by imagining yourself thirty years from now and looking back. Would you be able to say that this was truly worth doing? Indeed, that's what makes a great Core Group great: the ability to divine what the noble purpose of the organization might be, and move persistently in that direction.

"It's a sense of a higher order," says Richard Pascale, one of the few management strategists who has recognized the value of this kind of thinking. "When you see it, you begin to mobilize people and move people more correctly. The people in your company move their frame of reference; they manage the present from the future. They deal with the same crap that everyone else in business deals with, but they are sitting with a sense of possibility, and the problems show up differently."

I borrowed the phrase "noble purpose" from an oil company's information technology department. It was spinning itself off into a separate business, and the leaders of this new business decided that their new "noble purpose" would be to reinvent the use of technology in their industry.

It was pretty much business as usual, until a young technology manager (we'll call him James) confronted the leadership team by teleconference at a companywide meeting. Here is the story in James's own words, taken from a "learning history" I coauthored for this company (which, because of confidentiality agreements, could be labeled only as "OilCo:")

> The noble purpose had come through, in our organization, in a series of meetings where our bosses had explained it to us, just as they had heard it from their bosses. "This is your vision," they said. "We want everybody to buy in."
> In every meeting, I had said, "I don't understand what

'noble' means. Tell me." The response I got bothered me: "If you don't like the word 'noble,' just ignore it. Write in another word."

But the word meant something to me. Our current "noble purpose" was to revolutionize the energy industry. To me, that wasn't "noble" at all. It simply meant that we were interested in profits only; the mother company wanted us to return a certain amount of profit, and we would do it—one way or another. In my view, a truly noble purpose would address concerns larger than profits. It would allow me, as an individual, to get up and say, "I'm going to work today because I feel good about it. I know that OilCo is contributing to the world, the nation and the community, and it cares about people. It's taking care of the environment. I know, deep in my heart, that nothing like the *Exxon Valdez* would ever happen to us. And if it did, we wouldn't respond in the same way that Exxon did."

So, at this teleconference, I finally asked the President of the business unit about it. That was a somewhat frightening thing to do. To speak on closed-circuit TV, they have you go in a room with a telephone. You can hear what's been said, but you can't see anything, so you don't know exactly what's going on.

When my turn came, I said that I appreciated the opportunity to speak. "I very much appreciate the openness that our company has moved towards." But I told them that I didn't see the nobility in our noble purpose. "What does the word 'noble' mean?" I asked.

"I don't know," said the President. "To tell you the truth, I haven't thought much about it."

At that moment, James's microphone went dead. So he didn't hear the end of the President's comment, or the applause that followed. This particular President had been known, in the past, for his abrupt, abrasive manner; but this time he simply admitted before the whole company that he didn't know the answer. It was a cathartic moment for everyone. Only James was left to learn about it later:

> Remember, I was in a closed-off room with a telephone. When I came back out, they told me that people had cheered and clapped, and they were still discussing the noble purpose.
>
> I didn't feel like much of a hero. I wasn't the first one to ever notice that there was no definition behind "noble." I was just the first one to say it out loud.
>
> For weeks thereafter, people I didn't know would stop me and shake my hand. That made me feel like I had done the right thing.

That incident took place in the mid-1990s. James is still at OilCo, and for a while thereafter he enjoyed a series of invitations to take part in high-level discussions about strategy. But within about two years, there was another reorganization. Most of the senior executives left; the consulting firm retreated back within OilCo. A new wave of cost-cutting ate into the budget for experimentation and collaboration. Ironically, however, the purpose that James had championed—the idea of embracing environmental sustainability—now seemed more important than ever. This new "purpose" resonated with the new management priorities at OilCo. And fascinatingly enough, the story of James's moment in the video control room (his "Jerry Maguire" moment, as it were) continued to linger in the memory of people who were there. It turned out that the feeling was fairly widespread, even at this hard-nosed oil company: nobility should refer to something more than merely making money.

The concept of a "noble purpose" stems from feudal society, where lords and royalty needed to prove that they were responsible to God, who had (through their birthright) granted them a privileged place in society. When Napoleon created the Order of the Légion d'Honneur in 1802, it was the first such honor whose recipients did not need to be hereditary nobles. "The French are not changed by ten years of revolution," the emperor said. "They care for only one thing: honor. So this sentiment must be fed; they must be given distinctions."

In organizations today, honor is still the driving force underlying a noble purpose. But there is no longer an influential, universal aristocracy to tell us what is noble and what is not. Instead, we must do that for ourselves. And in organizations, honor has come to mean a sense of purpose that transcends merely "winning," "fulfilling the assignment," "making money," or "pleasing the Core Group." A truly honorable sense of purpose is one in which the organization seeks to leave the world a much better place, in some way closely related to the organization's own integrated learning base.

For example: Many of our deepest technological and political challenges—including the "leapfrogging" of the developing countries into postindustrial society, the exploration and ultimate colonization of space, and the restoration of enough natural environment to protect the remaining diversity of species on Earth— are also significant organizational challenges. Then there's the problem of billions of disaffected young people in impoverished nations (including nations that breed terrorists), the enormous inequalities between rich and poor (and the devastating impact this could have on the global middle class), the continuing misery of new urban areas with inadequate sewage and traffic infrastructure, the expansion of health care costs, and the decline of educational quality.

Every organization will be able to deal with only one or two of these imperatives—not as an add-on, but as a redefinition of its key business. Giving money (or even time) to charity is not an example of a noble purpose; for a separate charity has nothing to do with the company's own integrated learning base or the power and energy of its Core Group. A truly noble purpose, in short, is one that requires a company to dedicate its greatest resources to an end that transcends its purposes to date. And since this will tax and challenge all of the organization's constituents, it will require enormous presence of mind to persevere.

Indeed, there is already a clear example of the pitfalls that await any organization that tries. Lord John Browne, CEO of what was then called the British Petroleum Oil Company, was lauded in 1997 for his speeches acknowledging that global climate change was a serious problem and that fossil fuels had produced that problem. Driven in part by his awareness of the growing environmental concern among BP employees, he promised that BP would adjust its business to do something about global climate change.

In 1998, Browne got more specific: He announced targets for carbon emissions reductions for BP by 2010 that were, as journalist Darcy Frey put it, "far more ambitious than the Kyoto Protocol." The company spent $200 million launching what they called "the new brand," but which was actually a name change to "Beyond Petroleum": a promise that BP would innovate its way out of the fossil fuel energy business into a much more diversified and resilient energy business, involving (potentially) a wide range of new fuels and technologies. This was a gutsy move for a highly safety conscious (indeed, somewhat risk-averse) engineering culture with enormous investments in the massive infrastructure of petroleum exploration, production, refining, and transportation.

Almost immediately, severe criticism came from two quarters. On one hand, Greenpeace and other environmental groups charged that the company hadn't gone far enough. If BP were really serious, it would give up its Alaska pipelines and drilling and put a lot more money into solar research. Therefore, this must just be greenwashing.

On the other hand, the City of London and other stock market analysts responded by downgrading BP's buy ratings, and shareholders acted accordingly. They sold. It was a big enough vote of no confidence in the new brand that it shocked BP insiders. The basic attitude around the City about BP was much like the skepticism of an unnamed American scientist whom Frey interviewed:

"Whether [BP] will have any chance of successfully outcompeting newcomers in renewable energy is a very big question. Because historically, once those transformations have happened, the existing companies have not held the edge." In other words, analysts doubted that a company with 100,000 employees could reinvent itself. You can't teach an old dog new tricks.

The result of these two bouts of criticism was an immediate halt to the momentum within the company. The new brand, with its appealing green solar logo, could not be withdrawn, but even casual visitors to BP noticed a sudden reluctance to talk about it. It was seen by some employees as a hyped-up promise that their company had naively made to the world. There were more demands for immediate performance, particularly from operations like renewable energy.

And yet it was obvious, for those who probed beneath the surface, that there was still a strong sense of commitment to the original imperative. Environmentalism was as strong within the company as ever. It just wasn't obvious how BP would get there. "At BP," a manager there told me, "we don't change the ship, but we do change the sea. There is nothing that even John Browne could do to stop what we're doing with the 'green' aspect of the new brand. It's already under way and it can't be stopped. Too many people have too much invested in it to let it drop away now."

Essentially, BP has run up against the inexorable reality of noble purpose time frames. These initiatives require steadfast patience, because they operate on feedback cycles that move much more slowly than the feedback cycles involving the Core Group (or even the feedback cycle involving customers).

For instance, if you propose the launch of a new product, you will learn almost immediately (through office gossip) about how well it meshes with the Core Group's priorities. It could take a year or two more to learn how it is received in the marketplace. But it may be fifty years or more before the impact of your decision on the larger world is fully understood.

Under the pressure of day-to-day business urgencies, and even more so under the kind of pressure that Greenpeace and the City of London can muster, it is far easier to ignore the still small voices of that far-off, seventh-generation time frame. After all, it took more than fifty years for the consequences of Plan B to come home to roost for tobacco companies. No wonder so few companies get as far as BP did. And yet if the company doesn't act on a noble purpose, sooner or later its best people will drift away—or at least their hearts will become numb as their passion drains into more noble engagements elsewhere.

Which is where the Core Group comes in. It's one thing to feel a calling, or even a sense of noble aspiration, as an individual. When it happens through an organization, then it requires the sponsorship of the Core Group, or else the rest of the organization will not embrace it. Perhaps the Core Group doesn't see the noble purpose that is calling it forward. Otherwise, they'd already be embarked

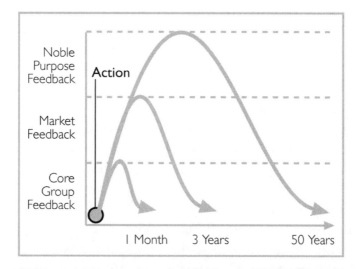

Typical time passage before the results of a decision become obvious to the decision-maker. In most cases, the Core Group feedback can enter consciousness months before the feedback from the marketplace, and years before the effect of an organization's noble purpose becomes evident—if it ever does. This creates enormous pressure in favor of decisions that favor Core Group priorities over nobler, longer-term priorities. Part of being noble is learning to stay the course: to hold fast to the original intention until the long-term effects become evident.

on it. Or perhaps they see it and have decided that it's not for them, and the organization, at this time. Too difficult. Too much opposition. Too many priorities. Or perhaps they think they *are* doing something about it, when anyone else would perceive them as just treading water.

There may well be a shadow Core Group in your organization, holding a noble purpose in mind that the rest of the organization doesn't yet see. When you cultivate this kind of group, things start to happen. The power of the organization starts to get unleashed.

Finally, we can never be sure if our sense of the organization's noble purpose is correct. In the end, we may feel betrayed by it; most lofty aspirations, sooner or later, fail to live up to the hopes of those who pursue them. But even if we can't get a definitive answer, the question is still worth asking. What *is* the greatest unfulfilled potential of our system? Those who take that question seriously seem to go places, useful and valuable places, that other people miss.

Diagnostic Exercise 11
The Core Group Theory of Life

Nick Zeniuk, formerly a car launch planning team manager at Ford Motor Company, tells the story of a postmortem after a highly successful car launch in the early 1990s. The senior executive, several layers of hierarchy above the team, said, "You guys were eighteen months behind schedule. Yet you brought it in on time and under budget. How?"

"Well," said the team leaders, "we were in a crisis, so we had to ignore the usual corporate garbage. We let the engineers do their own testing and revisions and didn't second-guess them. We worked closely with our suppliers. We practiced servant leadership. And we let go of the feeling that we had to be in control all the time."

"Yes," he said, "but what were the new processes you used?"

"We didn't have any," said the team.

"Then what were the new control measures?"

"We had none of those either."

"Then what *was* it?"

"It was just a group of people working together and trusting each other. It was mind-boggling."

The vice president stared at the team blankly for a minute. Then he thanked and dismissed them. None of them were invited to tell other teams what they had done. To this day, the VP probably feels that they were holding out on him. He might as well have said it explicitly: "We may espouse the idea of teamwork. But when you get right down to it, teamwork and trust won't get you very far. If you really want to improve, you need 'hard' innovations—process designs, incentives, and controls, ideally in a form that can be rolled out to other working groups."

As individuals, we all hold innate theories about the way the world works—so ingrained in us that we barely notice them, and powerful because they color our perception. We doubt and ignore any aspect of reality that contradicts them, and the actions we take instinctively tend to be based on them.

For example: If I believe that people are basically well-intentioned, I will notice when people take initiative or contribute to the quality of the work. Attuned to those moments, I will encourage them, and more of them will happen around me. On the other hand, if I believe that people are treacherous and out to take whatever they can get, I will tend to notice every act of betrayal and every moment when people slack off. Intent on not being taken advantage of, I will humiliate and threaten people. The resulting resentment and fear will, of course, produce more treachery. No matter what I *say* out loud about fostering trust, my theory will produce actions that speak much louder.

Theories held by the Core Group are doubly powerful. The entire organization, acting to fulfill perceived priorities and interests, routinely amplifies them. Everyone comes to believe them—or act as if they did. The organization as a whole seeks, at least in part, to demonstrate that the Core Group's view of the "right thing to do" is accurate, that we collectively know what we're doing, and that therefore we should keep barreling ahead in the same direction. It takes great strength of character, under those circumstances, to open one's mind to other possibilities.

Hence this diagnostic. To "make a better world," we must be aware of the theories that keep our world as it is. What are the theories held by the Core Group—and the organization—as implicit answers for each of these questions?

1. What's the best way to get things done? Is it through processes and control measures (as Nick's boss suggested)? Or through "ignoring the usual garbage," servant leadership, and trusting each other?

2. What's the basic character of people as employees? Are they fundamentally trustworthy, treacherous, or somewhere in between? To what extent are they eager to contribute? To what extent are they eager to exploit, or to take whatever they can get away with?

3. What's the appropriate kind of authority? Should decisions be handed down from the top? Decided from the bottom? Or does it depend on the circumstances (or even the mood) of the moment?

4. How does an organization create a good workforce? Should you recruit the most skilled, best-educated people available, no matter how badly they get along? Or should you look for the kind of people whom you prefer to have around, and then train them in the necessary skills?

5. What's the organizational approach to ethics? Writer Annette Simmons recalls meeting a lawyer who had generalized the principle of client advocacy into a universal credo: "It is my moral obligation if I see an advantage to take it. Life is an adversarial system, and my job is to be the best possible adversary I can be." He went on to offer one caveat: "In a worst-case scenario, you might have to try sincerity. If you're really good, you can fake that, too."

6. What's the right way to live? What does your Core Group believe about quality of life—the forms of community, family, environment, and material wealth that are healthiest for human beings? How much "stuff" do they own? How much travel do they do? How cosmopolitan are they? How do they balance the conflicting demands of their own work and family lives?

7. What's the right strategy for organizational success? To produce high-quality products? Or to gain market share and shelf space? Do schools succeed when they presume that all children in the district should be able to learn, or when they focus attention on just a few individual children?

8. What's the right way to lead? Have the answers? Show no fear? Be stoic? Be strong? Be a steward? Cultivate your people? Get results? Keep your eye on the ball? Be flexible? Be rational? Be emotional?

9. What's the right way to handle a crisis?

10. What are the ideas that you "just don't consider around here"? What kinds

of options are too risky to raise? What does the Core Group say (or not say) that prevents these things from being talked about? And what, exactly, is at risk for them—or for everybody else?

Now that you have some answers, what do you do with them?

You test them with other people. Is this truly what is believed around here?

Then you ask: Which of these theories is getting in the way of the type of world we want to create?

And then you ask: With whom do we want to talk about this?

CHAPTER 26

The Body
Politic

For the past decade or so, there has been a great hunger in the business world for corporations to take on the ambience of small-town communities. You sometimes hear managers yearning for this ideal when they discover that their most "dead weight" employees, slacking off in cubicles, are church group or community leaders. "Why can't we set things up around here," they ask, "so people bring that same kind of volunteer spirit and energy to work?" Why can't people bolster each other's success, instead of competing for clients or resources? Why can't decisions be made more democratically, with less bureaucracy? Why can't companies operate, in short, not like communities as they are, but like the small-town communities of our imagination, the way we would like them to be?

Because organizations have another purpose. They can't simultaneously foster community and fulfill their Core Group imperatives. If you want community, then set up your own, within the workplace if you like. But don't expect the organization to recognize or help foster it just because you've created it. And if your goal is to make a workplace based on fostering learning, competence, and justice, you'll need a Core Group member involved. If the Core Group believes wholeheartedly in community as a goal, then community becomes the purpose of the organization—just as raising the share price becomes the purpose if the Core Group wholeheartedly believes in *that.*

But what, then, about actual communities—the places that people enter, not when they take on a job, but when they are born or move into an area? Do they have Core Groups? And if they do, is that a natural state of affairs, or does it represent an inherent pattern of abuse?

To answer these questions, let's distinguish communities from organizations according to the nature of their Core Groups.

First of all, organizations are by and large the most powerful entities in most communities. Organizations draw their power from the intensity of purpose and quality of action—which in turn stems from the fact that they aren't answerable to everyone equally. In following the perceived needs and priorities of a narrower Core Group, they make themselves powerful.

Second, civic society needs that power. It needs the participation of all the organizations within it—corporations, government agencies, and nonprofits. Their role is not to dominate, but to provide the strength and capability that they have in service of the whole body politic.

Third, it's appropriate for organizations within civic society to have varied and varying Core Groups. But there is only one appropriate Core Group for civic society as a whole, and that is everyone who lives there.

In an organization, decisions should be made on behalf of the perceived needs and priorities of the leadership. In a civic society—a community of any size from a village to a nation—civic decisions should be made on behalf of the life, liberty, and pursuit of happiness of all the people who live within its boundaries. If you live there, you should be seen as part of the Core Group.

Here, then, is the great political challenge of our time: to devise a system of democratic government in a world full of Core Groups. Powerful organizations must exist with their Core Groups intact, but they must be given both the incentives and the wherewithal so that, in aggregate, they can act on behalf of every one of the people in a community. Not because they are forced to, but because it is natural to want to. Such a system would have to allow Core

Groups to continue to exist, and allow the rest of us to draw upon the benefits of life with powerful organizations—without sacrificing the whole of the body politic to them.

In other words: Core Groups of organizations would no longer be confused with the Core Group of a society. The people *on whose behalf* organizations operate would no longer be confused with the people *on whose behalf* society operates.

Until we have a civilization that can reconcile the contradiction between the Core Group nature of organizations and the open nature of community, we won't have a viable political culture.

In the end, perhaps it's not just a corporation or organization that is great because it has a great Core Group. Perhaps the quality of a community or a nation depends on the quality of the Core Groups of the organizations within it—and their ability to maintain a respect for the global and local citizenry as a whole. How do we foster *that?*

Many of the ideals that people have about governance today came to us from the Enlightenment—the period of intellectual questioning and ferment that took place in Europe during the seventeenth and eighteenth centuries. Before that time, Western rulers saw themselves as the heads of the "body politic," making all the decisions for the people who comprised its mass, with authority descended through divine right, direct from God. The great political accomplishment of the Enlightenment was to conceive and forge a transition: from a governance philosophy of unassailable authority, handed down from God through royalty, feudal nobility, and church to a government of authority that was granted by the consent of the governed.

After the Enlightenment, the people of the West saw rulers as their public servants, whose legitimacy could be taken away at any time. People around the world have since come to recognize the "body politic" as the source, not the recipient, of power. This is a profound transition, and in many ways, it has only begun. As Paul

Berman has noted, it is this transition, from a concept of God as authority to a concept of secular authority, that is provoking radical Islamic movements like Al Qaeda to respond with terrorism.

We may be on the verge of a whole new wave in this transition today, with Core Group dynamics at the heart of it.

In today's civil society, just as within organizations, the voice of organizational Core Groups is amplified. They drown out other voices and priorities. This doesn't happen just because organizational Core Group members are wealthy individuals who can make (for example) campaign contributions or bequests to political institutes. Core Group members are powerful because they work through organizations. Each of these organizations contains skillful professionals working on their behalf: buttonholing each other, making deals, visiting sites, starting projects, asking questions, dropping off gifts, establishing relationships, and proposing ideas.

When an organization operates on behalf of the perceived needs and priorities of a Core Group, that's appropriate. But when a community or society in general operates on behalf of the perceived needs and priorities of a Core Group and pays scant attention to the rest of its members, it represents a return to feudalism—abusive, barbaric, faster-than-the-speed-of-the-Internet contemporary feudalism. When a community or society is split into two or more parts, each paying allegiance to a different Core Group with very little overlap, then the result is disruption and polarization, with all the dangers and frustrations that occur when neighbors don't understand each other. Both of these conditions are prevalent in the body politic of the United States today, and presumably in Europe and Asia as well.

The Core Group status of most communities is often described in terms of class conflict: The elite wealthy upper class is the Core Group. Everyone else, whether middle class or part of the impoverished underclass, is mostly invisible, or at best a "citizen of mutual consent." But Core Group realities are more complex than that. In the late 1950s, Yale sociologist Robert Dahl mapped the networks of influence in the small city of New Haven, Connecticut, looking for evidence of a single "power elite" that controlled the whole community. Instead, he found a board of assessors that routinely granted illegal property tax breaks to their friends. He found school principals giving preferential treatment to the children of their PTA leaders. He found an aristocratic New Haven society, long since retired from city politics, and two local political parties dominated by recently assimilated ethnic groups (then, mostly Italian and Irish). Altogether, he found a dozen or so separate political communities, each with its own Core Group of people at the center. Although New Haven is not that large a city, they were only vaguely aware of each other, except when their interests clashed.

Dahl's book (called *Who Governs?*) reminded me of the 1980s-era New York that Tom Wolfe portrayed in *The Bonfire of the Vanities*, a novel based on extensive reporting about New York's body politic. There, too, different constituencies seem almost unaware of each other, except when the Manhattan-meets-Bronx hit-and-run accident at the heart of the novel brings them together. Then the various Core Groups come into focus: the "harps" of the criminal justice system versus the financial "masters of the universe" versus the "social X rays" of Park Avenue versus the "firebrands" of the black churches versus the "mouse" who owns the tabloid newspaper.

At first glance, organizations don't seem very important in either book, but in fact, if you look between the lines, they are the most powerful players—more powerful by far than any "ruling elite." New Haven's political landscape—and its literal landscape as well, in an era of urban development—are determined by the interests of corporations, Yale University, real estate development groups, political parties, churches, and emerging ethnic organizations. In *The Bonfire of the Vanities*, the individuals navigate a perpetually spinning machine whose cogs include investment banks, Bronx courts, Harlem churches, Park Avenue foundations, charter airline corporations, and the ubiquitous tabloid newspaper.

On a national and international level, things are similarly convoluted. The Core Groups of the most powerful global organizations become the Core Groups of society as a whole, but they are not just the rich organizations. Advocacy groups, environmental groups, media networks, professional networks, and many other kinds of networks all have distinct and influential Core Groups. The "have-nots" are those who are not plugged in in some informal way; they are the ones who are further away than six degrees of separation from the organizational sources of power.

It is telling that people on all sides of the political spectrum (including the very wealthy and even some of the conventionally powerful) feel themselves to be not well-enough plugged in. Everyone is aware of some Core Group with influence over their political realities—a Core Group that they would like to circumvent or alter, but in which they are not welcome as a member. And they blame the institutions whose Core Groups they detest. Conservatives blame the civil service and unions. Liberals blame corporations and lobbyists. Secular organizations blame religious organizations, and vice versa. Each set of organizations has its own record of abuses, stemming from its own Core Group dynamics. As each set of institutions defends itself, our collective political will is squandered.

The problem is not with organizations and their Core Groups per se. The basic problem is a political structure that was never designed for them, and that is inadequate for containing them—not in New Haven, not in New York, not in any national governance system, and not on a global level. Perhaps it's time to redesign the governance structure of democracies at all these levels to explicitly recognize the importance of these new entities called organizations, and to pay closer attention to their legal and moral status.

An appropriate governance structure in such a society might resemble the current United States system of checks and balances— not just among three branches of government, but among hundreds of thousands of organizations, corporations, and agencies, all interrelated with each other and with the government, all changing continually and managing themselves.

Such a system would probably have several qualities:

1. It would cultivate transparency—bringing covert organizations, such as lobbyists and financial networks, as much as possible to the surface, so people could judge more easily (for instance) the quality of Core Groups, their activity behind the scenes, and their tendencies toward parasite behavior.
2. It would put a very few, clear limits on Core Groups grounded in ongoing values and customs. There might be limits, for instance, on the amount of cash that can be extracted from organizations by Core Group members.
3. It would make it easier for people to start organizations (and thus Core Groups), and to raise capital for legitimate purposes.

In his book *The Invisible Continent,* the Japanese management expert and politician Kenichi Ohmae suggests that the ability to easily start organizations is a hallmark of a strong economy. He compares Japan, where entrepreneurs must pay close attention to a thousand state regulations that govern all aspects of their business—for instance, they have to make sure that amusement parks are equally fair to all forty-eight prefectures—with America, which is relatively laissez-faire. The Core Group theory suggests that the ability to found organizations easily is also a hallmark of democracy. People learn to be citizens in organizations where they can operate in Core Groups and can experience what it means to have an organization exist on their behalf—and yet take part in a body politic greater than any individual organization.

In the United States, the path from here to there seems particularly frustrating. Political discourse is dominated by the fiercely virulent Core Groups of the Republican and Democratic parties. Their actions betray their essential purposes: to embed their gangs in positions of power and influence, and to weaken the institutions that support the other side. The government itself is a separate set of organizations, with a widely divergent set of Core Groups of its own, each with their own spheres of influence. None of these entities have any interest in a new system of governance; they've mastered the old one too well.

I can imagine a new kind of constitutional convention, conducted perhaps over the Internet (which itself has fascinating Core Group dynamics that are not fully understood yet). But perhaps the whole idea of a constitution, or any change in political governance, is not right either. Perhaps what we really need is a cultural change, a change in people's hearts and minds, so that they recognize, when they start an organization or enter a Core Group, how much the rest of us depend on them.

For I don't think I truly understood Core Groups until my daughters were born. Before then, my wife and I both had fulfilling and highly regarded careers. But we were also relatively rootless. We went our own way, and society was content to let us drift.

Now society has a real stake in us. We are parents of three of its future members. Frances, Elizabeth, and Constance (who are all under five years old as I write this) are our children, but they are not just "our" children. In a small but real way, we are raising them on behalf of everyone. And "everyone" doesn't hesitate to remind us of this. Walk down the street with an infant in a stroller who is underdressed for the weather—and see how many people give you advice about buying the child a sweater. We are responsible for them (and relinquish that responsibility, bit by bit, only to our children themselves as they get older), but everyone has a valid interest in their development.

Similarly, an organization doesn't "belong" only to its Core Group. In a small but real way, it belongs to all of us. We all have a valid interest in the well-being and development of the World Wildlife Fund, Procter & Gamble, the U.S. military, BP, Ford, Boeing, the Coast Guard, Delta, the other organizations I've picked on in this book—and all the rest. They are giant, immensely powerful toddlers, being wheeled by their Core Groups in immense strollers the size of city blocks. But if they're chronically prone to tantrums, or starved, or catching their death of cold, it's a concern to all of us.

We need a culture that can help people live up to the spirit of this kind of custodianship. We need attitudes and laws that pro mote and foster the best possible Core Groups for the best possible organizations. Most of all, we need to cultivate a new kind of awareness in ourselves, our organizations, and the culture at large. There are times and places when it is just and right to act on behalf of the Core Group. But there are other times and places when it is not. We need the wisdom to tell the difference—to know when it's right to put aside our loyalty to the Core Group, and act instead as if it's everyone who really matters.

A NOTE TO THE READER

I had a difficult choice to make in this book. When I first conceived of it, I decided that I would eschew "blind" references—all the companies and organizations I wrote about would be named, and I would not hide behind anonymous references, which by their nature could not be checked. However, as I got into the work, I began to realize that some of the key points could not be made *except* through anonymous stories. Otherwise, they would compromise the careers of people who told the stories, and in some cases they would unfairly reverberate on the organizations themselves. Small but telling events would be blown out of proportion.

When anonymity is required, I have not changed crucial details; I have only omitted them. I have identified every organization by its general category and size, and identified every individual by his or her correct position in the hierarchy.

In this way, I hope I have been true to the need for veracity and credibility, while avoiding unnecessary blame and disproportion.

Inevitably, there will be a need for additions, corrections, and follow-up to this book. Please see my website at http://www.well.com/user/art or http://www.artkleiner.com.

—Art Kleiner

GLOSSARY

Here is a quick index to the ideas of Core Group theory. It should also serve as a review of the terrain covered in this book, from community to careers to corporate governance, and the influence of Core Groups on the way the world works. —Art Kleiner

Core Group: The group of people in any organization who set the direction of the enterprise, because decisions (from top to bottom of the hierarchy) are made on behalf of their perceived needs, desires, and priorities. The Core Group is "who really matters" in organizations, but not in communities. *(Chapter 1: The Customer Comes Eighth)*

Amplification: The recurring phenomenon in which casual statements by Core Group members in an organization become louder, stronger, and more influential than anybody, including the Core Group, ever intended. *(Chapter 8: Guesswork)*

Body politic: The collected citizenry on whose behalf a nation or community ought to make collective decisions. The great political challenge of our time is designing democratic societies that allow organizations to be powerful but not to dominate at the expense of the body politic. *(Chapter 26: The Body Politic)*

Bureaucracy: A Core Group insulated from objective measures of its own performance. *(Chapter 10: Welchism)*

Community: The kind of human enterprise, *unlike* organizations, in which decisions are (or should be) made on behalf of all of its members. *(Chapter 26: The Body Politic)*

Core Group enablers: People in organizations who adopt attitudes and practices that they know are wrong, but that keep dysfunctional Core Groups in place. *(Chapter 15: Core Group Enablers)*

Core Group envy: Continual covetousness of Core Group status by those who don't have it; leads to passive-aggressive behavior (by people inside organizations) or presumptuousness (by outsiders). *(Chapter 6: Employees of Mutual Consent; Chapter 21: Management Consultants)*

Core Group feud: Phenomenon in which Core Group factions are most focused on beating or defeating each other; leads to paranoid, hebephrenic, and catatonic behavior at all levels of the hierarchy. *(Chapter 18: Core Group Feuds and Maladaptive Companies)*

Disabled bystanders: A phrase coined by David Kantor. People who see dysfunctional Core Group behavior and can't, or won't, say or do anything about it. *(Chapter 15: Core Group Enablers)*

Doggie treats: Incentive, targets, measurements, and any other numerical signals of direction. These tend to trump all other Core Group signals as drivers of organizational behavior. *(Chapter 9: "Doggie Treats": Incentives, Targets, and Measurements)*

Employee of mutual consent: Anyone drawing a salary or other payment in an organization who is not a member of the Core Group. In most organizations, this includes ninety percent or more of the population. Employees of mutual consent are characterized by their contractual relationship. *(Chapter 6: Employees of Mutual Consent)*

Equity: Any share of accumulated wealth, including such intangible forms of social capital as reputation and relationships; it also includes financial equity, organizational stock (conventional equity), the ability to "make rain," credentials, capability, health, fitness, family, love, awareness, sensitivity, and spirit. Building up a diversified portfolio of equity is a prerequisite for dealing effectively with Core Group dynamics. *(Chapter 16: A Portfolio of Equity)*

Expanded-Core-Group organization: An organization deliberately designed so that decisions are made on behalf of all, or most, of the people working there. These tend to be either stifling bureaucracies, or great places to work. *(Chapter 12: The Expanded-Core-Group Organization)*

Fiduciary model of corporate governance: The pervasive fiction that corporations should (or do) operate on behalf of their shareholders. *(Chapter 24: Corporate Governance)*

Glass ceiling: The barrier that makes it difficult (or impossible) for some people to get into the Core Group, no matter how qualified, because of a feature like ethnic background, gender, habitual appearance, lack of a particular skill, sexual orientation, political point of view, economic class, level of education, or disability. *(Chapter 13: The Glass Ceilings)*

Guesswork: Habitual pattern of organizational behavior in which employees anticipate and estimate Core Group needs and priorities, rather than asking directly about them. *(Chapter 8: Guesswork)*

Hidden curriculum: The unwritten body of knowledge about Core Groups and their behavior that comprises the most pervasive and well-retained lesson taught in most schools. *(Chapter 22: Schools and the "Hidden Curriculum")*

Hierarchy: The formal structures of organizational command and control, which influence, but do not fully determine, the membership of the Core Group. *(Chapter 3: A Field Guide to Some Common Core Groups)*

Inner Core Group: Mental image or model, held by each individual, of those "on whose behalf I should make decisions." Cultivating a mature inner Core Group is a highly effective strategy for dealing with dysfunctional Core Group dynamics—and building a life. *(Chapter 14: Your Inner Core Group)*

Integrated learning base: A phrase coined by historian Alfred D. Chandler, Jr. The unique body of knowledge that provides each organization with its distinctive competence. This is taken most seriously when members of the organization see the Core Group paying attention to it. *(Chapter 7: A Core Group Way of Knowledge)*

Leadership: The ability to get others in an organization to confer legitimacy on you and thus put you in the Core Group. *(Chapter 5: Power and Legitimacy)*

Legitimacy: The kind of power that derives from the consent of the governed. In organizations, legitimacy derives from the commitment of decision-makers. *(Chapter 5: Power and Legitimacy)*

Noble purpose: The unfulfilled potential of an organization, or the destiny that it might fulfill on behalf of future generations or the broader world. When it is unseen by the Core Group, it will go unrealized. *(Chapter 25: The Cycle of Noble Purpose)*

Organization: A sentient creature composed of human thought and activity, whose passion and purpose is determined by its Core Group. *(Chapter 4: A Very Special Kind of Love)*

Parasitic Core Groups: A concept developed by Arie de Geus. Core Groups which serve their own self-interest at the expense of the natural functions of the host organization. During the 2001–2002 Christmas season, the collapse of Enron brought Parasitic Core Groups to international attention. *(Chapter 17: Parasitic Core Groups)*

Rankism: A word coined by Robert Fuller. The attitude, internalized by many people, that some people are intrinsically worth less than others; in organizations, this often translates into behavior that treats employees of mutual consent with less dignity than members of the Core Group. *(Chapter 13: The Glass Ceilings)*

Shadow Core Group: A group within an organization that has assembled itself as a practice body to hold and develop alternative ways of thinking and acting that the real Core Group could adapt or adopt someday. *(Chapter 23: The Shadow Core Group)*

Threshold of confidence: The point at which people become aware that they are reliably capable of generating some equity. *(Chapter 16: A Portfolio of Equity)*

Threshold of sustainability: The point at which equity begins to replenish itself reliably. *(Chapter 16: A Portfolio of Equity)*

Welchism: A management approach based on streamlining bureaucratic organizations by reshaping the Core Group into a smaller, leaner, more performance-driven entity. *(Chapter 10: Welchism)*

NOTES

Note: This book draws heavily on articles that I have written during the last three years for *strategy+business*, the quarterly published by Booz Allen Hamilton; you will find many such references herein.

Chapter 1: The Customer Comes Eighth

The Exxon story comes from a personal conversation with a former HR executive there. It has been quote-checked with that individual.

My preferred source on the word "core" is Eric Partridge, *Origins: A Short Etymological Dictionary of Modern English*, New York: Greenwich House, 1983, p. 121. The de Geus quote is from conversation, but it echoes themes in *The Living Company*, particularly pages 98–128.

As for the population growth of organizations, I have found no single comprehensive source, but there are a variety of partial references, which all tend to establish the same basic growth rate: a doubling of the number every twenty-five years. The U.S. Statistical Abstract, for example, lists Internal Revenue Service figures for the number of active (i.e., taxpaying) proprietorships, partnerships, and corporations since 1980. The number grows faster in boom times and slower in recessions, but essentially it has almost doubled in the years since 1980, from 13 million to 24 million (U.S. Census Bureau, *Statistical Abstract of the United States: 2001* [Washington, D.C.: U.S. Census Bureau] Section 15: Business Enterprise, table 710: Number of Returns, Receipts, and Net Income by Type of Business: 1980 to 1998, p. 473). During the same period of time, the U.S. population grew by only about forty percent (U.S. Census Bureau, *Statistical Abstract: 2001*, table 4, page 9, www.census.gov/prod/2002pubs/01statab/pop.pdf), which is one basis for my assertion that the population growth of organizations is eclipsing that of people. Further statistics: A separate table from the U.S. historical census shows the total number of business enterprises rising from about 2 million in 1940 to 12 million in 1970. A strikingly similar pattern emerges in the Foundation Center's count of Foundations, which more than doubled from 21,000 to 50,000 between 1976 and 1999 (Global Business Network, "Many More Foundations" [Emeryville, Calif.: 2001]). For perspective on this, see Drucker, *Post-Capitalist Society*. No doubt there should be an economic study sometime of the relationship between (for instance) organizational population and the unemployment rate. If there's a glut of organizations, then even during relatively moribund economic times, it should be easier to find work than it would otherwise be.

Here is one bit of substantiation (among many) for the point that behind every great organization is a great Core Group: "Shares of Corporate Nice Guys Can Finish First," by Gretchen Morgenstern, *New York Times*, April 27, 2003.

Chapter 2: How Organizations Think

Kevin Kelly describes the "hive mind" and Cinematrix in the first few pages of *Out of Control: The Rise of Neo-Biological Civilization* (New York: Addison-Wesley, 1994). A photo of the game session I attended appears on page 122 of *The Whole Earth Review*, no. 48 (Fall 1985). It shows Kevin, Sun Computer pioneer John Gilmore, and John "Cap'n Crunch" Draper manipulating their paddles at the 1984 Hacker's Conference at Marin County's Golden Gate National Recreation Area. Mary Douglas describes her "thought world" concept in the last chapter of *How Institutions Think*.

The Cisco quote is from SMART Letter #73, by David S. Isenberg (June 26, 2002), at http://isen.com. Apparently it refers to several Core Group members by name: CEO John Chambers, chief financial officer Larry Carter, and senior vice president Kevin Kennedy.

Chapter 3: A Field Guide to Some Common Core Groups

Sources on Procter & Gamble include "The House That Ivory Built: 150 Years of Procter & Gamble," *Advertising Age* (August 20, 1987); Alicia Swazy, *Soap Opera: The Inside Story of Procter & Gamble* (New York: Times Books, 1993), especially around page 20; and my own *Age of Heretics*, Chapter 3 ("Reformists"), as well as some of my own interviews. Boeing sources include "Investors Prefer Deal Over Strike—Analysts: Boeing Had No Choice, But Was Edge Against Airbus Lost?" by Stanley Holmes, *Seattle Times*, August 30, 1999; "Why Engineers Strike—The Boeing Story," by Woodruff Imberman, *Business*

Horizons 44, 6, 35(10) (November-December 2001); "A Casualty of Boeing Strike: Friendships Forged over Years," by Erik Lacitis, *Seattle Times,* April 14, 2000; "Strike Cost Boeing Some of Its Workers—Resignations Climbed; Jet Deliveries Stalled," by Kyung M. Song, *Seattle Times,* April 5, 2000; "Boeing's 'Brains'' Showing Brawn—75% of Engineers, Technicians Strike," by Kyung M. Song, *Seattle Times,* February 10, 2000; and conversations with Boeing employees and observers. The Microsoft quote is from "The Colossus of Redmond Suddenly Seems More Human," by John Markoff, *New York Times,* June 10, 2000. Also see the fabulous and culture-revealing "Microsoft Lexicon" compiled and edited by Ken Barnes, at http://www.cinepad.com/mslex.htm. Bill O'Brien is quoted at length in Peter Senge, *The Fifth Discipline: The Art and Practice of the Learning Organization,* (New York: Doubleday/Currency, 1990). You can also learn about his approach in O'Brien et al., "Precepts for Mentors . . . and those being mentored," in Senge et al., *The Dance of Change,* page 128. Barbara Waugh's quote is from an e-mail exchange. Ex-PFC Wintergreen is a character in Joseph Heller's *Catch-22* (New York: Simon & Schuster, 1961). And the concept of the Core Group model derives directly from writing about the network mapping research of Karen Stephenson—see Art Kleiner, "Karen Stephenson's Quantum Theory of Trust," *strategy+business,* (Fourth Quarter 2002): page 54.

Chapter 4: A Very Special Kind of Love

The Gail Bentley quotes appear in "What to Do When Your Life Falls Apart," originally published in WorkingWeekly.com, July 11, 2000, no longer available online. Also see "Can This Publication Be Saved?" by Andy Bourland, in the web newsletter *ClickZ,* July 21, 2000, http://www.clickz.com/design/profit_pub/print.php/826711; and "Tragic CEO moans over corpse of online venture," by Jon Rhine and Todd Stine, *San Francisco Business,* July 21, 2000; and "Last laugh: Collectors gobble scandal-corp swag," by Lisa Provence, *The Hook,* October 3, 2002 (http://www.readthehook.com/stories/2002/10/02/coverStoryLastLaughCollect.html). The Royal Dutch/Shell quote comes from an interview with a senior executive of that company. The McCaw story is from Mark Anderson, "Two Rivers," *Strategic News Service* (March 9, 2000), http://www.tapsns.com. The corporate relocation research comes from William H. Whyte, *City: Rediscovering the Center* (New York: Doubleday, 1988), page 289. Graef Crystal's cogent complaint about executive pay is from *In Search of Excess: The Overcompensation of American Executives* (New York: W. W. Norton, 1991), page 173. The quote about John Reed is from Ferguson, *High Stakes, No Prisoners,* page 128. The reference to the dragon and Jackie Paper is (of course) to "Puff, the Magic Dragon," by Peter Yarrow and Leonard Tipton,

1963; recorded on Peter, Paul and Mary, *Moving, In Concert,* and *10 Years;* copyright © 1963, Pepamar Music.

Chapter 5: Power and Legitimacy

My understanding of enthusiasm and commitment, and its power in conferring legitimacy, owes a great deal to Peter Senge, *The Fifth Discipline: The Art and Practice of The Learning Organization,* New York: Doubleday/Currency, 1990, particularly pp. 218–22 (on the various forms of commitment and compliance that characterize decisions). A nice survey of theories of authority and legitimacy is "Social Theories of Authority," by Eduardo Zambrano, an essay prepared for the *International Encyclopedia of the Social and Behavioral Sciences* (South Bend, Ind.: University of Notre Dame, Department of Finance and Business Economics). The "FNG" story is from "The Very Real Dangers of Executive Coaching," by Steven Berglas, *Harvard Business Review* (June 2002): page 89. The French "work-to-rule" strike example comes from "How to Fire Your Boss: A Worker's Guide to Direct Action," by the Bay Area Industrial Workers of the World, at http://www.iww.org/direction_action/s2.html. Linda Pierce's autobiographical essay is "Learning What We're Worth: The Path to Relevance at Shell Oil Company," in Peter Senge, et al., *The Dance of Change,* page 177. Also see "Opening Doorways to a Better Life at Work: A Conversation with Bill McQuillen," by Karen Ayas (with commentary by Linda Pierce), *Reflections,* Spring 2003, page 22.

Chapter 6: Employees of Mutual Consent

The Rex Stout quote is from *Death of a Doxy* (New York: Macmillan, 1966), page 86. The information about Betty Lehan Harragan comes from an interview with her and from her two books, *Games Mother Never Taught You* (New York: Warner Books, 1977); and *Knowing the Score: Play-by-Play Directions for Women on the Job* (New York: St. Martin's Press, 1983). The "Brand Called You" concept was put forth in Tom Peters, "The Brand Called You," *Fast Company* (August/September 1997). Also see Art Kleiner, "Strike Up the Brand," *strategy +business* (Second Quarter 2001).

Chapter 7: A Core Group Way of Knowledge

The winery story comes from Mary Douglas, *How Institutions Think,* pages 106–8. The Drucker quote comes from Peter Drucker, *Management Challenges for the Twenty-First Century* (New York: HarperCollins, 1999), page 158. Core

Competence is defined in Gary Hamel and C. K. Prahalad, "The Core Competence of the Corporation," *Harvard Business Review* (May–June 1990). Alfred Chandler's "Integrated Learning Base" concept appears in *Inventing the Electronic Century*, pages 3–5. Anyone interested in developing an integrated learning base should look there. Also see Art Kleiner, "Professor Chandler's Revolution," *strategy+business* (Second Quarter 2002): page 84; the Sony and Philips story is taken from both sources. As for the Coca-Cola formula, the actual number of executives who know it is apparently between two and five. Sources include William Poundstone, *Big Secrets* (New York: William Morrow, 1985) (Poundstone says two), and The Sleuth website: "Super Secrets Under Lock and Key," http://www.topsecretrecipes.com/sleuth/sleuth1.htm. John Sculley's book was *Odyssey: Pepsi to Apple...A Journey of Adventure, Ideas, and the Future* (New York: HarperCollins, 1988). Information on Delta's last great crisis came from " 'So Be It': Why Delta Air Lines Decided It Was Time for CEO to Take Off," *Wall Street Journal,* May 30, 1997; the background on the future of the airline industry comes from Tom Hansson, Jürgen Ringbeck, and Marcus Franke, "Flight for Survival: A New Operating Model for Airlines," *Booz Allen Hamilton eNews,* December 2002; Hansson, Ringbeck, and Franke, "Airlines: A New Operating Model: Providing Service and Coverage Without the Cost Penalty" (Booz Allen Hamilton, 2002); Peter Schwartz, *Inevitable Surprises* (New York: Penguin Books, 2003); and James Fallows, *Free Flight: From Airline Hell to a New Age of Travel* (New York: Public Affairs/Perseus, 2001). For more about Elliot Jaques's view of cognitive complexity as a managerial prerequisite, see Elliott Jaques and Kathryn Cason, *Human Capability: A Study of Individual Potential and Its Application,* (Arlington, Va.: Cason Hall Publishers, 1994); and Art Kleiner, "Elliott Jaques Levels With You," *strategy+business* (First Quarter 2001): page 126.

Chapter 8: Guesswork

The Becket story comes from several sources, but I ended up using the version in Will and Ariel Durant, *The Age of Faith* (New York: MJF Books, 1950), page 671. The description of "amplification" comes from conversation with Charles Hampden-Turner; also, "Through the Looking Glass," a report written for Royal Dutch/Shell (1986). The line, "I promoted you because I believed we thought alike" comes from Demack, *The Modern Machiavelli,* pages 82–83. The Jack Welch quote is from an unpublished interview conducted by *Fortune* magazine writer Stratford Sherman in 1990. The Mickey Kaus/Katharine Graham quote is from the weblog "kf rallies after setback," kausfiles.com, July 24, 2002. The older/younger manager anecdote borrows names from the casts of *Space Cowboys* and *Apollo 13,* respectively.

Chapter 9: "Doggie Treats" (Incentives, Targets, and Measurements)

Balanced Scorecard sources include Robert S. Kaplan and David P. Norton, *The Balanced Scorecard: Translating Strategy Into Action* (Cambridge, Mass.: Harvard Business School Press, 1996) and a variety of other works by Kaplan, Norton, and Robin Cooper. Opposing sources include N. Thomas Johnson and Anders Bröms, *Profit Beyond Measure: Extraordinary Results Through Attention to Work and People* (New York: The Free Press, 2000). My own article making sense of the matter is Art Kleiner, "What Are the Measures That Matter?" *strategy+business* (First Quarter 2002). For Taylor, Sloan, and Brown, my preferred sources are Andrea Gabor, *The Capitalist Philosophers* (New York: Three Rivers Press, 2002), Alfred D. Chandler, Jr., *The Visible Hand: The Managerial Revolution in American Business* (Cambridge, Mass: Belknap Press, 1977); and Peter Drucker, *Adventures of a Bystander* (New York: Harper and Row, 1978). The Fred Kofman quotes are from Kofman, "Double-Loop Accounting," in Peter Senge et al., *The Fifth Discipline Fieldbook* (New York: Doubleday/Currency, 1994), pages 287–88. The Richard Foster quote is from Al Vogl, "Excellence Won't Save You," *Across the Board* (March/April 2002): page 41. His book is Richard Foster and Sarah Kaplan, *Creative Destruction: Why Companies That Are Built to Last Underperform the Market—And How to Successfully Transform Them* (New York: Doubleday, 2001).

Chapter 10: Welchism

The Peter Block quote comes from an unpublished interview I conducted with him in the mid-1990s. The GE statistic comes from *General Electric's Century: A History of the General Electric Company from Its Origins to 1986*, an unpublished manuscript by George Wise, page 8. The material about GE comes from a variety of sources, including about fifteen interviews I conducted with managers at GE; one critical source was Noel Tichy and Stratford Sherman, *Control Your Destiny or Someone Else Will* (New York: Doubleday/Currency, 1992). The "number one or number two" policy was rescinded several years ago. The material on the vitality curve and the Welch quote come from Welch, *Straight From the Gut*, page 160 and environs. The "on the team or off the team" quote is from an unpublished interview of Welch by Stratford Sherman. The Robert Jacoby material is from Art Kleiner, "Bare Knuckles on Madison Avenue," *New York Times Magazine*, November 8, 1987. The material about Jacques Nasser and Ford comes largely from interviews I conducted. Wayne Cascio's research and thinking on downsizing can be found in his book *Responsible Restructuring* (San Francisco: Berrett-Koehler, 2002).

Chapter 11: The CEO's Choices

Peter Senge writes about the Leader as Designer in *The Fifth Discipline* (New York: Doubleday/Currency, 1990), page 341ff. The four BP questions were described in Dominic Emery, Andreas Priestland, and Robert Hanig, as told to Art Kleiner: "Dialogos Working Paper #1: First Level Leaders: Engagement & Design Story" (BP and Dialogos, March 2002). The questions were developed by Kate Owen and John Manzoni. For Karen Stephenson's work see Art Kleiner, "Karen Stephenson's Quantum Theory of Trust," *strategy+business* (Fourth Quarter 2002): page 54. For Isaacs's work, see *Dialogue and the Art of Thinking Together.*

Chapter 12: The Expanded-Core-Group Organization

Some quick sources on the companies mentioned at the beginning: Diane Lindquist, "There's No 'I' in this Team: CEO Bob Beyster Steers SAIC through Recession and Terrorist Attacks," *Chief Executive* (March 2002); Jody Hoffer Gittell, *The Southwest Airlines Way: Using the Power of Relationships to Achieve High Performance* (New York: McGraw-Hill, 2002); Lamar Muse, *Southwest Passage: The Inside Story of Southwest Airlines' Formative Years* (Eakin Publications, 2003); Andy Law, *Creative Company: How St. Luke's Became the "Advertising Agency to End All Advertising Agencies"* (New York: John Wiley and Sons, 1999); for W. L. Gore, Michael Kaplan, "You Have No Boss," *Fast Company* (October/November 1997): page 226, and John Naisbitt and Patricia Aburdene, *Reinventing the Corporation* (New York: Warner Books, 1986); for Toyota, N. Thomas Johnson and Anders Bröms, *Profit Beyond Measure: Extraordinary Results Through Attention to Work and People* (New York: The Free Press, 2000). Also see Gates, *The Ownership Solution.* Finally, Robert Levering and Milton Moskowitz, *The 100 Best Companies to Work for in America* (New York: Plume, 1995), contains descriptions of W. L. Gore, Southwest Airlines, and Springfield Remanufacturing.

Diane Burton's research is presented in M. Diane Burton, *How Start-Ups Hire, Organize and Keep Their Employees* (Cambridge, Mass.: Sloan School of Management, MIT, April 2001), slides. Jack Stack's story is told in *A Stake in the Outcome;* in Stack and Bo Burlingham, *The Great Game of Business* (New York: Doubleday/Currency, 1992); and in Art Kleiner, "Jack Stack's Story is an Open Book," *strategy+business* (Third Quarter 2001): page 76. For Jaques's Requisite Design, see Elliott Jaques, *Requisite Organization: A Total System for Effective Managerial Organization and Managerial Leadership for the Twenty-First Century* (Arlington, Va.: Cason-Hall, 1988).

Chapter 13: The Glass Ceilings

Sources on the history of the "glass ceiling" concept: Sarah I. Hartwell, "Breaking the Glass Ceiling," *Executive Female* (January–February 1988): page 72; Louis Papa and Henry Holtzman, "Breaking the Glass Ceiling," *Modern Office Technology* (October 1987); Ann M. Morrison, Randall F. White, Ellen Van Velsor, and the Center for Creative Leadership, *Breaking the Glass Ceiling* (Reading, Mass.: Addison-Wesley, 1987). The Robert Fuller reference is to *Somebodies and Nobodies.* The Deming anecdote comes from an interview with long-standing quality consultant Harold S. Haller; see his company's website at http://www.haroldhaller.com.

Chapter 14: Your Inner Core Group

The book described is Stewart Brand, *The Whole Earth Software Catalog* (New York: Doubleday, 1985, 1986). The magazine was called the *Whole Earth Software Review;* it lasted only three issues. Editor was Richard Dalton, then Art Kleiner. The Diana Durham quote is from *To Finish the Quest: The Chalice of Our Collective Sovereignty,* 2003, unpublished manuscript. The Isaacs quote is from conversation, but reflects some of the insights in his book *Dialogue and the Art of Thinking Together.* This chapter also builds heavily on insights from Peter Garrett and Jane Ball.

Chapter 16: A Portfolio of Equity

The "Frederick" story was derived from a private learning history conducted by Charlotte Roberts, Nina Kruschwitz, and myself for Bluefire Partners, Charlotte, N.C. The company whose story is told has been disguised, but the essentials are correct. Probably the best description of "natural capital" and "social capital" is in Paul Hawken, Amory Lovins, and L. Hunter Lovins, *Natural Capitalism* (New York: Little, Brown & Company, 1999). The Pound quote is from Ezra Pound, *ABC of Reading* (Toronto: New Directions, 1934), page 25. The Paul Revere story is from Malcolm Gladwell, *The Tipping Point.* Gladwell in turn builds upon David Hackett Fischer, *Paul Revere's Ride* (New York: Oxford University Press, 1994). The scene with O. J. Simpson's mother and sister is in Dominick Dunne, *Another City, Not My Own* (New York: Ballantine, 1997), pages 243–44. The Isaacs quote is from a letter published in Mark Anderson's e-mail newsletter, *Strategic News Service* (April 30, 2002). There are also references to Robert T. Kiyosaki and Sharon L. Lechter, *Rich Dad, Poor Dad* (New York: Warner Books, 2000), and to Joe Dominguez and Vicki Robin, *Your Money or Your Life* (New York: Viking Penguin, 1992). I will let you, dear reader, research your own editions of the three coming-of-age stories I mention: The Harry Potter novels written by J. K. Rowling, *Charlotte's Web* by E. B. White, and *Franny and Zooey* by J. D. Salinger. Finally, if you want an academic study of one form of equity, here's one from a legal scholar, no less: Karl S. Okamoto, "Reputation and the Value of Lawyers," *Oregon Law Review* (Spring 1995).

Chapter 17: Parasitic Core Groups

The concept of parasites comes directly from Arie de Geus, *The Living Company*, page 165ff; his quote is on page 166. I also drew on the following Enron sources: Malcolm Gladwell, "The Talent Myth," *The New Yorker* (July 22, 2002) (free rein); David Lane and Professor Pankaj Ghemawat, *Enron: Entrepreneurial Energy*, Harvard Business School Case Study N9-700-079 (Cambridge, Mass.: Harvard Business School Publishing, August 14, 2000) (adoration before the crash); Rebecca Smith and Richard B. Schmitt, "Enron Pays Millions to 'Critical' Staff: Sum Dwarfs Payments to More than 5,000 Dismissed Workers," *Wall Street Journal*, December 12, 2001 (first wave of shock); "Letters to the Editor from Former and Current Enron Employees," *Houston Chronicle*, December 4, 2001 (Vietnam letter); Kurt Eichenwald with Diana B. Henriques, "Web of Details Did Enron In as Warnings Went Unheeded," *New York Times*, February 9, 2002; Gretchen Morgenson, "How 287 Turned Into 7: Lessons in Fuzzy Math," *New York Times*, February 9, 2002 (Enron sales record); Reuters News Service, "Enron Sends California Garbage," March 20, 2002 (discarded Kleenexes); William Greider, "The Enron Nine," *The Nation* (May 13, 2002).

Chapter 18: Core Group Feuds and Maladaptive Companies

The Barbara Waugh quote about Carly Fiorina comes from *The Soul in the Computer*, page 147. Also see Art Kleiner, "Diary of a Change Agent," *strategy +business* (Third Quarter 2002): page 18. Sources on the HP feud included Mark R. Anderson, "Intellectual Honesty," *Strategic News Service*, August 28, 2002; Yahoo's "HewlettPackardEmployees" message board; "If Wall Street Knew What HP Knows," posted on Dave Farber's Interesting-People Message Board, March 1, 2002; Bob Batchelor, "Downsize This: The Hewlett-Packard Merger with Compaq Won't Produce Any Winners," *The American Prospect* (March 25, 2002); Ken Popovich, "Fiorina, Others Could See Merger Windfall," *Ziff Davis eWeek*, April 5, 2002; "HP, Compaq CEOs Reject $22M in Merger Bonuses," Associated Press, November 16, 2001; Larry Dignan, "Fiorina Fires Back Against Charges," and "Hewlett: Rumor Played a Part in Case," *CNET*

News.Com, April 24, 2002; Dignan, "HP Lawsuit Reveals Hardball Tactics, Warts," *CNET News.Com*, April 25, 2002; "HP-Compaq: Where's The Upside," *BusinessWeek* (September 17, 2001); Excerpts from *The HP Way* on the Hewlett-Packard website; and excerpts from a transcript of an internal speech given by Barbara Waugh at Hewlett-Packard. Also note Michael Maccoby, *The Gamesman* (New York: Simon & Schuster, 1976). The cognitive double bind is an adaptation and updating of Gregory Bateson's double bind theory of schizophrenia, drawing on information from Dr. Faith Florer of Marymount College, Manhattan, and on Charles Hampton-Turner, *Maps of the Mind* (London: Mitchell Beazley Publishers, 1981), page 49ff. The final Waugh quote is from page 193 of *Soul in the Computer*.

Chapter 19: Government Agencies

The first Wilson quote is from James Q. Wilson, *Bureaucracy*, page 367. The second is from page 369. The reference to public service outside the United States derives from e-mail from Bill Godfrey. My information on the FCC comes from several sources, but most directly from Peter Schwartz. The Schwartz quote comes from Peter Schwartz, *Inevitable Surprises* (New York: Penguin, 2003), Chapter 5, page 92.

Chapter 20: Labor Unions

The Geoghegan quote is from *Which Side Are You On?*, pages 251–52. A telling reference on United Airlines is Daniel Gross, "ESOP's Fable: United's Employees Own Most of the Airline. So Why Are They Helping to Kill It?" *Slate*, August 13, 2002, http://slate.msn.com/id/2069362/. The "never give an inch" novel is Ken Kesey, *Sometimes a Great Notion* (New York: Viking/Penguin, 1963). For Irving Bluestone's labor perspective on companies' integrated learning bases, see Barry Bluestone, *Negotiating the Future: A Labor Perspective on American Business* (New York: Basic Books, 1994). The story about the school union emerged from a program developed at Dialogos called "Stepping Stones." For more information, see http://www.dialogos.com.

Chapter 21: Management Consultants

For more information about Reflection Learning Associates and learning histories, see the website http://www.learninghistories.com. In writing this chapter I found myself going back to some of the classic management books written by consultants. It was fascinating to read them, between the lines, as guides to the consulting business. They included: Bruce Henderson, *Henderson on Corporate Strategy* (Cambridge, Mass.: Abt Books, 1979) (learning and experience curve, BCG); Thomas Hout, *Competing Against Time* (New York: The Free Press, 1990) (also BCG); Tom Peters and Robert Waterman, Jr., *In Search of Excellence* (New York: Harper & Row, 1982) (Seven-S framework, McKinsey); John R. Katzenbach and Douglas A. Smith, *The Wisdom of Teams* (Cambridge, Mass.: Harvard Business School Press, 1993) (McKinsey); Michael Porter, *Competitive Advantage* (New York: The Free Press, 1985) (Monitor). For more about Heiner Kopperman and ChangeWorks, see http://www.changeworks.de.

Chapter 22: Schools and the "Hidden Curriculum"

My information on the teacher shortage comes from Edward Guttman, "The U.S. Teacher Shortage, Its Causes and Impacts," New York University Interactive Telecommunications Program, 2003. The "Preps, Freaks, Hicks, and Gangstas" story is told in Nathan Dutton, Rick Quantz, and Nolan Dutton, "The Great Game of High School," in Peter Senge, Nelda Cambron-McCabe, Timothy Lucas, Bryan Smith, Janis Dutton, and Art Kleiner, *Schools That Learn* (New York: Doubleday/Currency, 2001), page 370. Also see Snyder, *The Hidden Curriculum*, and Penelope Eckert, *Jocks and Burnouts: Social Categories and Identity in the High School* (New York: Teachers College Press 1989).

Chapter 23: The Shadow Core Group

In mentioning Stanley Bing I am of course thinking of his book *What Would Machiavelli Do?—The Ends Justify the Meanness* (New York: HarperBusiness, 2000). For the story of Lew Veraldi, see Mary Walton, *Car*, pages 15–20. For the Topeka story, see Art Kleiner, *The Age of Heretics*, page 74ff. For the story of Steve Jobs, see Frank Rose, *West of Eden: The End of Innocence at Apple Computer* (New York: Penguin, 1990), or a variety of other books. (I'm partial to Steven Levy's book *Insanely Great*, but it doesn't really focus on the Apple Core Group story.) The section on intervention is influenced by (and derived directly from) the ongoing experimentation and thinking associated with the Dialogos organization in Cambridge, Massachusetts, particularly the work of: William Isaacs, Peter Garrett, Robert Hanig, Kelvy Bird, Skip Griffin, Glennifer Gillespie, and David Kantor. For more about Dialogos, see the website: http://www.dialogos.com. A Working Paper on the "Spiral Model" goes into this model of practice in more detail: http://www.dialogos.com/spiralmodel/. Also see Senge, et al., *The Dance of Change*. "Amplifying Positive Deviance" is described in Barbara Waugh, *Soul in the Computer*, page 32ff.

Chapter 24: Corporate Governance

There are a number of sources for the Ford/Dodge brothers story. I found
two most helpful: Richard S. Tedlow, *Giants of Enterprise: Seven Business
Innovators and the Empires They Built* (New York: HarperBusiness, 2001), pages
119–20; and Peter Collier and David Horowitz, *The Fords: An American Epic*
(New York: Summit Books, 1987), page 83. For the movement to "take back the
charter," see especially Marjorie Kelly, *The Divine Right of Capital*, page 174ff.
My comment on *Grant's Interest Rate Observer* reflects a reading of James
Grant, *Minding Mr. Market: Ten Years on Wall Street With* Grant's Interest Rate
Observer (New York: HarperCollins, 1993). The Margaret Blair comment is
from *Ownership and Control*, page 58. The stakeholder material draws on
Richard Marens and Andrew Wicks, "Getting Real: Stakeholder Theory,
Managerial Practice, and the General Irrelevance of Fiduciary Duties owed to
Shareholders," *Business Ethics Quarterly* (April 1999): pages 273–93. It also
draws on Elaine Sternberg, *Just Business*, particularly pages 49–53 (with one
disagreement: She argues that business managers like stakeholder theory, because it lets them avoid accountability; that may be true somewhere, but I've
never seen it).

Re stock prices rarely predicting future performance: This is practically a
cliché. In finding the courage to write this seemingly innocuous sentence, I was
influenced by Henwood, *Wall Street*, especially Chapter 4 (a very full discussion);
Alfred Rappaport and Michael J. Mauboussin, *Expectations Investing: Reading
Stock Prices for Better Returns* (Cambridge, Mass.: Harvard Business School
Press, 2001) (actually, they suggest that stock prices *do* predict future returns,
but not by themselves); Leon Levy and Eugene Linden, *The Mind of Wall
Street: A Legendary Financier on the Perils of Greed and the Mysteries of the
Market* (New York: PublicAffairs, 2002); by correspondence with Flavia
Cymbalista; and by a mid-2002 report in *BusinessWeek* (whose citation, alas, I
can't find!) tracking the poor performance record of high-tech stocks. The op-ed
cited on short-term abuses is Steve Galbraith, "With Guidance Like This," *Wall
Street Journal*, January 7, 2003. Galbraith, who is Morgan Stanley's chief market strategist, also wrote that "many on the Street [lose] sight of the most powerful force in investing—reversion to the mean—simply because the upcoming
quarter [is] in the bag." And in a bear market, people overlook the potential of
companies with great Core Groups.

The Hawken phrases come from Paul Hawken, Amory Lovins, and L.
Hunter Lovins, *Natural Capitalism* (Boston: Little, Brown & Company, 1999),
page 4. The Dunlap story comes primarily from John Byrne, *Chainsaw*. The
Monks-Minow/Sears, Roebuck anecdote is in Monks and Minow, *Corporate*

Governance, page 181ff and page 408. Their suggestion about electing all board members is in the same book, page 500. The Blair and Porter(!) suggestions are in Blair, *Ownership and Control*, pages 191–92, quoting from Michael Porter, *Capital Choices: Changing the Way America Invests in Industry* (Washington, D.C.: Council on Competitiveness, 1992), page 86. This chapter emerged in part from an article I coauthored with Bryan Smith, "Is the Purpose of a Corporation Return on Investment to Shareholders?" *The Systems Thinker* (April 1995).

Chapter 25: The Cycle of Noble Purpose

In fact, research *did* cross the desk of cigarette company officials in 1963 or earlier, pinpointing cancer and addiction. See Stanton A. Glantz, John Slade, Lisa A. Bero, Peter Hanauer, and Deborah E. Barnes, *The Cigarette Papers* (Berkeley: University of California Press, 1996), page 15 (they say 1963); Philip J. Hilts, *Smokescreen: The Truth Behind the Tobacco Industry Cover-Up* (Reading, Mass.: Addison-Wesley, 1996), page 4ff (he says 1953); and Richard Kluger, *Ashes to Ashes* (New York: Vintage, 1996), page 132ff (he traces a trajectory of research from 1950 through 1959 and beyond). The Philip Morris consent decree is described in "Former Smoker Wins $28 Billion," Associated Press, October 4, 2002. The adaptation to cellular phones, the Lief Salfold study, and the follow-up suggestions by Mark Anderson appear in several issues of Anderson's *Strategic News Service*, especially the issues of February 5, 2003; February 18, 2003; February 25, 2003 (which includes a letter, by me, that anticipates the opening of this chapter, along with Mark's reply that I quote in part); and March 18, 2003 (which mentions further studies). The original study appeared in *Environmental Health Perspectives*. The Larry Fink material on Dow Chemical was adapted from Art Kleiner, "The Three Faces of Dow," *Garbage* (July/August 1991). The EPA report (and a lawsuit against Dow) were cited in Kathie Marchlewski, "Dow Responds to Dioxin Suit," *Midland Daily News*, May 17, 2003. The Mehmet Sarikaya quote is from Peter Schwartz, *Inevitable Surprises* (New York: Penguin Books, 2003). The Richard Pascale quote comes from an interview I conducted with him in the mid-1990s. The oil company "noble purpose" story was told in two places: In Art Kleiner and George Roth, *Oil Change: Perspectives on Corporate Transformation* (New York: Oxford University Press, 2000), page 94ff; and in Art Kleiner, George Roth, and Nina Kruschwitz, "Should a Company Have a Noble Purpose?" *Across the Board* (January 2001): page 18. The Napoleon quote is from an 1803 address to the French Council of State, quoted in "The Nobiliary Element in the Order of the Légion d'Honneur," a piece of web scholarship authored by "Dr. Pangloss," who cites, in turn, as his sources: "Napoléon et la Noblesse d'Empire" by Jean Tulard; "Quest-ce que la Noblesse," by Alain Texier, "Ordres et décorations" by Claude Ducourtial and the French "Quid." It appears on the Maine World News Service website: www.maineworldnewsservice.com/caltrap/nobiliar.htm. The BP story is documented in Terry Macalister, "Big Oil's Green Evangelist," *Guardian*, April 27, 2002; and Darcy Frey, "How Green is BP?" *New York Times Magazine*, December 8, 2002.

Chapter 26: The Body Politic

The three workplace goals, "learning, competence, and justice," were suggested in e-mail correspondence by Daniel Wilson. The Paul Berman paraphrase is to Paul Berman, "The Philosopher of Islamic Terror," *New York Times Magazine*, March 23, 2003. Robert Dahl's book *Who Governs?* describes his sociological surveys; see especially Chapter 13, "Specialization of Influence: Subleaders." I also mention Tom Wolfe, *The Bonfire of the Vanities* (New York: Farrar, Straus & Giroux, 1987). Ohmae's comparison of Japanese and American restrictions on entrepreneurialism is in Kenichi Ohmae, *The Invisible Continent* (New York: HarperBusiness, 1999), pages 126–27. On the fascinating Core Group dynamics of the Internet, see for example, Clay Shirky, "Power Laws, Weblogs, and Inequality," February 8, 2003, in Shirky's weblog at http://www.shirky.com/writings/powerlaw_weblog.html. In the discussion of "getting from here to there" I drew on Noam Scheiber, "Business School: Enron and the Irrelevance of Campaign Finance Reform," *The New Republic* (February 4, 2002).

BIBLIOGRAPHY

The following books were indispensable to me in building an understanding of the issues in *Who Really Matters*—sometimes directly, sometimes obliquely, often because I internalized a part of them without fully realizing it until later. This is hardly a comprehensive bibliography of relevant "Core Group" observation and thinking; that would be a life's work. It is biased toward books that I would recommend to others.

Badaracco, Joseph L. *Leading Quietly: An Unorthodox Guide to Doing the Right Thing*. Cambridge, Mass.: Harvard Business School Press, 2002. From a Core Group perspective, this is the best book on leadership I have seen, and one of the most inspiring books imaginable for employees of mutual consent. It starts where *Who Really Matters* starts: with the idea that every decision matters. How then to make the right decisions? Slowly, thoughtfully, experimentally, with an eye toward the goals you truly want to achieve.

Bennis, Warren. *Why Leaders Can't Lead: The Unconscious Conspiracy Continues*. San Francisco: Jossey-Bass, 1989. More than any other management writer, I suspect, Warren Bennis understands Core Groups from the inside out.

Bennis, Warren, and Patricia Ward Biederman. *Organizing Genius: The Secrets of Creative Collaboration*. New York: Addison-Wesley, 1997. Almost in passing, this book elegantly lays out the basic governance issue facing Skunk Works and other creative teams: balancing autonomy with larger Core Group priorities.

Black, Edwin. *IBM and the Holocaust: The Strategic Alliance Between Nazi Germany and America's Most Powerful Corporation*. New York: Crown, 2001. What the Core Group wants will happen, even if it is deadly and traitorous—in part because the Core Group defines deadliness and treachery.

Blair, Margaret. *Ownership and Control: Rethinking Corporate Governance for the Twenty-First Century.* Washington, D.C.: The Brookings Institution, 1995. Beneath this sober book of plain and imaginative advice one imagines a lively, gay, party-animal-of-a-book-on-corporate-governance just waiting to kick up its heels. It's authoritative, skeptical, and inspiring; Core Group reformers will find it bolsters their courage.

Byrne, John A. *Chainsaw: The Notorious Career of Al Dunlap in the Era of Profit-at-Any-Price.* New York: HarperCollins, 1999. In this rollicking organizational tragedy, Byrne (one of the best business journalists of our era) unpacks the story of a maniacal meta-Welchist who destroyed a Core Group and then a company.

Chandler, Alfred D., Jr. *Inventing the Electronic Century: The Epic Story of the Consumer Electronics and Computer Industries.* New York: The Free Press, 2001. Part One of a two-part theoretical culmination to Chandler's lifelong study of corporations and their influence, this book provided a pivotal introduction to the concept of an "integrated learning base."

Collins, Jim. *Good to Great.* New York: HarperCollins, 2001. This book establishes both the essential and undefinable nature of greatness in organizations and Core Groups. It shows that we can know it, measure it, and replicate it—explicitly in the unforgiving arena of profit-making, but implicitly everywhere.

Coupland, Douglas. *Microserfs.* New York: HarperCollins, 1995. Coupland's best novel is about a small group of employees of mutual consent who move from Microsoft (where only one of them is in the Core Group) to start their own Core Group, which (like many start-up Core Groups) resembles a family.

Dahl, Robert A. *Who Governs?—Democracy and Power in an American City.* New Haven: Yale University Press, 1961. The best in-depth description I found of multilayered Core Group dynamics in a local community.

de Geus, Arie. *The Living Company: Habits for Survival in a Turbulent Business Environment.* Boston: Harvard Business School Press, 1997. A manifesto for Core Groups that see their companies as more than merely economic entities. To de Geus, a company's source of cohesion is the relationship between its Core Group and the rest of the organization.

Demack, Ian. *The Modern Machiavelli: Power and Influence at Work.* Warriewood, Australia: Woodslane, 2001. From Australia (which is emerging as a critical center of management thinking) comes this incisive, worldly fable of a power seeker who apprentices himself to a sardonic top executive.

Douglas, Mary. *How Institutions Think.* Syracuse: Syracuse University Press, 1986. This dense and evocative set of lectures on anthropological philosophy describes how institutions and individuals learn to think from exposure to each other; how organizations and professions engender "thought-worlds" that make it difficult to sustain an outside perspective, even for those who recognize the value of one; and how the antidote is to keep building and rebuilding organizations—in effect, trying on different Core Groups until you find one that fits.

Drucker, Peter F. *Post-Capitalist Society.* New York: HarperCollins, 1993. Compelling, authoritative evidence that the world has moved toward a "society of organizations." And an overview of the principles that would be necessary in designing an appropriate governance system for that kind of world.

Ehrenfeld, Tom, *The Startup Garden.* New York: McGraw-Hill, 2001. A guide to creating the kind of small businesses that cultivate great Core Groups.

Ellison, Ralph. *Invisible Man.* New York: Random House, 1947. Embedded in this famous postwar novel of American racism is a keen and unrestrained recognition of Core Group dynamics.

Ferguson, Charles F. *High Stakes, No Prisoners: A Winner's Tale of Greed and Glory in the Internet Wars.* New York: Times Business, 1999. What happens when several Core Groups collide in the personal computer software business—Vermeer (a start-up producing a web designer's program), Microsoft (which bought it), Netscape (which flubbed it), and several venture capitalists (who dominated it). Gripping. Revealing.

Fligstein, Neil. *The Transformation of Corporate Control.* Cambridge, Mass.: Harvard University Press, 1990. History of the evolution of Core Group cultures in corporations from the nineteenth century through the 1980s, and the structural forces that influenced them.

Fuller, Robert. *Somebodies and Nobodies: Overcoming the Abuse of Rank.* Gabriola Island, B.C.: New Society Publishers, 2003. The problem isn't Core Groups; the problem is the denigration of dignity of non–Core Group members, by themselves and others. Calling it "rankism," Fuller nails this concept. I suspect that it is a harbinger of a new kind of cognitive politics. (I would like to think the Core Group is another such harbinger.)

Gates, Jeff. *Democracy at Risk: Rescuing Main Street from Wall Street.* New York: Perseus, 2000. The tragic and frightening large-scale impact ("legalized looting," he calls it) of every bit of Core Group indulgence, added up over time.

Gates, Jeff. *The Ownership Solution: Toward a Shared Capitalism for the Twenty-First Century.* New York: Perseus, 1998. Critically valuable guide to ESOPs and other methods for creating an Expanded-Core-Group organization.

Geoghegan, Thomas. *Which Side Are You On?—Trying to Be for Labor When*

It's Flat on Its Back. New York: Farrar, Straus & Giroux, 1992. Poignant and hilarious dissection of the role played by labor in America and the consequences of American antilabor politics, written with lots of heart and swear words, and a keen eye for Core Group dynamics.

Gladwell, Malcolm. *The Tipping Point: How Little Things Can Make a Big Difference.* New York: Little, Brown & Company, 2000. How small shifts get amplified in human networks to create significant social change. His "connectors, mavens, and salesmen" map interestingly onto common Core Group roles.

Harvey, Jerry. *The Abilene Paradox and Other Meditations on Management.* New York: Lexington/Macmillan, 1988, particularly Chapter 6, "Eichmann in the Organization." How come people collude with the totalitarianism of their bosses? How come there are "Core Group Enablers"? In one of several extremely powerful essays in this book, Harvey draws on Hannah Arendt's theory of totalitarianism to come up with—if not an answer (for there is no easy answer), then an extremely important deepening of the question.

Henwood, Doug. *Wall Street: How It Works and For Whom.* London: Verso, 1997. Finance capitalism has its own social and political structure, with its own Core Groups, influential beyond its own boundaries. Henwood, editor of the *Left Business Observer,* sheds one of the brightest lights on it.

Hillman, James. *Kinds of Power: A Guide to Its Intelligent Uses.* New York: Doubleday/Currency, 1995. Frustrating because it is unintentionally oblique and opaque, this Baedeker of dominant behaviors, if truly understood, could nonetheless be an essential vehicle for learning to enter a Core Group or make a mediocre Core Group great.

Hirschman, Albert O. *Exit, Voice and Loyalty.* Cambridge, Mass.: Harvard University Press, 1970. People who despise a Core Group with influence over their lives have two choices: Exit (leaving the job or buying a different product) or Voice (trying to influence it to change for the better). In an age where Exit is relatively easy (like our time), a high-quality Core Group develops a healthy balance between Exit and Voice (in other words, it fosters Loyalty). But what kinds of legal constraints make it easier, or more difficult, for Core Groups to be healthy? A classic way of thinking with more relevance than ever.

Isaacs, William. *Dialogue and the Art of Thinking Together.* New York: Doubleday/Currency, 1999. Isaacs' research and practice is on the power of conversation to navigate between developing the "inner Core Group" and orienting yourself with the "outer Core Group."

Jackall, Robert. *Moral Mazes: The World of Corporate Managers.* Oxford:

Oxford University Press, 1988. Less poetic than Earl Shorris's *Scenes from Corporate Life,* more grounded in academic research, and equally damning of parasitic Core Groups.

Jacobs, Jane. *Systems of Survival: A Dialogue on the Moral Foundations of Commerce and Politics.* New York: Random House, 1991. A dialogue exploring two chains of Core Group values, wending their way through history, opposed to each other: the political morality of "guardians" (soldiers) and the economic morality of "commerce" (traders).

Jensen, Michael C. *The Theory of the Firm.* Cambridge, Mass.: Harvard University Press, 2000, especially Chapter 8, "The Distribution of Power among Corporate Managers, Shareholders, and Directors." From a major proponent of the fiduciary view, an overview of the research on the relationship between corporate structure (who owns what form of stock, etc.) and corporate performance, leading to a conclusion that (if I read it correctly) suggests that structures that promote great Core Groups lead to better performance.

Kelly, Marjorie. *The Divine Right of Capital: Dethroning The Corporate Aristocracy.* San Francisco: Barrett-Koehler, 2001. Many of the features that I see as inherent to organizations, Kelly sees as artifacts of legal machinations—artifacts that can be changed through better governance laws. Our views seem opposed, but I think we are both raising the kinds of issues that, with any luck, would lead a society to rethink its governance structure in light of the dangers *and* benefits of disproportionately powerful Core Groups.

Klein, Naomi. *No Logo.* London: Flamingo, 2000. This is the rallying cry for a movement against global corporations, seeing them as invisible behemoths, stamping the earth, with brands instead of human faces. That perception is correct. The book could have been called "Consumers of Mutual Consent." But because the movement ignores Core Groups, and doesn't explicitly acknowledge them (in either corporations or its own organizations), it makes itself weaker.

Kleiner, Art. *The Age of Heretics.* New York: Doubleday/Currency, 1996. Some nice Core Group stories here.

Kleiner, Art, and George Roth. *Oil Change: Perspectives on Corporate Transformation.* New York: Oxford University Press, 2000. Many Core Group dynamics are revealed in the three-year period covered by this in-depth oral history of a large American oil company.

Kramer, Joel, and Diana Alstad. *The Guru Papers: Masks of Authoritarian Power.* Berkeley, Calif.: Frog, Ltd., 1993. The worst thing you can be in an organization is "out of control." Here, a pair of researchers into cult psychology demonstrate the connection between the desire for control in religion, addiction, and . . . organizations. If we want to understand how we choose our bosses, one place to look is among those who have literally chosen their bosses by seeking out a guru.

Kremer, Chuck, with Ron Rizzuto and John Case. *Managing by the Numbers.* New York: Perseus, 2000. The commitment of a great Core Group translated into everyday financials (which is typical of financial literacy).

Lodge, David. *Nice Work.* Middlesex, England: Penguin, 1988. Two cultures that misunderstand each other—corporate and university—confront each other in the persons of a factory manager and a professor, each with Core Group issues and doomed romantic intrigues.

McKnight, John. *The Careless Society: Community and its Counterfeits.* New York: Basic Books, 1995. An overview of the ways in which organizations hijack the body politic. His prescriptions are all about expanding the number of Core Groups available for people to join.

Milgram, Stanley. *Obedience to Authority: An Experimental View.* New York: Harper & Row, 1974. You go into the room. The Core Group member there tells you to administer a test to an employee, who receives electric shocks when he gets an answer wrong. The employee pleads with you to stop. Do you stop? The conclusion: It depends on the legitimacy of the Core Group, and that in turn depends partly on you.

Monks, Robert A. G. and Nell Minow. *Corporate Governance.* Cambridge, Mass.: Blackwell, 1995. The text, from a pair of activist/authorities, that I found most useful in coming to terms with the corporate governance issues described in this book.

Monks, Robert. *The New Global Investors.* Oxford: Capstone, 2001. How to set up governance structures that might yield a better world by influencing the makeup of corporate Core Groups. Three key principles: disclosure of corporate impact on the rest of the world, disclosure of lobbying activity, and setting up long-term investors as Core Group overseers.

Nocera, Joseph. *A Piece of the Action: How the Middle Class Joined the Money Class.* New York: Simon & Schuster, 1994. History of the evolution of autonomous mass finance, with enormous implications (I think) for designing a postorganization world democratic society.

Oshry, Barry. *Seeing Systems: Unlocking the Mysteries of Organizational Life.* San Francisco: Barrett-Koehler, 1995, 1996. Oshry brings people together in weekend workshops, disorients them, assigns places in the hierarchy to them, and watches the Core Group dynamics emerge as if he were a compassionate poet-entymologist.

Roth, George, and Art Kleiner. *Car Launch: The Human Side of Managing*

Change. Oxford: Oxford University Press, 1999. This oral-history-style "learning history," which I developed with MIT business researcher George Roth, describes the fate of a product launch team that confronted Core Group dynamics at a major auto company.

Sampson, Anthony. *Company Man: The Rise and Fall of Corporate Life.* London: HarperCollins, 1995. A history of Welchism—the transition throughout the corporate world from 1960s-style managerial bureaucracy to 1990s-style lean Core Groups.

Saul, John Ralston. *Voltaire's Bastards: The Dictatorship of Reason in the West.* New York: Vintage, 1992. Great Core Groups believe in the value of autonomous people; terrible Core Groups start by seeking control over the people they manage. Ralston traces the evolution of modern-day terrible Core Groups from the tensions of the Enlightenment. He says our world is in thrall to them. *Who Really Matters* was written in hopes that the way out of Ralston's dilemma may start inside organizations.

Schein, Edgar H. *The Corporate Culture Survival Guide.* San Francisco: Jossey-Bass, 1999. Want to diagnose the values underlying the actions of an organizational Core Group? You could do worse than follow the sequence of discovery that Schein, our preeminent expert in corporate culture, lays out here.

Senge, Peter, Art Kleiner, Charlotte Roberts, Rick Ross, George Roth, and Bryan Smith. *The Dance of Change.* New York: Doubleday/Currency, 1999. This book, part of the *Fifth Discipline Fieldbook* series, could be thought of as a campaign manual for the ongoing sort of initiative described in Chapter 23, "The Shadow Core Group."

Shorris, Earl. *Scenes From Corporate Life: The Politics of Middle Management.* New York: Anchor Press, Doubleday, 1981. Modern management, argues Shorris in forty extremely compelling bits of short fiction, has begun to use the methods of totalitarian states like Nazi Germany and Stalinist Russia. In many ways, *Who Really Matters* is a personal answer to the conundrums raised by Shorris in this book.

Snyder, Benson R. *The Hidden Curriculum.* New York: Knopf, 1971. How schools and universities teach, first and foremost, Core Group realities and the conventional ways of addressing them.

Stack, Jack, and Bo Burlingham. *A Stake in the Outcome.* New York: Doubleday, 2002. The full story of Springfield Remanufacturing Corporation, with particular emphasis on the benefits and methods for designing an Expanded-Core-Group organization.

Sternberg, Elaine. *Just Business: Business Ethics in Action.* London: Little, Brown & Company, 1994. A utopian view of business purpose—"to maximize owner value over the long term by selling goods or services"—leads to some very highly principled and pragmatic views of stakeholders, corporate governance, and the enlightened self-interest of great Core Groups.

Thurber, James. *The Years With Ross*. Boston: Little, Brown & Company, 1957. Possibly the best Core Group history ever, of the central characters at the *New Yorker* from 1927 through 1951.

Trompenaars, Fons, and Charles Hampden-Turner. *Riding the Waves of Culture*. New York: McGraw-Hill, 1998. A masterful look at the values of varied cultures opens the door to understanding the differences among Core Groups of varied organizations.

Tuchman, Barbara A. *The March of Folly: From Troy to Vietnam*. New York: Knopf, 1984. Isolated, willful Core Groups (mostly in government) have changed the course of history, all the way back to Rehoboam's council (which split Israel and ultimately led to its dispersal), and all the way forward to Lyndon Johnson's administration (and perhaps George W. Bush's as well).

Walton, Mary. *Car: A Drama of the American Workplace*. New York: W. W. Norton, 1997. A great guesswork story, in one of America's best-known companies (Ford), in which a great car (the Taurus) with passionate advocates is shaved, bit by bit, down to mediocrity.

Waugh, Barbara, with Margot Silk Forrest. *Soul in the Computer: The Story of a Corporate Revolutionary*. Makawo Maui, Hawaii: Inner Ocean, 2001. How can an employee of mutual consent, seeking to make a better world, go far in a large organization? How far can that employee go? Barbara Waugh, moving step by step through Hewlett-Packard, found out and offers significant principles and an inspirational example.

Welch, Jack, with John A. Byrne. *Jack: Straight from the Gut*. New York: Warner Books, 2001. If you're going to be a Welchist, do it right. Do everything he says, not everything he does.

Wilson, James Q. *Bureaucracy: What Government Agencies Do and Why They Do It*. New York: Basic Books, 1989, 2000. Masterful study of government as it actually works, not as it is espoused to work, in the United States, with the impact of great and terrible Core Groups lurking behind every paragraph.

Young, Iris Marion. *Inclusion and Democracy*. Oxford: Oxford University Press, 2000, particularly Chapter 5, "Civil Society and Its Limits." Every society faces the implicit political question: how to apportion legal power (power to put people in jail), economic power (power to employ), and social power (power to shame). Young's survey of the field, in service of a search for inclusive democracy, seems a good starting point for considering these issues in light of a society of organizations.

ACKNOWLEDGMENTS

When I consider the help and friendship extended to me over the course of this book's gestation, I realize how wealthy an individual I am. I would like to gratefully express thanks to all the following people, who took time to read, convene, or advise in ways that made an enormous difference to the quality and value of *Who Really Matters*.

People who worked directly on the book:

Kelvy Bird created all of the diagrams for the book, and much of the creative force behind the "diagnostic exercises" is hers as well. The quality of both speaks for itself.

As my on-the-ground associates, Maggie Piper and Emily Freidberg provided superlative support, insight, and enthusiasm without which this book would not have been possible. Maggie also designed the Core Group website (http://www. well.com/user/art), and Emily organized the book's promotion—and much more.

Nina Kruschwitz contributed much-valued editorial support at the beginning stages and much-valued perspective and thinking all the way through.

Sharon Harkey (Purple Shark Transcriptions) transcribed the tapes of the interviews on which this book is based. Ellen Bork conducted background research; Catherine Russo, Justin Lamberto, Katy Harper, and Erica Giokas provided clerical work that made a difference.

Literary agent Joe Spieler, of Joe Spieler and Associates, helped conceive, develop, and care for this project at every stage; he is a Core Group avatar.

Editors Roger Scholl (Doubleday) and Nicholas Brealey (Nicholas Brealey) each left a valued mark on the book. I am also grateful at Doubleday to Michael Palgon, Sarah Rainone, David Drake, Chris Welch, and others (to whom I have not yet been introduced as I write this).

People who provided a context of support for the book as a whole:
Randall Rothenberg and Ann Graham, editors of *strategy+business,* saw the value of this work early (especially in Ann's case) and created a space where the ideas herein could be nurtured and developed.

William Isaacs and others at Dialogos (Cambridge, MA) were supportive at every step of the way, in more ways than I can say. Dialogos, in effect, became a staging ground for give-and-take that contributed to every aspect of these ideas. I am grateful to Peter Garrett and Jane Ball (now of Dialogue Associates), Robert Hanig, Kelvy Bird, Skip Griffin, Marianne Picard, Glennifer Gillespie, Diane Nakashian, Tang Sayabovorn, Jess Kelty, Paul Milledge, Bruce Allyn, and others I have met through this organization. I also wish to acknowledge my fellow participants in the 2002–2003 Leadership for Collective Intelligence course given by Dialogos, where I learned much of relevance to this book.

Red Burns, George Agudow, Martin Elton, Tom Igoe, Midori Yasuda, and others at New York University's Interactive Telecommunications Program have provided me an intellectual home for years—a place where the Core Group concept first emerged in a course I taught on the Future of the Infrastructure.

This book came to life in a series of conversations organized by:
Lisa Kimball, Starla King, Frank Burns, and others at Caucus Systems (Collaborate '99, where I first broached the Core Group concept publicly); LeAnne Grillo, Dan Kim, and Peter Senge at Pegasus Communications/The Society for Organizational Learning, where I delivered the first public Core Group talk; Karen Otazo and John Hofmeister, who opened their home to one such conversation; Nancy Murphy, Peter Schwartz, Napier Collyns, Sophia Liang, Erik Smith, and others at Global Business Network; Michael Chender, David Sable, Hal Richman, Susan Szpakowski, Bob Ziegler, Tony Lamport, and others at Shambhala Institute; Amiel Handelsman, Business Ethics Conference; Teddy Zmrhal (Columbia University Executive MBA Program); Neal Goldsmith, Carriage House Talks; Sergio Lub, Friendly Favors; Michael Bokeno, in the Journal of Organizational Change Management; Robin Sacrafamilia, Sandra Ross, Deanna Heggie, and the various people at T. W. Branum; Cheryl Rhodes, Tony Bove, Carolyn Cooke, and Randall Babtkis; Audrey Cohen, Marymount College; Richard Kreutzer and Vitz Baltero at EARCOS; Peter Schutte, Anne Starr, Peter Senge, Guus Geisen, and others at the Learning Schools Conference in the Netherlands; Mark Anderson, *Strategic News Service;* Sonja Radatz, First International Congress for Systemic Management; and Linkage's Organization Development Conference.

People whose time, thought, advice, and interest made a
much-appreciated difference:

Cliff Barry and Susan DeGenring, Myrna Casebolt, Flavia Cymbalista, Jim Collins, Napier Collyns, Diane Coutu at *Harvard Business Review*, Arie de Geus, Jim Evers, Robert W. Fuller, Joel Garreau, Jeff Gates, Mark Gerzon, Toni Gregory, Christy Hudgins, David Hudnut, David Isenberg, Joe Katzman, Julius Kleiner, Barnett Lipton, Tim Lucas, Nancy Murphy, Roberta Myers, Karen Otazo, Vincent X. Potenza, Hal Richman, Charlotte Roberts, George Roth, Tom Ryan, Edgar Schein at *Reflections*, Clay Shirky, Annette Simmons, Karen Stephenson, Michael Stone, Chiawat Thirapantu, Fons Trompenaars, Louis van der Merwe, Al Vogl and Matthew Budman at *Across the Board*, Diana Van der Woude, Barbara Waugh, and Daniel Wilson.

People whose comments, insights, help, and encouragement contributed
to the shape and direction of Core Group theory:

Tom Abeles, Michael Agard, Mary Ann Allison, Cindie Baker, J. Baldwin, Ron Bean, Dan Berkowitz, Eric Best, John Blackwell, Gary A. Bolles, Hilary Bradbury, Steven G. Brant, Debra Brosan, Marilyn Brown, David Bubna-Litic, Michael Burns, Nelda Cambron-McCabe, Phil Candreva, Marty Castleberg, Alfred D. Chandler, Jr., David Coghlan, Janet Coleman, Angela and Bob Cox, Kenneth Craddock, Stuart Crainer, Joanie Davis, Eric deLuca, Ian Demack, David Derby, Robert Dickman, Evan Dudik, Janis Dutton, John Edwards, Tom Ehrenfeld, Richard Elsner, Dominic Emery, Chris Ertel, Richard Farmer, Larry Frascella, Rick Frazier, Stephanie George, Tom Gilmore, Bill Godfrey, Bill Gordon, Diana Guilbert, Edward Guttman, Michelle Halsell, Jody Hankinson, Bill Harris, Peter Hill, John Hofmeister, Linda and Martin Horowitz, Jean Horstman, B. C. Huselton, Dennis Jaffe, Dennis Jaffe, Joe Jaworski, N. Thomas Johnson, Adam Kahane, Philipp Kauffmann, Barbara Kleiner, Max and Helen Kleiner, Victoria Kniewel, Richard Kohl, Heiner Koppermann, Petra Kuenkel, William Lambert, Bob Lee, Woody Liswood, Cheri Lovre, Ralph Martin, David Mason, Ian McAuley, Debra Meyerson, Robert Monles, Brian Mulconrey, Pauline Ores, Ruby Payne, Hugh Pidgeon, Linda Pierce, Anu Ponnamma, Ruthann Prange, Brian Rathjen, Lew Rhodes, Judy Rodgers, Wendy Rogovin, Rick Ross, Harriet Rubin, Patricia Sachs, Roger Saillant and others at Plug Power, Mary Scheetz, Michael Schrage, Barbara L. Schultz, Alisa Schwartz, Peter Senge, Andrea Shapiro, Eric Siegel, Bruce and Ellen Singleton, George Smart, Bryan Smith, John Smith, Chris Soderquist, Deb Soholt, Jack Stack and others at the SRC enterprises, Mark Stahlman, Ross Stapleton-Gray, John Sumser, David Taber, Ann Thomas, Margaret Thorpe, Bill Torbert, Leslie Tremaine, Myron Tribus, Candido Trujillo, Fred Turner, William Tyler, Liisa Valikangas, Gerhard van den Top, Drew Walter,

Doug Weinfield, Siegfried Woldhek, Peter Woolliams, Don Yates, Ian Yolles, John Zavacki, Nick Zeniuk, and undoubtedly some critical people I've overlooked here (but not, in the end, forgotten).

During the time I was working on this book, several people influential to it passed away. I hope that *Who Really Matters* will honor the memory of Donald Michael, William O'Brien, Cliff Havener, Elliott Jaques, and Leon Levy.

...and finally...

I can never be grateful enough to my family, whose wholehearted and enduring love and support continues to really matter: Julius, Irene, and Edward Kleiner; Linda and Cal Heusser; the Rev. Herb Florer; Herb and Ben Florer; and most of all, Faith L. Florer, Frances Kleiner, Elizabeth Kleiner, and Constance Kleiner.

INDEX

Page numbers of illustrations appear in italics.